CW01654581

# Constructing Realities

# Constructing Realities: Identity, Discourse and Englishness

BY

**STUART CARTLAND**

*University of Sussex, UK*

emerald
PUBLISHING

United Kingdom – North America – Japan – India – Malaysia – China

Emerald Publishing Limited
Emerald Publishing, Floor 5, Northspring, 21-23 Wellington Street, Leeds LS1 4DL

First edition 2024

Copyright © 2024 Stuart Cartland.
Published under exclusive licence by Emerald Publishing Limited.

**Reprints and permissions service**
Contact: www.copyright.com

No part of this book may be reproduced, stored in a retrieval system, transmitted in any form or by any means electronic, mechanical, photocopying, recording or otherwise without either the prior written permission of the publisher or a licence permitting restricted copying issued in the UK by The Copyright Licensing Agency and in the USA by The Copyright Clearance Center. Any opinions expressed in the chapters are those of the authors. Whilst Emerald makes every effort to ensure the quality and accuracy of its content, Emerald makes no representation implied or otherwise, as to the chapters' suitability and application and disclaims any warranties, express or implied, to their use.

**British Library Cataloguing in Publication Data**
A catalogue record for this book is available from the British Library

ISBN: 978-1-83797-546-4 (Print)
ISBN: 978-1-83797-545-7 (Online)
ISBN: 978-1-83797-547-1 (Epub)

Printed and bound by CPI Group (UK) Ltd, Croydon, CR0 4YY

INVESTOR IN PEOPLE

# Contents

Acknowledgements *vii*

**Introduction** *1*

**Chapter 1 Discourse, Narrative and National Identity** *11*

**Chapter 2 Globalisation and Discourses of Englishness** *27*

**Chapter 3 The Ideologically Constructed Myth of Englishness** *51*

**Chapter 4 Racialised Discourses and Cosmopolitan Existences** *83*

**Chapter 5 Discourses of Englishness and Multiculturalism** *111*

**Chapter 6 Englishness and Discourses of Europe** *135*

**Chapter 7 Devolution and Discourses of Englishness** *163*

**Conclusions** *191*

Bibliography *195*

# Acknowledgements

First and foremost I'd like to thank my family, Jacindy and Elieh for tolerating me for the duration of this project, not to mention help with unending editing. A special thank you also to Paul Hopper for helping me with this work from the very beginning. I would also like to thank my colleagues within the University of Sussex and the University of Brighton who have always been supportive and helpful. Thank you to the editors and staff at the journals who have accepted my work over recent years in particular Culture Matters and Compass. Finally, I would like to thank my students both at the University of Brighton and the University of Sussex who have inadvertently been subject of opinion and attitudinal observation, and who have always constructively challenged my assertions.

# Introduction

This body of work will critically investigate contemporary concepts and constructions of English national identity, or rather, Englishness. It will suggest that within the contemporary context, discourses of English national identity are dominated and characterised by a prevailing and assertive conservative approach. This work will examine theoretical and conceptual approaches to national identity and nationalism from a particular conservative interpretation of Englishness in relation to key contemporary themes. It will then suggest that within the contemporary context and in relation to relevant topic areas of investigation, Englishness is dominated by a specific sense of insecurity of identity, one that is characterised by a sense of defensive exclusivism.

The aim of this body of work is not to produce a reductionist account of what constitutes English national identity; instead, it is a critical, empirical and theoretical examination of determining themes behind dominant conceptualisations of Englishness in the contemporary period. Within this context, it will be argued that discourses of Englishness are overwhelmingly dominated by a conservative interpretation and understanding. These discursive articulations are constituted by a predominantly ethno-nationalist and deeply historicised account of national identity that are largely ideologically informed by a defensive account towards long-term and ongoing processes such as globalisation and immigration and operate as exclusive rather than inclusive identity signifiers. Relatively recent developments and themes such as devolution, the European Union and a wider context of political and social flux, fluidity and uncertainty are symbolically used to further an ideologically conservative interpretation of Englishness within a context of identity insecurity and anxiety.

When locating discourses of Englishness in the contemporary era, this specifically refers to discursive representation, narratives and understanding of Englishness informed by ongoing and recent events, developments and processes that can widely be viewed as political, ideological, social and cultural. Moreover, the central element of investigation concerns the specific development of a politically and ideologically constructed sense of Englishness that has been formed and has coalesced since the late 1990s but more specifically from the late-2000s. Arguably, there has never been such interest, debate, discussion and confusion over what it means to be English. The fluidity and multidirectional

**Constructing Realities, 1–10**
**Copyright © 2024 Stuart Cartland**
**Published under exclusive licence by Emerald Publishing Limited**
**doi:10.1108/978-1-83797-545-720231001**

politics of identity within the English context requires an urgent need for critical investigation and demystification of this subject area. Concepts of Englishness, or constructs of English national identity, are not based upon fixed or singular meanings. They are both fluid and contested; however, in the current discursive environment, they have become dominated by a particularly conservative ideological interpretation and narrative.

The methodological approach adopted within this body of work will be to employ an underlying use of discourse analysis to critically investigate the characteristics and the constructed nature of discursively constituted ideological and empirical articulations of Englishness. Although this research is predominantly a theoretical and conceptual analysis of competing narratives, it will utilise empirical evidence to substantiate these claims and the tangible effects of ideologically constructed conceptualisations of national community. These empirical forms of evidence will be drawn from a range of sources, such as opinion polls, voting behaviour, interviews and public attitudinal surveys, media coverage and the politicised approach taken by large sections of the media, political and social commentary and the wider national public, political and social debate concerning issues relative to the constructed conceptualisation of Englishness.

This body of work will draw upon and engage with key social, cultural and political theorists of nationalism and national identity such as: Umut Ozmirkiri, John Breuilly, Tom Nairn, Thomas Hyland Eriksen and Benedict Anderson. This will not seek to be an exhaustive account of identity; it will instead be situated within the contemporary English experience and will utilise writers and theorists within this specific area such as: Craig Calhoun, Arthur Aughey, Bridget Byrne and Krishnan Kumar. This work will also be heavily informed by the use of discourse as a means to analyse and examine dominant national narratives and understanding around concepts of Englishness, particularly from theorists Ernesto Laclau and Chantal Mouffe but also drawing upon the work of Jacob Torfing, Thomas Diez and Frederic Jameson to facilitate an evaluative understanding of the character of a dominant narrative within this field of enquiry.

Brexit, devolution and immigration reflect politicised narratives shaping the conceptualisation of Englishness. These ongoing developments require discursive analysis to examine their influence on identity formation. This subject area requires investigation to understand how these processes inform a specific politicised identity. Identity, particularly concepts of national identity projected in the public realm, is political. Arguably, England is in the midst of a crisis of political, social and cultural identity, however, lost in this conjuncture seems to be that identity, particularly a sense of national identity is something that is created and constructed not empirically given.

It will be argued that England is dominated and held to account by a narrow conservative social, cultural and political imagination and narrative. The emphasis and targeting of issues such as immigration, multiculturalism and Europe are presented as 'denaturing' (Balibar, 2002) in terms of a specific interpretation of national identity from a conservative ideological perspective. These key issues are used as sites for ideological and discursive affirmation and legitimacy for a conservative dominated conceptual account of Englishness.

In an era of ongoing processes such as the break-up of Britain and a disassociation with Europe, England has become exposed both politically and in terms of identity, and is forced to come to terms with a position of unpreparedness, yet this debate and national conversation has become dominated by exclusionary and divisive rhetoric and discourse dominated by a sense of English grievance, loss and anxiety. England has become dominated by a very tangible form of conservatism, not just discursively but also politically, a vote to leave the European Union which was most notable within England, an overwhelming dominance of Conservative MPs within England, the rise and legacy of the United Kingdom Independence Party (UKIP) and its deep incursions into the political environment. Coupled with this is the fundamental split of the United Kingdom along political and ideological grounds with the SNP constituting an overwhelmingly dominant position within Scotland while the Conservative Party maintain a similar position within England.

A mediated understanding of Englishness and English national identity is dominated by a specific conservative interpolation, interpretation and narrative. Dominant conservative concepts of Englishness can be characterised by an archaic and backwards looking position driven by a decline in a primacy of Britishness, yet tentatively opposed to the break-up of Britain, motivated by a deep-seated Euroscepticism and driven on by cultural and social reactionism. Thereby, being an inextricable link between the intersectionality of conservative positions towards key contemporary themes of devolution, Europe, immigration, multiculturalism and dominant discourses of Englishness whereby exceptionalism and separateness has become naturalised and normalised to the point that it is almost impossible to reimagine it any other way.

Within the context of a post-Scottish independence referendum, post-European referendum, post-'end-of-multiculturalism', post-UKIP ideological terrain of social commentary and national imagining, national discourses have hardened and have become receptive to a politics of exclusion, a sense of loss and political incorrectness. Concepts such as a politics of exclusion are crucial when analysing the discursive representation of a dominant conservative Englishness. The creation, belief and dominance of this form of Englishness can be viewed as a means to systematically rationalise and come to terms, in a self-serving form of coherence what it means to identify as English and how and where this is situated in the context of present challenges. This process also enables a vernacular of 'injured Englishness' acting as a vehicle for a shift towards a more ethno-nationalist identity of disaffection and resentment.

Although it is difficult to disentangle Englishness from Britishness, particularly in an historical context, what has become clear is that the present era represents an historic moment when the English are becoming to discover a clear conception about a distinction between Englishness and Britishness, even if this choice has been impelled rather unwillingly. Dominant discursive forms of Englishness are often formed and informed against a plural and highly multicultural society that is experiencing a relatively high degree of flux, yet this background has helped create social and cultural anxieties which have become manifested politically. Concepts of Englishness, therefore, can be viewed as experiencing a paradoxical relationship between identity and cultural imagination. This can also be viewed as a means of informing national narratives of perceived decline and perceptions of the present and the use of narratives of nostalgia.

Contemporary conservative discourses of Englishness validate an ontology of identity within a narrow ideological framework. It becomes the dominant lens through which the entire social, cultural and political landscape is interpreted. Simplistic narratives and ideological accounts of complex sociocultural lives have long been contested, but in our post-truth hyperreality, discursive representations of belonging and place have become highly politicised. These representations are driven by narratives of fear, uncertainty and anxiety, often detached from reality. This body of work will critically examine theoretical constructions of English national identity, exploring their mediation through place and experience; it will also investigate the impact of ideologically driven narratives on public discourse and concepts of identity, particularly in relation to belonging and exclusion. It will be suggested that dominant conservative discourses are often contradictory and confused while at the same time marginalise the everyday experiences of many within contemporary English society.

## Why Discourse Theory

Discourse is the construction of a framework for understanding a particular subject area within a particular context. As a general working definition of the term, discourse can be described as the creation and articulation of dominant forms of narrative used to give an understanding of our social, cultural and political world, located within an ideological framework. Discourse is the articulation of knowledge, and knowledge is located within discourse Therefore, it is constantly fluid and open to contestation and manipulation. Discourse is primarily linked or concerned with meaning; this is crucial when discussing or critically analysing concepts of identity and narrative.

What is common throughout all definitions of discourse is that it is something that frames experience and understanding and gives meaning to experience. Discourse provides a medium through which thought, meaning and action, and alternately, action, meaning and thought take place. Hence, such significance can be placed upon discourse when considering concepts of nation, nationalism and national identity. These conceptual realms cannot exist outside of discourse.

Discourse is the ideological symbolic representation of place, people, institutions, behavioural codes and norms. In this sense, it is a mediation of understanding experience both as lived reality but also as part of an imagined social community. It is, therefore, inescapable within the realm of national identity and the conceptualisation of place, inclusion and exclusion. In a specific conservative and right-wing context, it relies upon a particular historicised national narrative; it also relies upon the use of a mythscape binding landscape to a specific symbolic representation.

Discursive narratives form an important resource for individuals and groups in the construction of identity. It provides a self-legitimising and often self-replicating feedback loop of understanding and meaning which happens on both an individual and group level, making narrative a critical cognitive instrument for making one's own lived experience legible. Nationalist narratives, to be effective and to resonate, are often characterised by persuasion. Carefully cultivated national narratives seek to resonate with existing social norms and values but also operate within an ideological framework for understanding and providing action towards desired conclusions. Crucially, in terms of a conservative discourse of Englishness, narrative can operate as a discourse of defensiveness or loss which can therefore be easily identified and located within conservative forms of nationalism informed by specifically historicised or radicalised understandings and interpretations.

Discourses of nationalism and national identity provide a space for unlimited ideological social significance and imaginary. Theoretical conceptualisations surrounding discourse will be used in conjunction with other approaches to critically engage with Englishness in the contemporary period. Discourse theory is explored here as a tool to unpack contested and challenged political and ideological conceptualisations of identity. Moreover, the contested, debated and challenged nature of discourse and the substantive content in which people identify with it is what makes national identity an area of investigation so vital to evaluate and understand, particularly within the context of a contested conceptualisation of Englishness.

Discourse is the articulation and practice of ideology; therefore, it would be meaningless to focus solely upon ideology alone. Discourse also highlights the constant state of contested meaning; it operates as a system of belief. Indeed, political ideology is expressed through discourse, and this in itself defines contested meanings of nationalism and national identity. Discourse analysis is particularly important when considering concepts of Englishness as discourse informs and leads us in how we interpret and understand national identity but is also a manifestation and expression of identity; in other words, national identity and nationalism are a direct product of discourse around the topic or subject of nation. At the same time, as there can be no complete, unified and entirely suitable national identity, there can be no complete, unified or entirely whole discourse. Likewise, all identities can also be viewed as being relational and dependent to varying extents on systems of difference within which they reside or operate.

Discourse presents (an often simplified) understanding of 'truth', 'fact' and 'reality'. As Foucault observed, 'each society has its regime of truth, its 'general politics' of truth; that is the types of discourse which it accepts and makes function as true' (Foucault, 1980:131). Discourse is never just a mere description; discourse is pre-loaded with what we already know about the world in order to give some sort of explanation or understanding. Discourse is also often pre-loaded with certain purposes, aims, objectives, motives, interests and strategies, all of which are almost never consciously apparent, but all of which make the analysis and examination of discourse in this context particularly necessary.

Discourse is constitutive of social relations in that all knowledge, all discussion, all argument takes place within a discursive context; this is of central importance when considering concepts of identity and community within a national context. This also helps explain why discourse theory, and particularly as a critical analytical approach, is so specifically valuable within the context and in relation to the topic of Englishness or constructions of dominant narratives of English national identity.

Central to this idea of discourse and discursive articulation is the idea of cultural politics and dominance of the debate and discussion which Stuart Hall et al discuss in terms of hegemony or the practise of theory, translation and audience. Through this particular interpretation, discourse operates as a form of verification. Through repetition and reaffirmation, a particular discursive representation becomes legitimised as a justified 'common sense' means of understanding.

Laclau and Mouffe's analytical approach to the social constructivism of discourse is central here to understanding why an ideological approach to particular topics and attitudes frame understanding, particularly the competition for meaning within the social and different forms of articulation.

A wide selection of content and an ideologically generated discursive output will be critically analysed and examined within this body of work. Locations of discourse such as powerful and influential sections of the media, high profile political and social debate and discussion including social and political commentary will be utilised and examined as specific locations of discourse. However, this will also be accompanied by public opinion and attitudinal reactions and responses from sources such as opinion polls, surveys and interviews alongside analysis and interpretation of public displays of mood and opinion such as voting behaviour in relation to areas pertinent to this research.

The ideologically directed nature and the specific focus on particular ideological characteristics is why the arguments and ideas of political figures and commentators form an important and relevant unit of analysis alongside and as part of a wider discursive field relative to their intended area of focus. As Guy Debord (1998) suggests, once one achieves dominance over the methods of social and political discourse, one achieves a social and political verification for the universal recognition and verification of their views. In a disjunctive field of analysis, political and social commentators express particular ideologically constructed approaches to inclusivity/exclusivity and direct debate and produce a narrative in a contested field of meaning, yet they also reflexively articulate populist mood. This often operates in a symbiotic discursive feedback loop of message meaning and motive. One cannot view discourse through determinist or reductionist means as a simple top-down process; however, it is neither simply as bottom-up and instructive process either. Throughout this body of work, discourse will be discussed and understood as a complex, multidirectional and reflexive means to understand debate, discussion and the construction of contested conceptualisations of Englishness within the contemporary era which deeply inform understandings and interpretations of self, others and community.

## Contribution to Field of Knowledge

The crux of this research is not to try to find some definable sense of Englishness or essence of English national identity but instead to uncover and demystify the dominant defining characteristics of the discursive forces and symbolic positioning that this topic is situated within. To create, maintain and further a dominant sense of Englishness is a social, cultural, political and ideological process underpinned by a normalised and naturalised understanding and interpretation of place, history, community and people. Dominant discursive articulations of identity propose such a symbolic order. This is particularly applicable in the current case of Englishness and its discursive relationship to conservative representations of it as a naturalised and reified symbolic account. This work will develop the argument that within England, conservative ideological representations have almost become unquestioned and naturalised in its relationship and representation of Englishness.

Contained here is a synthesis of previous academic and empirical research and theory that will be applied to contemporary developments concerning identity politics within England. It will be suggested that developments and challenges to the British nation state such as devolution, debates around Europe, ongoing processes of multiculturalism, immigration and a wider context of globalisation have become dominated by a conservative response and narrative and have exposed and problematised conceptual definitions of England, English national identity and a sense of Englishness more than ever before. The culmination of these factors has made the question of Englishness unavoidable, immediate, confusing, contested and overtly ideologically motivated.

Conservative discourses of Englishness can be viewed as being informed by an anxiety of loss, a loss of empire, global position but also an anxiety of a sense of powerlessness in relation to a wider development of globalisation which includes processes of ongoing migration, a perceived blurring of cultural boundaries and economic uncertainty. Englishness has become reimagined within and in relation to a series of contemporary and long running processes and developments. This provides an ideological narrative through an essentialisation of culture, geography, history and a sense of nostalgia within a popular imagination and becomes a reterritorialised identity.

Although this can be viewed as an analysis of contemporary accounts of English nationalism, it is far more complex and nuanced than a simple study of nationalism. It draws from a series of unique and complex social, cultural and political developments particular to the geo-political environment and a very specific response and interpretation to these from a particular ideological standpoint.

A renegotiation of Britain has provided an opportunity for the conservative right to solidify its discursively dominant position within a reimagining of England. The inherent vagueness of Englishness has been left to be defined by reactionary forces on the political right. England or Englishness has largely become positioned as a political and cultural reactionary response to conceptions of Britishness associated with notions of cosmopolitanism, multiculturalism and outwardly directed civic and cultural values of inclusion. In other words, Britishness can be viewed relatively as more receptive to a differentiated population (arguably, this being historically a colonial necessity), whereas Englishness through a conservative dominated discourse has become far more exclusive. The paradox being that England is a very multicultural and pluralist society of immense and longstanding diversity.

Within the contemporary era, an Englishness based upon a liberal, modern, outward looking sense of inclusivity has arguably become sidelined, instead a narrative of essentialised dualistic myth, traditionalist conservatism has firmly established itself. Concepts of Englishness are arguably abstract, contextual and unstable entities, often contradictory, ambiguous and are constructed in a conceptual sense through the presence of ideologically constituted discourses. Discourses of identity and a perceived 'common sense' have become fundamentally entwined and dominated by a conservative interpretive position, one that relates to a deeply symbolic manner where meaning is attached to varying ideological reference points. In this regard, a national identity or narrative is discourse. It is a way of constructing meaning which influences and organises both our actions and the way we conceptualise ourselves, others and the community in which we live. This is the fundamental importance of why these social and political constructs must be examined and held to account.

It will be postulated that Englishness has developed into a particular conservative nationalism whose construction has led to an exclusive rather than inclusive identity. This has been reinforced and has positioned itself as the dominant narrative and means to conceptualise Englishness as an ideologically based identity. As Stuart Hall suggested, 'we only know what it means to be "English" because of the way "Englishness" has come to be represented, as a set of meanings' (Hall, 1995). To identify with being English instead of British (as research suggests the majority of English now do) is to imagine oneself metaphorically as there is nothing natural or genetic about this categorisation. It is a cultural, social and political process which becomes part of our essential narratives and natures. What these symbolic meanings are, how and why they are produced and are then able to carry such purpose is the very point of this body of work. This is not a top-down or bottom-up determinist process; it is one where the English as the symbolic community participates.

## Theoretically Situated Within Existing Body of Literature

In analytical terms, Englishness can be viewed as an empty signifier rather than an ideologically fixed category. Moreover, as a signifier, it is complex and fluid. It has been associated and expressed through a variety of different ideological and political approaches including socialist, radical and liberal representations. However, within a contemporary context, Englishness has become dominated by a defensive and insular conservatism. This does not necessarily equate to a manifestation at the ballot box; indeed, the political aspect is just one of a multi-level and interdisciplinary element that this work will consider. What is crucial is that as a dominant and normalised meta-narrative, this position incorporates the political as just one of its intersectional characteristics. Discourses surrounding Englishness constitute forms of national identity, yet these are informed by wider discursive processes taking place.

This body of research draws from and synthesises concepts of discourse theory from Laclau and Mouffe with post-structuralist concepts of identity and nationalism such as 'banal nationalism' by Michael Billig and 'imagined communities' by Benedict Anderson as a means to understand the conceptualisation of the nation in an abstract sense. At the same time, this research is concurrently informed by and located within specific social and cultural elements and political articulations within the English experience from cultural theorists such as Stuart Hall.

The particular interpretation towards discourse within this body of work is firmly located within the Laclau and Mouffe post-Marxist social and cultural analysis of discourse, not an economically reductionist or essentialist account. What is important to highlight here is that struggles over discourse concerning nationalism or national identity are not just about presenting the most attractive or representative perspective; it is about normalising a political position, idea or myth and establishing it as an intelligible ingrained characteristic. Therefore, the constitution of a social identity is an act of power, identity as such is power. From this perspective and relating back to the work of Stuart Hall but also Antonio Gramsci, hegemony operates as a dominant framework that rules out alternatives as being incoherent, illegitimate, incompatible, irrational or alien.

The theoretical application of discourse is necessary as it is primarily concerned with the production of knowledge. Knowledge is produced through the application of meaning within specific conceptual frameworks of understanding. Discourse is used to frame subjects or topics and how they are then viewed and imagined. This knowledge and understanding about a particular subject or topic produces very real consequences and effects. They establish normative modes, theories and perspectives of understanding, interpreting and verifying representations of reality. In this regard, all identities are open to contestation; thus, discourse becomes the means and method to establish a dominant sense of identity within a field of competing meanings.

Theoretical concepts of ideology and how it informs and constructs particular interpretations and understandings of identity formation will be applied, particularly from theorists in this field relevant to the context of identity such as Slavoj Zizek, Tariq Modood and Immanuel Wallerstein. This will not be an analysis of ideology, but rather, ideology will be situated within a post-political discourse dominated by a narrative of conservatism and characterised by an ideological normativeness of insularity, exclusion and a sense of defensive anxiety. In other words, Englishness will be analysed as a 'reactive identity' (Modood, 2013:52) within the context of ideological articulation through discourse.

It will be argued that a dominant sense of Englishness legitimises ideological structures of unrepresentativeness, inequality and exclusivity. Ideology and discourse determines how we can conceptualise identity or at least forms the boundaries of our imaginations however contested, nuanced and contingent this process is. Ethnicity, within a context of a dominant conservative social, cultural and political exclusive, discourse will be explored and applied from research carried out by writers such as Stuart Hall, Michael Skey and Gail Lewis. It will be demonstrated how discursive concepts of a conservative Englishness both feed upon feelings of anxiety, flux and perceptions of change and crisis while also relying upon and perpetuating these narratives to maintain its position of a dominant social and political discourse.

This body of work will also develop and apply the concept of 'symbolic demarcation lines' (Balibar, 2002:52) which are ideologically managed to provide a dominant sense of what England is and what Englishness means. A dominant conservative discourse of Englishness has become the taken-for-granted and illusionary, 'common sense' position. It also takes the position of an assumed empirical and objective view of society, politics and discursive concepts of Englishness.

Discourses of Englishness have become reliant upon, and are constructed around historically and culturally determinist and essentialist narratives. For social historians Linda Colley (1992) and Krishnan Kumar (2003), the historical submerging and potential emergence of a confident and assertive, cultural, social and political sense of Englishness is indeed indexed respectively to the decline of a sense of Britishness within a wider political and social context. It will be argued that as a general process, Britishness as a primary identity has become abandoned; meanwhile we are witnessing a concurrent prevailing dominance of a sense of Englishness within England. As an analysis and development of this perspective, the exploration of a dialectical relationship between processes of cultural hybridity and concepts of national identity from Jan Nederveen Pieterse and Pnina Werbner will be drawn upon while developing the paradoxical relationship between the existence of a highly multicultural society within a post-PC conservative discursive context from theorists such as Tariq Modood, Susan Condor, Roshi Naidoo and Partha Chatterjee.

Analytical concepts of traditionalism inform understandings of Englishness through a politicised historiographical identity. Writers such as Eric Hobsbawm, Helen Baxendale, Etienne Balibar and Gary Day will be applied and referred to as a means of contextualising what is meant when 'conservatism' is utilised in an ideological sense. However, from a theoretical approach of understanding and contextualising conservatism from post-imperial and post-colonial social and cultural discourses of British and English identity, Paul Gilroy, Ben Wellings, Colin Wright, Arthur Aughey and Simon Gikandi among others will be utilised to provide a framework of analytical reference points.

Chapter 1

# Discourse, Narrative and National Identity

This chapter will provide an analysis of the intrinsic links between identity, representations of national identity and ideologically created constructs that are informed and experienced through discourse and narrative. In particular, constructs of belonging and identity will be explored. National identity will be evaluated as an artificially and ideologically constructed articulation alongside discourses and narratives as expression of national belonging and ownership. The production of knowledge around space, place and nation will be investigated within the context of identity, community and lived experience. A perceived 'crisis of identity' and the construction of narratives in which this is viewed and responded to will be examined alongside constructions of 'common sense'. In essence, the overall theme will explore a sense of nation as narrative and the construction of naturalised and normalised narratives of identity.

## Discourse

Before we can begin to critically engage with how theories of discourse can help inform and conceptualise perspectives of nation, nationalism and national understanding in the context of Englishness in the early 21st century, we first need to explore understandings of what discourse actually might mean, entail or be constructed as. This section will outline the theoretical parameters of the term discourse, present aspects of the debate surrounding this concept and offer a way to negotiate the discourse or ideology argument. Contained within this section will be an ongoing analysis of the intrinsic links between identity, nationalism, ideology concepts of common sense and theory surrounding discourse. The intent here is to discuss the importance of analysing discourse and its use as a means to critically engage and understand contemporary concepts of Englishness in relation to and within the context of the following chapters and finally offer an insight and an analysis of the relationship between discourse, nationalism and identity formation.

**Constructing Realities, 11–25**
**Copyright © 2024 Stuart Cartland**
**Published under exclusive licence by Emerald Publishing Limited**
**doi:10.1108/978-1-83797-545-720231002**

## Discourse and Narrative

Discourse is the construction of a framework for understanding a particular subject area within a particular context. Discourses located within nationalist narratives provide a sense of belonging to a community or individual with an identity which one may find supportive in times of perceived uncertainty, difficulty or crisis. Stories and myths (often linked to place) are essential to the construction of identity; however, they often operate in a realm of ambiguity leaving room to function in a range of contexts. Indeed, these narratives, as Michael Morden (2016) points out, can be treated as unifying paradigms. Often when narratives are referred to within the subject matter and context of nationalism, it has a strong relationship to emotional structures and responses. It can ignite emotive responses individually and collectively, and therefore, 'narrative is especially central in the cognitive organisation of the self and individual identity' (Morden, 2016:452).

Developments and ongoing processes such as Brexit, devolution and immigration frame a specific politicised narrative through which these contemporary, but also historical, topics are viewed but also deeply inform a specific identity narrative and ideologically motivated national discourse. The focus on specific subject areas facilitates the construction and maintenance of an ideologically and politically conservative paradigm for understanding Englishness and concepts of national identity within a wider context.

Narratives form an important resource for individuals and groups in the construction of identity. It provides a self-legitimising and often self-replicating feedback loop of understanding and meaning which happens on both an individual and group level, making narrative a critical cognitive instrument for making one's own lived experience legible. Nationalist narratives, to be effective and to resonate, are often characterised by persuasion. Carefully cultivated national narratives seek to resonate with existing social norms and values but also operate within an ideological framework for understanding and providing action towards desired conclusions.

Crucially, in terms of a conservative discourse of Englishness, narrative can operate as a discourse of defensiveness or loss which can therefore be easily identified within conservative forms of nationalism. In this format, 'nationalists observe societal change and lament the collapse of the known order. National triumph is identified only in the distant past, ever more obscured by the irresponsible transformations wrought-often- by the Other' (Morden, 2016:459). For example, this can therefore be used to characterise overly simplistic prevailing dominant anti-immigration and anti-EU discourses within conservative conceptualisations of Englishness in the early 21st century. Alternatively, this can also be applied to almost all aspects of understanding our sociocultural lives from art and music to international relations.

## Discourse and Nationalism

Discourses of nationalism and national identity provide a space for unlimited ideological social significance. Concepts and theory surrounding discourse will be used in conjunction with other theoretical and conceptual means to critically engage with Englishness in the contemporary period. Discourse theory is explored within this chapter as a tool to unpack contested and challenged political and ideological conceptualisations of identity. Arguably, all identities are open to contestation, thus in regards to nationalism discourse becomes the means and the method to establish a dominant or hegemonic sense of national identity. Nationalism and concepts of national identity can be viewed as an expression of ideology; in fact, nationalist rhetoric can be seen to cloak the ideological core. The contested, debated and challenged nature of discourse and the substantive content in which people identify with it is what makes national identity an area of investigation so vital to evaluate and understand.

Discourse informs and leads us in how we interpret and understand national identity but is also a manifestation and expression of identity; in other words, national identity and nationalism are a direct product of discourse around the topic or subject of nation. At the same time, as there can be no complete, unified and entirely suitable national identity, there can be no complete, unified or entirely whole discourse, 'all discourses and articulations are necessarily open ended or fuzzy' (Oswell, 2006:56). All identities can also be viewed as being relational and dependent to varying extents on systems of difference within which they reside or operate.

As a general working definition of the term, discourse (in relation to concepts of nation and national identity) can be described as the creation and articulation of dominant forms of narrative used to give an understanding of our social, cultural and political world, couched within an ideological framework. To widen this theoretical conceptualisation of discourse even further, Ernesto Laclau and Chantal Mouffe (1985) would argue that in fact all knowledge is located within discourse whereupon one could insist that through application and articulation it is therefore always open to interpretation and manipulation. The term discourse is primarily concerned with meaning or, as Laclau and Mouffe (1985) refer to it as, the structured totality resulting from articulatory practice; in other words, discourse is 'real' not just theoretical or ideological in character.

What is significant is that concepts of discourse offered by theorists such as Laclau and Mouffe are not hamstrung by purely economically determinist conceptual frameworks yet refer to theories of a more cultural and social-oriented discourse. This can prove to be of vital significance when trying to understand forces behind the persistence of national identities in the 21st century.

Discourse, especially in relation to concepts of nation and nationalism, is significantly involved with the specific attachment and meaning of signs and practices, or as Purvis and Hunt state, 'the individual social networks of communication through the medium of language or non-verbal sign-systems' (Purvis and Hunt, 1993:485). Along these same theoretical lines, Stuart Hall offers the following definition of discourse to mean: 'sets of ready-made and pre constituted "experiencings" displayed and arranged through language' (Hall, 1977:322). What is common throughout all definitions of discourse is that it is something that frames experience and understanding and gives meaning to experience. Discourse provides a medium through which thought, meaning and action and alternately, action, meaning and thought take place, hence why such significance can be placed upon discourse when considering concepts of nation, nationalism and national identity.

It is important to be aware, however, that discourse is not a closed concept. Laclau and Mouffe (1985) refer to discourse in a post-structuralist sense in that it is a concentration of floating signifiers which actors compete to mould into meaningful configurations. Concurrently, Purvis and Hunt (1993) describe it as constituting a system or structure with variably open boundaries between itself and other discourses. To put it quite simply, discourse is primarily concerned with meaning and representation which is constantly contested through competing discourses. As Stuart Hall suggests:

> Discourse is a group of statements which provide a language for talking about– i.e. a way of representing– a particular kind of knowledge about a topic. When statements about a topic are made within a particular discourse, the discourse makes it possible to construct the topic in a certain way. It also limits the other way in which the topic can be constructed.
>
> (Hall, 1994:291)

Discourse, therefore, is not just one statement but many statements working together to form a 'discursive formation' according to Foucault (1972). Often these statements work together because they imply a relationship to one another and support one another. 'Discourse is about the production of knowledge through language' (ibid); however, this production of knowledge is itself also produced through social practice, or in other words, meaning is attached through practice. It is ideological and political in character. As arguably all social practices entail meaning, all social practices have an element or aspect of discourse and therefore discourse enters into and influences all such practice. In this sense, class, gender, sexuality and ethnic background don't have any essential identity and meaning. The exercise of power implies the attempt to construct lines of inclusion and exclusion, to articulate one identity with another but also to separate one identity from a particular constructed other image of society.

Discourse is about making sense in different positions, situations and perspectives and often discourse can be produced by many individuals in a range of different institutional environments and contexts. Discourse essentially frames subjects or topics and how we view them, imagine them or discuss them. Key to understanding the position taken by Foucault is to realise that discourse always draws from, incorporates or subsumes other discourses and are always in one way or another in a process of evolution or change. The relationship between the different statements within a discursive formation must be systematic and follow rationally; Foucault describes this as a 'system of dispersion': whenever one can describe, between a number of statements, such a system of dispersion, whenever... one can define a regularity... we will say... that we are dealing with a discursive formation' (Foucault, 1972:38).

## Discourse and Ideology

Discourse and ideology generally describe a means to analyse and understand our social worlds, experiences and existences. It can therefore be suggested that, 'ideology and discourse refer to [...] social life, the idea that human individuals participate in forms of understanding, comprehension or consciousness of the relations and activities in which they are involved' (Purvis and Hunt, 1993:474). This simplistic analysis or interpretation can mask quite significant and important differences. In essence, by using 'ideology', we are limiting ourselves to a partial understanding. Ideology can be interpreted as conceptualisation, whereas discourse can be viewed as conceptualisation but also articulation and practice. Discourse is the articulation and practice of ideology; therefore, it would be meaningless to focus solely upon ideology. Discourse also highlights the constant state of contested meaning, whereas 'ideology is a vain attempt to impose closure on a social world whose essential characteristic is the infinite play of differences and the impossibility of any ultimate fixing of meaning' (Barrett, 1994:260).

Discourse operates in the realm of nationalism in what Hastings (1998) calls, a 'system of belief'. An example of the political discursive position is provided by Stuart Hall's analysis of Thatcherism in that it, 'combines the resonant themes of organic Toryism – nation, family, duty, authority, standards, traditionalism-with the aggressive themes of a revived neoliberalism – self-interest, competitive individualism, anti-statism' (Hall, 1979:29 in Hall, 1988). To take this example further, although Thatcherism was hegemonic in its intention (in regards to political ideological developments and 'real' lived conditions and experiences), its aim as a project was to (successfully or not) 'restructure the whole texture of social life, to alter the entire formation of subjectivity and political identity, rather than simply to push through some economic policies' (Barrett, 1994:243). Examples of political ideology expressed through hegemonic political discourse are not unique to certain or particular geographical location or historical epochs; it defines the very essence of nationalism and national identity. However, in this instance, conservative ideological hegemonic political discourse is engaged directly in contemporary struggles and claims over 'Englishness'.

Foucault believed that ideology was based on false statements, or rather, ideology is largely based in and around social, political and moral statements which are rarely ever simply true or false. The way we describe 'the truth' or 'the facts' interferes with deciding what is true or false and is bound up with subjective values or normative assumptions. Ideology is therefore littered with such attached meaning, as Stuart Hall points out, 'most social scientists now accept that our values enter into all our descriptions of the social world, and therefore most of our statements, however factual, have an ideological dimension' (Hall, 1994:293). Discourse can therefore be viewed as ideology and ideology as being manifested as or through discourse. By referring to ideology alone, we are only giving half of the process of articulation or representation.

Discourse is not ideologically neutral as this would be impossible even though any given particular discourse could be used and adopted by various groups with different backgrounds or interests; hence, a discourse does not necessarily simply reflect interests of any particular class or gender. Discourse presents (an often oversimplified) understanding of 'truth', 'fact' and 'reality'; moreover, 'each society has its regime of truth, its "general politics" of truth; that is the types of discourse which it accepts and makes function as true' (Foucault, 1980:131). Discourse is never just a mere description; discourse is pre-loaded with what we already know about the world in order to give some sort of explanation or understanding. Discourse is also often pre-loaded with certain purposes, aims, objectives, motives, interests and strategies, all of which are almost never consciously apparent. All objects of inquiry or knowledge are then discursive but importantly not everything is discursive, only that which can be seen as or presented as knowledge. Discourse is constitutive of social relations in that all knowledge, all discussion, all argument takes place within a discursive context; this is of central importance when considering concepts of identity and community within a national context.

A good explanation of understanding the post-Marxist (and to a varying degree, postmodernist) perspective on ideology and discourse is given by Jacob Torfing when he summarises the work of Laclau as, 'we do not have any access to the real world except through its construction as a discursive form within more or less ideological systems of representation' (Torfing, 1999:113). Discourse can, therefore, be viewed as the negotiated, differential and signifying attachment of meaning and symbolism, and this informs social interaction and provisional and relative understanding particularly in relation to concepts of identity and national narratives. In others words, it is a means of creating truth or certainty in an environment where this is absent.

## Discourse and Power

In a Foucauldian sense, discourse can be viewed as power, and discourse is a means of articulating and exercising power. Competing discourses fight over how something can be viewed, interpreted or discussed and is directly linked into a contest over power. Discourse can be viewed as always operating in relation to power and contestation. Accordingly, truth doesn't necessarily need to be 'true' to be seen as the most valid argument or option when discussing discourse, more often than not it is the more persuasive or convincing argument or play to emotions, popular assumption or stereotypes, for instance. It is not just empirical evidence that can make something 'true' or as accepted knowledge but rather power. As Foucault points out:

> We should admit that power produces knowledge... that power and knowledge directly imply one another; that there is no power relation without the correlative constitution of a field of knowledge, nor any knowledge that does not presuppose and constitute... power relations.
>
> (Foucault, 1980:27)

In other words, 'those who produce the discourse also have the power to make it true – i.e. to enforce its validity, its scientific status' (Hall, 1994:295). This can be why Foucault believed in an intimate and integral relationship between discourse, knowledge and power. Foucault famously stated that 'knowledge is power', but what can be viewed as equally important to highlight is that 'truth' is power and discourse is an exercise of power through using and organising concepts of 'truth'.

The early 21st century has been widely termed a post-truth era. Indeed, this has been hailed and even used by those on the right to foster narratives that have very little resemblance to events with much success. Truth or fact can be either inconvenient or created to provide validation. When we apply this to competing discourses of Englishness for instance, it becomes recognisable how deeply this impacts upon concepts of legitimising and justifying differing interpretations of what Englishness or English national identity might be. For example, it was not just the message of 'get Brexit done' that provided such an overwhelming majority for the Conservatives in the 2019 general election, arguably it was through dominating the national narrative and control of cultural experiences that enabled the Tories to pick up so many seats, including in former Labour strongholds. Elections are not won on practical manifesto pledges but rather through dominating the national narrative, regardless of the real life experiences or the seemingly counter-intuitive support given.

Discourse is the practice of power and meaning (and for producing truth or fact if so desired). Power (particularly according to Foucault) is in everything we do; discourse is a means of expressing this. Truth is also a provisional aspect of our social existences and the relationship between truth and power is intrinsic, 'truth isn't outside power' (Foucault, 1980:131), but also power produces 'truth' or an accepted version of 'truth', and this is the function of discourse. Providing 'knowledge' or 'truth' is also the power to define identity through the control or use of discourse, hence why knowledge can be viewed as power. Discourses are ways of talking, thinking or representing a particular topic, position or situation. They produce 'knowledge' about a particular subject; this knowledge then influences social practices and attitudes and therefore has real effects and consequences, 'in other words, power is inscribed within discourses, not outside them' (Purvis and Hunt, 1993:488).

Frederic Jameson (2007) expands upon this understanding of identity in that the concept of the image of the self and identity asserts and enforces the conviction that it corresponds to the concept, to its object as a self-perpetuating and self-understood being. This relationship is conceived and plays across a broad variety of epistemological fantasies and illusions, from notions that it represents some inner truth and knowledge represented and imagined through signposts and markers to the way that it is self-legitimising and justified within itself.

Competing discourses as articulations of ideology, politics and a world view, for instance, therefore fight over how something can be viewed or interpreted and presented as factual knowledge. Those that prevail determine what is viewed as 'truth' of a particular situation; this can be viewed as the production of hegemony or discursive dominance. Hegemony, in short, creates, establishes and maintains dominant normative modes of thought, perspective and understanding, without necessary evidence or substance to support it, the EU referendum campaign being a case in point here. Wild and unfounded claims such as being able to deliver £350 million to the NHS per week or the inevitability of Turkey's secession to the European Union and the implied freedom of all Turkish citizens to live and work in the United Kingdom became fact. Claims, in this regard, become truth irrespective of evidence to the contrary. 'Truth' is created through fantasy, symbolism and simplistic binary understandings; this is where its power lies.

Michele Barrett neatly states, 'hegemony is best understood as the organisation of consent – the processes through which subordinated forms of consciousness are constructed without recourse to violence or coercion' (Barrett, 1994:238). In a classic Marxist sense, this is viewed as existing for economic reductionist purposes alone; however, to apply theories concerning discourse to conceptualisations of nation and national identity, we should move away from such a perspective and take more of a Gramscian view of hegemony as existing in the political, cultural and social authority sense of the word.

This Gramscian theory of hegemony can thus be viewed as the production of a collective identity instead of a collection or collaboration of pre-constituted identities. Through the use of hegemonic discourse and the articulation of values, judgements and normative ethics, distinct boundaries are reinforced; this can be referred to as a process of 'discursive homogenisation' (Koobak and Thapar-Bjorkert, 2012). This notion of a normalisation of hegemonic discourse can be viewed as a similar process to Banal Nationalism as raised by Micheal Billig (1995) in that a certain sense of dominance is created and maintained by everyday exchanges and structural relations, but also it borrows from Benedict Anderson's *Imagined Communities* (1983) as it is the dominant fantasies or illusions which narrate our social existence. As Stuart Hall notes, 'in a world of competing discourses, ideology is an expression of meaning's contingency. Paradoxically, however, ideology's ultimate ambition is to achieve banality or "common sense"' (Hall, 1998:1062).

From the Gramscian perspective, hegemony corresponds to or represents the consensual aspect of authority; this can be conceptualised through the idea of 'the organisation of consent' as articulated by Gramsci. This refers to the promotion of a particular hegemonic structure or framework of interpretation and the normalisation and acceptance of basic values and meaning which is also achieved at the same time as the marginalisation and stigmatisation of opposing positions or discourses. Such a process is historically relative and contingent as certain symbols or meaning can change and fluctuate. Acceptance or rejection of certain ideas, groups, lifestyles and politics can change. Hegemony, then, is not domination as a physical or repressive force. It can be viewed as working through consensus, through gaining and organising consent, this can be referred back to Adorno and Horkheimer (1944) and the culture industry.

Cornell West highlights the structural dynamics of modern political discourse in its quest for truth, knowledge and dominance within the realm of identity and representity (identity expressed and articulated through representation) within the politics of modern nationalism, 'the structure of modern discourse [is] to be the controlling metaphors, notions, categories and norms that shape the predominant conceptions of truth and knowledge in the modern West' (West, 2003:300). Discourse is thus a power struggle over the framework and structure of what influences, shapes, informs and legitimises concepts of national belonging, direction, nationalism and national identity. In other words, the hegemonic project of today's politics of the conservative right represents an example of '"hegemony-as-normalisation" as opposed to a "hegemony-of-domination"' (Smith, 1994:40). What is critical here is that struggles over discourse concerning nationalism or national identity are not just about presenting the most attractive or representative perspective; it is about normalising a political position, idea or myth and establishing it as an intelligible ingrained characteristic.

Discourse equates to the limiting of acceptability and the construction of frameworks of structural positioning. As Anna Marie Smith suggests, 'hegemonic social structures condition identity formation – by normalising some subject positions and excluding others' (Smith, 1998:157). Hegemonic positioning in regards to social structures such as the mass media or the education system normalises accepted or unaccepted norms and roles or rather a naturalised structural positioning. It can be viewed as evident that social structures such as the mass media, 'help to establish and maintain the hegemony of specific political groups by producing and promulgating social myths and imaginaries' (Torfing, 1999:210). Laclau (1990) furthers this position by commenting that the constitution of a social identity is an act of power, identity as such is power. Hegemony as a dominant framework in this sense therefore rules out alternatives as being incoherent, illegitimate, incompatible, irrational or alien.

In the event of a perceived 'crisis of identity', the dominant discourse must aim to position itself not just as one alternative among many but as the only possible framework for the resolution of the crises (Smith, 1998). In this sense, such a framework seeks to explain, to compensate and to abolish whatever crisis it claims to be able to solve. It will seek to be organically linked as a 'common sense' choice in the given situation, it will become a metaphorical dimension, it will as Laclau comments, be the 'principle of reconstruction of the entire ideological domain' (Laclau, 1977: 103). In crises of identity subjects may look to identify with certain political or ideological positions, not just because of certain exhibited virtues or values but also a sense of continuity. This could help to explain why in times of crisis conservative, reactionary or traditionalist positions can widely exert influence.

Once identity is institutionalised, it therefore becomes a means of a popular interpretive framework through which social reality and individual social positioning is lived. However, the work of hegemonic or dominant discourse is never finished; it remains endlessly challenged by alternatives (other discourses) and is engaged in a constant state of maintenance of its authority, which will in turn from time to time include incorporating elements of competing discourses. In a postmodern sense, this is why discursive power is so important – it frames the argument before the argument has even begun. This process is a battle over political, social and cultural symbolism and meaning in relation to identity.

## Discourses of Common Sense

Concepts of common sense, much like related concepts of truth, are sites of discursive dominance. Common sense is a contestation for an accepted and normalised subjective ideological positioning, particularly in relation towards the interpretation of key social, political and cultural subject areas. Hegemony can be used to describe the ways and methods which consent is generated and organised, which in turn is directly related to the mechanisms and processes which knowledge and beliefs are first, produced, and second, disseminated. As Benedetto Fontana (2005) explains, the hegemonic or dominant conception is one that becomes established as the 'common sense' of the people. This conceptualisation forms the dominant discourse of civic life, social understanding and national narrative. It is a political concept; it states the organisation of culture and is at once the organisation of power. Common sense as an organising conceptual principle, 'proves exceedingly difficult to challenge as it is the manifestation of conceptual hegemony and antagonistic practices at the empirical level' (Sutherland, 2005:197). The struggle for the 'common sense' position is an integral part of the constant struggle for the dominant or rather hegemonic ideological position as it marks 'the moment at which an ideology triumphantly becomes "banal"' (Sutherland, 2005:194).

Common sense also operates in terms of a myth of national identity or community. For example, Prime Minister Boris Johnson referring to a 'good solid British common sense' (BBC, 2020). The point being that he is stating that there is firstly an agreed upon common sense that applies to all 66 million people in the United Kingdom, secondly that it is distinct from other nations concepts of common sense and thirdly, he is making a value judgement on a moral case for 'good' here. This is clearly very problematic and is indeed a fantasy. Moreover, Johnson is probably aware that such a thing is a fantasy, yet 'common sense' is a useful tool, operating both as instructions to 'do the right thing' (entirely subjective reasoning) and as norms and codes within society-constructed values enforced and normalised through dominant discourses of how things or instances are politically positioned.

Dominant narratives are essentially political ideologies, but they're also vague common norms and values that can be hijacked and manipulated for political ends. When Johnson refers to a distinct British common sense, it can be interpreted that he is relaying and reinforcing his Brexit narrative of a superior, self-reliant and distinct nation. On the other hand, this could easily be laughed off as conjecture, but only maybe by those who actually believe and buy into the message and image that Johnson is conveying. The point being is that the message of a 'good solid British common sense' is largely accepted and dominant within wider society, so to question this is a political and ideological act in itself. Indeed, if you are not deferential to prevailing values then ergo, you have no common sense.

The struggle for hegemony, or rather, discursive dominance is a political and ideological struggle. Politics in this sense consists of the ongoing attempt to construct identities and mobilise them around discursive 'tropes' (Leggett, 2013).

Common sense is the ground upon which ideological battles can be viewed as being fought and contested for dominant or popular acceptance or consent. This operates as the practice of hegemony, or rather, the creation and maintenance of hegemonic national narratives and discourse. Laclau and Mouffe (1985) insist hegemony must be viewed as the articulation of identities in the context of antagonistic social relations. This directly relates to contestation over discursive dominance. Hegemony, therefore, must always be viewed as being contingent and relative to opposing discourses. As Leggett (2013) highlights, identities are relational, that as such they always hold the potential for antagonism. In this sense, discourses therefore over identity are always contested but always project an element of pluralism.

Common sense, as an ideological conceptualisation, is often positioned against an 'other' or an oppositional position. When common sense is positioned within a conservative discursive realm, it is often symbolically positioned against pejorative understandings of competing discourses and groups such as; 'the looney-left', 'political correctness-gone-mad', 'wokeism' or 'metropolitan elites'. Although aimed as competing discursive positions, this 'other' is located outside of a conservative dominated conceptualisation of common sense however illusionary and contradictory it might be. To narrow this group down even further, north London boroughs such as Highbury and Islington are often referred to by the conservative right, in socio-economic-political terms, as a centre for so-called metropolitan elites or as Conservative Home Secretary Suella Braverman described as 'tofu-eating, Guardian-reading, wokerati' yet, 'Islington is the 14th most deprived local authority in England' (Lewis, 2016:9). On the other hand, 'elites' are also conflated with faceless and unaccountable bureaucracy, often with the added caveat of 'unelected'. For example, during the Brexit campaign, the European Union and MEPs were the ire of such oversimplified discourse; however compared with the House of Lords, for example, MEPs do face a public vote. In essence, common sense is another means of creating a reality to fit within an ideological agenda.

It is often right-wing and conservative commentators that are most likely to decry the influence of the elites and their supposed sway of unaccountable power over the population, indeed social media and independent TV channels (such as GB News in the United Kingdom) have turbocharged these accounts, yet politicians or political commentators from this persuasion are the most likely to be from the most privileged backgrounds and are located nearest to social, cultural, economic and political power. It can be suggested that the dominant discursive representation of so-called elites from a conservative perspective operates as an ideological foil and facilitates a rhetoric and narrative of an illusionary common sense position. However, from an entirely contradictory context, for instance, 'Jeremy Clarkson, leading his Bloke Battalions from a big house in Oxfordshire, or the privately educated former City trader Nigel Farage, leading his People's Army from the pub' (ibid). This attempt at being perceived to be in-touch with ordinary people and being diametrically opposed to unaccountable elites is mere symbolic posturing and positioning, yet posturing and positioning that is entirely politically and ideologically based and couched within a dominant conservative conceptualisation of a specifically constructed common sense.

Within this context, a Gramscian approach to discourse, politics and ideology can be used to understand concepts of 'common sense' in relation to and contextualised within everyday practices and assumed social and political understandings. This can be used as a means to conceptualise concentrations of discursive power within a contemporary social and cultural environment. Common sense is a highly political and ideological tool used in conjunction with a particular political and ideological world view. It is not an objective and rational account or approach; indeed, it can be viewed as exactly the very opposite yet this is how a dominant discourse portrays its interpretation and understanding of it. The use of common sense within the context of national identity is an articulation of ideological, political, social and cultural hegemony. It is an appeal to or represents a naturalised, dominant, social, cultural, political narrative or understanding. It also is used in conjunction with an illusional moral community built around and containing specific values. Symbols, institutions, associations and rhetoric become identified with and 'internalised to such an extent that they constitute common sense, the ultimate goal of any movement pursuing a nationalist project' (Sutherland, 2005:193) or to be commonly considered as the legitimate position of understanding and interpretation by a wider audience.

Through this understanding, common sense does not and cannot exist in an objective manner. However, this is how it is appealed to within the creation or maintenance of a particular discourse or narrative. It is an appeal to an illusionary objective and common understanding of a topic or subject, yet this is ideologically constructed within a discursive realm. In this regard, it is important to point out that rationality or logic and common sense have little to do with one another and therefore must not be reduced as such; however, this is precisely what they are discursively and rhetorically reduced to and are equated to.

## Rhetorical Constructions

The use of emotive and symbolically charged language is key in the construction of dominant forms of discourse in relation to concepts of common sense. Rhetoric is used as a vehicle for the articulation of discourse; it engages in a power struggle with competing discourses to represent a legitimate dominant narrative – this can be clearly identified, for example, within contemporary Conservative government policy proposals and statements regarding the welfare state and the distribution of benefit payments or an approach to illegal migration. A clear rhetorical and symbolic link is made between government spending, debt, urban decline, poverty and a 'culture of dependency' on welfare payments and an implied link of choosing to not work and receive benefit payments as a social choice linked to a perception of moral decline and exploitation of the welfare system. As an example, this is an ideologically laden discourse in the clearest sense. It is an ideological attempt to attribute a subject position to the reader and to create an illusionary 'common sense' solution or position, readers are encourage to adopt this 'persuasive version of reality' (Hastings, 1998:209) as their own.

Rhetoric is often used in conjunction with concepts of common sense; it engenders belief and understanding without knowledge. It is also a form of communication that arises from emotive persuasion. Rhetoric cannot instruct and teach by means of reason or logic; rather, it is the technique by which the many or the populous is persuaded by myths and stories (Fontana, 2005). In other words, rhetoric is much like concepts of common sense. Through rhetoric, dominant discourses can be articulated, achieved, maintained and naturalised. Dominant discourses concerning Europe or immigration for instance are dominated by appeals to an assumed common sense through the use of rhetoric. These are entirely politically and ideologically created concepts. Statements or headlines such as 'a victory for common sense' are political and ideological discursive positions. Regardless if the 'victory' makes any rational or economic sense, the point is that it legitimises, justifies and naturalises a specific discursive position and therefore becomes hegemonic and dominant.

Concepts of nation and the attachment of national identity provide the theoretical space and the vehicle for the attachment of meaning, legitimacy, representativeness and 'truth'. Discourse is (in relation to this) the expression and articulation of identity, and dominant forms of nationalism are expressions of hegemonic discourse on the nation. As discussed earlier, hegemonic or dominant discursive frameworks do not necessarily need to contain truth or knowledge but what they do possess is power. Through this use of power, discourses of nationalism and identity can be used to perpetuate mythical social hierarchies and dominate not only how we view ourselves but also each other, or rather nationalist discourses play a central role in providing the myths and social imaginaries that organise and guide social, cultural and political action and meaning.

It can be argued that the creation and perpetuation of social imaginaries can dominate discourse on the topics of nation and national identity. As highlighted, the nation is a mythical and illusionary space where through discourse meaning and symbolism is attached. Through political discourse significance, value, character and legitimacy become politically charged in relation to competing discourse. Political symbolism and the attachment of meaning become sites of struggle and contestation for dominant forms of identity. Dominant discursive positions condition the formation of identity by normalising specific positions and excluding or de-legitimising others. Just as Foucault described the relationship between power and discourse – power creates discourse to perpetuate and maintain specific knowledge and understanding which in turn validates through the exercise of such dominant or hegemonic discursive positions certain truths.

One of the key issues regarding the theoretical debate around the use and application of discourse theory is that, in effect, it can end up viewing everything as discursive or as discourse. As Oswell comments, 'if the difference between one discursive system and another is itself discursive, then all difference is discursive' (Oswell, 2006:60). In other words, we can become trapped within discourse itself which reduces all social practices to a formal equivalence. Discourse can be viewed as over-reliant upon a linguistic and post-Saussurian symbolic model; we can therefore find it difficult to refer to anything that is not discursive.

However, discourse is not just an objective neutral description or narrative and it is not just concerned with political ideology. Discourse is conceptualisation but also articulation and practice of identity and its contested nature. Discourse analysis provides a useful means for us to understand, conceptualise, experience, think and represent ourselves in relation to contested and created concepts of national identity. It informs us and provides us with 'knowledge' about the subject and frameworks for understanding (in particular) concepts of Englishness in the contemporary era and implementing a critical analytical interpretation of it. It affects how we think about it, how we view it and how we position ourselves in our social world.

## Narrating the Nation: Nation as Narrative

To critically understand the driving forces behind dominant discursive representations of Englishness, we must examine who is narrating the nation and by what means. In many respects, the nation exemplifies contemporary conceptualisations of social and cultural formation; however, these are often arbitrary social, cultural and historical inventions which are used specifically to serve symbolic purpose of representation. For example, 'the recurrent metaphor of landscape as the inscape of national identity' (Bhabha, 1990:295), serves to emphasise a naturalised quality of national affiliation and collective expression through a sense of naturalised topographical timelessness.

Nations are, according to Homi Bhabha (1990), narrational constructions. They are essentialist interpretations and constructions which attempt to define and naturalise nations by the means of drawing from ideological representations of homogenous, innate and historically continuous traditions and dominant cultural and social formations. Therefore, nations exist in an imaginative space, or as Bhabha (1990) suggests, they only fully realise their horizons in the mind's eye. However, it is from these traditions of political and social thought that the nation emerges as a powerful historical idea.

The nation, as a concept or as a political realisation, is not stable. It can only come into being through cultural signification and representation. Symbolism and meaning need to be 'fixed'. This 'fixing' of meaning provides an important element in the means of constructing a dominant national narrative or discourse. Instead of an element having multiple values or interpretations, it becomes fixed as a central discursive element such as the symbolism of Europe, immigration or the welfare state within conservative discourses of Englishness. This operates as an ideological articulation through such specific attachment and therefore utilises ideologically potent symbolic elements which are relative to the subject and concepts of Englishness. Moreover, what is also required within this process is the performativity of language in the narratives of the nation (Bhabha, 1990). Language is used as the articulation of ideology. It is appropriated, consolidated and used to naturalise much the same as Judith Butler (1990) theorised in relation to gender. The arbitrary sign of language is historicised. According to Anderson (1983), this is the process of signification which he suggests comes before narrative. National discourses are loaded with the weight of ideologically symbolised words; this emphasises its inherent instability. The concept of the nation and its corollary national identity is bound by such a constant struggle of instability which requires constant reaffirmation and reinforcement; therefore, the concept of nation or identity is always fluid and never stable.

Key elements are used to articulate and represent meaning. Often even the most mundane and banal become the most powerful and taken-for-granted symbols. According to Bhabha (1990), even the concept of the English weather 'encourages memories of the "deep" nation crafted in chalk and limestone; the quilted downs; the moors menaced by the wind; the quiet cathedral towns; that corner of a foreign field that is forever England' (Bhabha, 1990:319). This normalises a concept of the 'long past' and intertwines them with cultural articulations of national interest, national distinctiveness and establishes cultural and historical boundaries of the nation. The naturalised and normalised uniqueness of a relationship between idiosyncrasies of the weather and Englishness also informs and acts as a symbolic reference to historicity, exclusivity and a manifestation of the self against the other. These imaginative geographies which are encapsulated within relationships to weather yet are used to represent and personify the nation itself.

Moreover, this powerful form of emotive and relatable discourse makes Englishness a mediated reality in that it is constructed around particular and specific symbols and motifs where participation, involvement and engagement in our social, political and cultural environment is based largely around observing someone else's observations of what constitutes a desirable sense of reality. This concept relies and relates to Jean Baudrillard's (1994) theory that we inhabit an age of hyper-reality. Dominant forms of discourse impel a particular interpretation and understanding of our social world, and this is largely achieved through mediated means where we can contextualise our existence and give meaning to the complexities and contradictions to the world around us in an often overly simplified and easily manageable manner.

Chapter 2

# Globalisation and Discourses of Englishness

This chapter will look at how specific processes have affected and created essentialised notions of culture, nation and identity. Globalisation will be briefly sketched out and understood as a process of an increasingly interconnected, interdependent and interrelated world and experience. In particular, it will use two theoretical approaches to examine how discourses of identity have been shaped in this relation. Firstly, deterritorialisation will be examined as a general theory that interprets a process of globalisation as undermining the political, cultural sovereignty of the nation and has also accelerated a decline of national and local identities. This theoretical approach will be evaluated as informing responses to perceived threats such as large scale immigration but also attitudes towards Europe and a sense of English or British exceptionalism. This approach will be evaluated as a historically shallow and culturally narrow understanding of identity and belonging. The second theoretical approach that will be used here to counter this is reterritorialisation. This will be used to explain a rise in exclusionary identity politics as a response to a deterritorialisation understanding of globalisation. It will examine a specific rise in boundaries, borders and difference in lived experience but most notably within concepts of identity. This analysis will also explore the rise of nostalgia and the nation operating as 'mythscape'.

It will develop the idea that dominant discourses of Englishness in relation to globalisation are conservative, nostalgic and defensive, especially in regards to notions of cultural globalisation. This chapter will show that arguably the dominant perspective of globalisation in relation to concepts of Englishness is a negative one, particularly centred around the perceived effects upon society, culture and a sense of national distinctiveness within the context of a conservative discursive representation of immigration, social change and an increasingly hybridised society. By engaging with writers and theorists such as Tomlinson, Hutchinson, Cameron and Palan, Gills and Calhoun, it will be suggested that dominant conservative discourses of Englishness are essentially a defensive ideological narrative or position, operating as a reactionary response to a continual and often rapid process of globalisation.

This chapter is not intended to set about providing an exhaustive and definitive account of globalisation, suffice to say it is widely recognised that globalisation is indeed happening, is widespread and profound. What will be briefly sketched out

**Constructing Realities, 27–49**
**Copyright © 2024 Stuart Cartland**
**Published under exclusive licence by Emerald Publishing Limited**
**doi:10.1108/978-1-83797-545-720231003**

is a working understanding of the process commonly known as globalisation and then move on to its relationship with national identity, specifically how it interacts with contemporary notions of Englishness. This approach generally views globalisation first and foremost as a process rather than something that is achieved and that it is to varying degrees reversible and negotiable rather than predetermined (Hopper, 2006). What is also key to this understanding of such a specifically complex process is that it is a multidimensional, intersectional and interdisciplinary process not dominated by or predetermined by any one facet of contemporary social, political and economic life.

Moreover, it will examine how and why globalisation may be interpreted negatively from a conservative perspective and why such dominant notions of Englishness could be considered as being anti-globalising in nature yet also produce a particular contradictory and paradoxical relationship. It will be suggested that perceptions of anxiety and threat dominate contemporary understandings and discourses of Englishness in relation to globalisation. The assertion here is that such a position in fact reterritorialises notions of Englishness in relation to competing perspectives of globalisation while deterritorialising English national identity within a re-emergence of a popular essentialised notion of Englishness as essentially bound up with ideological concepts of belonging, longing, boundaries and nostalgia in an era of fluidity and modernity.

All nation states and various multiple nationalisms have wildly divergent relationships and interactions with a general process of globalisation. There is no one-size-fits-all universal experience or character of globalisation; however, what needs to be analysed and explored is the key theoretical approaches to globalisation alongside contemporary forms of nationalism, particularly in regards to a sense of English national identity. The initial part of this investigation will begin with how globalisation can be viewed as representing or signifying a transgression and the removal or significant erosion of boundaries (deterritorialisation) and the undermining of the nation state and national distinctiveness.

## Deterritorialisation

First wave theories of globalisation view this process as rapidly undermining the political and cultural sovereignty of the nation and predicting the demise of the nation state, erosion of cultural difference and the decline of national and local identity. It is very hard to pin down contextually what we specifically mean by these terms local, national and regional. In the case of national borders, this relates to political and also cultural perceptions and ideological reflections or aspirations, as Robert Holton comments, 'geography in short, is cultural as much as political' (Holton, 2005:106). Distinctions along national geographical lines are in fact sociopolitical matters and often products of cultural and political discourse. Normative cultural associations also affect how we view territorial distinction or how they are presented and represented, e.g. West and East. Therefore, it is difficult to separate and compartmentalise territory and those who inhabit it into neat distinctions, such ideological attempts often result in concepts of national cultural homogenisation and can then be viewed as sociopolitical reductionist narratives. In many respects, it can be argued that globalisation has actually helped to emphasise the futility of such an exercise and has highlighted the increased awareness of the world being a single place. John Tomlinson points out that, 'the way in which national identity is experienced within globalisation is, like everything else, in flux' (Tomlinson, 2003:276). This flux and contextualised subjectivity links back to Anderson's (1983) *imagined communities* and the social, cultural and political imaginary of dividing an interrelated, interdependent, cross fertilised place through the discursive language of adherence, classification and prescribed ideological boundaries between different peoples, places and histories.

Whether globalisation is perceived as a positive or negative force, process or phenomenon will directly affect the subjective analytical approach taken. In a conceptual and theoretical sense, this is the challenge posed, however what is key is understanding this challenge and not just assume a position of general polarisation. Holton (1998) points out that the underlying analytical challenge is to balance a sense of the dynamic significance, historical periodisation and enduring effects of globalisation with a sense of its limits, set by counter-trends. It is also important to understand when considering globalisation and its relationship with national identity is to contextualise globalisation as not being an all-conquering and homogenising force driven by a logic of capitalism or Western cultural imperialism. Often in debates, surrounding globalisation and its effects upon the nation polarised positions (globalisation as either being a positive or negative force, benign or hybridising, diversifying or homogenising) are often casually taken up. One of the most dominant analytical approaches to this relationship and process is termed as deterritorialisation.

This theoretical approach can be briefly defined as involving the declining significance of territorial borders in inhibiting the spread of interacting and interdependent global forms of economy, politics and culture (Martell, 2008). Globalisation is viewed as a process constituting a threat to national distinctiveness, independence or sovereignty and can be seen as embodying a conservative or traditionalist approach to or perception of the nation or national identity. Although it is also arguable that the reverse is also valid – that such an outlook would also promote a sense of reterritorialisation (which will be investigated later) in that a defensive position towards predominantly social and cultural forms of globalisation will generate the promotion and defence of certain specific aspects of national distinctiveness.

From this perspective, globalisation can be viewed as a general process of cultural decentralisation in which the nation state has become decentred through the proliferation of global flows and disjunctures in a transnational or deterritorialised fashion (Appadurai, 1996). The result can be seen as the emergence of a new social imaginary, one where imagined national communities (Anderson, 1983) have become imagined worlds and where globalisation has provincialised the national (particularly cultural) space. Globalisation in relation to culture can be viewed as, 'paving the way for a more open conception of place and culture challenging the bounded spaces of nation-states' (Hopper, 2007:18). Processes and impacts such as individualisation, detradititionalisation and deterritorialisation are a direct result of increased levels of globalisation. However, these more contemporary developments can be viewed as conflicting with much older established assumed structured notions and perceptions of histories and cultures. John Tomlinson (2004) points out that the key to its cultural impact is in the transformation of localities themselves. In other words, an accelerated process of deterritorialisation works to weaken fixed notions of the bond between culture and place. Globalisation challenges us to rethink old conceptions of culture; in this sense, culture cannot be thought of as having inevitable conceptual ties to location as meanings are equally generated by the flows and connections between peoples and cultures. Through this perspective, cultures exist in an environment of almost global fluidity, that borders do not confine culture to any one space or location.

David Held et al. (1999) describe globalisation as leading to an increasing deterritorialisation of politics, rule and governance, meaning that culture itself is increasingly deterritorialised. While the notion of deterritorialisation can be seen as problematic, globalisation can be seen as producing an opposite process, one of reterritorialisation. As a consequence, the result can be that a process of cultural deterritorialisation is or has taken place and that in this sense culture is not constrained, restricted or defined by place, indeed the cultural experience is in many ways 'lifted out' of its traditional locality (Pison, 2005). For example, increased levels of movement of peoples in the form of diaspora communities, migration or enforced asylum or exile have moved culture from the specificity of place. Meanwhile, a process of reterritorialisation offers an often reactionary response emphasising a specifically and often exclusive and bounded social and cultural experience and imagining.

A process of deterritorialisation has exposed culturally narrow concepts of national identity. In other words, perceptions of national identity being inherently grounded and bound up with the nation state, national cultural distinctiveness, homogeneity and notions of distinct boundaries have increasingly become undermined and contested. That is not to suggest that dominant discourses of national identity are not based on these factors. The perception that globalisation is leading to some degree of deterritorialisation has only served to foster a reassertion of a belief of such qualities; indeed, Tomlinson points out, 'the kernel of truth in the claim that national identity is threatened by globalisation lies in the fact that the proliferation of identity positions may be producing challenges to the dominance of national identity' (Tomlinson, 2003:274).

It can be suggested that there are a multitude of versions of the general theory that there was an assumed existence during the 19th and 20th century of a 'classical' nation state which was politically sovereign, militarily autonomous, territorially bounded, culturally homogenous and economically self-reliant. Therefore, all such versions of this perspective assume to one degree or another of an erosion, increasingly powerlessness, destruction or transformation of a 'classical' nation state in the contemporary era. It could also be suggested that there is a general weakening of the nation state through mass migration and the multicultural nature of societies – this recasts the identity of the nation state and creates internal 'others' and enemies of immigrants and refugees, for instance. However, globalisation can be viewed as really being the globalisation of modernity, and modernity being the harbinger of identity (Tomlinson, 2003). This harbinger of a modernist and inclusive identity can be viewed as a challenge to traditionalist or conservative concepts of such 'classical' concepts of national identity, and if this is indeed the case, then a strong reterritorialising backlash is therefore to be expected.

The theory of deterritorialisation operates as a powerful concept in relation to globalisation and national identity in that it conceptualises an increasingly fluid and borderless cultural, economic and political process but also it may indeed provoke many different responses. Responses such as 'localism' may become emphasised, also more general social developments such as cosmopolitanism and more open pluralistic societies, although arguably the dominant response in terms of English national identity is a defensive position and reassertion of a conservative and traditionalist concept of Englishness within the context of a 'classical' imagining of the nation state. Although a general process of deterritorialisation may be theorised to be undermining concepts of culture to be perceived through the prism of the nation state and the positive cultural acumen that this might generate (Appadurai et al.), what it arguably might actually provoke in terms of concepts of national identity is in fact the very opposite.

John Hutchinson points out that, 'nationalism as an ideological movement is episodic, triggered by a sense of crisis that the nation is in decline or under threat' (Hutchinson, 2005:135). Episodic resurgences are triggered by sudden perceived threats to the primary goals identified by Smith of autonomy, identity and territorial integrity of the nation. Such threats can be interpreted through contemporary conservative discursive contextualisations as: the European Union (autonomy), multiculturalism (identity), devolution (territorial integrity) and can be viewed as an explanation as to why concepts of Englishness in the contemporary era are viewed as being in crisis. A general perception from a conservative discursive position is that Englishness and England is situated within such crisis. Moreover, such crisis don't necessarily go away or disappear; they reconstitute themselves within evolving contexts and challenges to conservative discursive dominance.

As outlined in the previous chapter, it is theorised that the idea of nation and community allows people to imagine a community within the territory of a modern nation state, this being a relatively recent development. At the same time, the idea of 'nation' is the dominant way in which concepts of culture and society are imagined and characterised within the contemporary west. Therefore, cultural and political implications of globalisation are a primary concern when considering the impact of a process of globalisation. The oft-used terminology of post-nationalism, ethno-nationalism and transnationalism have become key analytical approaches as a means to evaluate and understand the impact of globalisation; however, the main question here is: are the cross-border flows of globalisation leading to a breakdown in the coherence of national identities or, quite the converse, their resurrection? Within the context of contemporary processes of globalisation, it is important to understand that how the 'nation' is imagined directly affects and can determine how positively or negatively we view the effects of a wider process of globalisation. How we imagine the nation, or more specifically in a modern political context, the nation state shapes and informs how we engage with it as essentialising and territiorialising cultural relations which will therefore be increasingly affected or impacted by (the theoretical view of) deterritorialising global flows.

What directly influences and affects nationalist discourse on the wide ranging topic of globalisation is how 'culture' is imagined and related to that of nationhood and nationalism. This is what Archer et al. terms, 'the whole "nation-state-to-international" matrix of cultural relations established by the globalisation of the terms of the Peace of Westphalia of 1648 as a result of Western imperialism' (Archer et al., 2007:116). Paradigmatic understandings of culture are, therefore, related to and embodied through national or nation-based understandings of culture, which inform the modern social imaginary. Nations provide the template for a general understanding of culture, and the nation state provides a context for cultural global relations; this informs the context concerning understandings of globalisation and national identity.

Such understandings and awareness refer to the *volksgeist* or the unique spirit of the nation which has been carefully constructed through discourse in terms of, 'romantic myths, histories and literary traditions, and which became widely communicated through the channels of the mass media of the time' (Habermas, 2000:286). Here, Habermas can be seen to draw from key theories such as the invention of traditions and national symbols (Hobsbawn and Ranger) and from imagined communities (Anderson). Crucially, Habermas highlights that the foundation to national cultural identity is artificially created as a national cultural narrative. In this regard, it can be said that nation states embody collective expressions of national self-ascription and development in an historical sense. As such, they act both as political and cultural boundaries.

Within the wider cultural context, processes of globalisation can also be viewed as challenging, embedded and dominant Eurocentric and Westernised concepts of cultural dominance. Craig Owens (1985) points out that globalisation (and in more general terms postmodernism) has provoked a crisis of cultural authority specifically of the authority vested in Western European culture and institutions. Theoretical interactions, conceptualisations and interpretations with contemporary globalisation can be termed as decentred, allegorical and schizophrenic. However, a discovery of the plurality of cultures is never a harmless experience, as Paul Ricoeur comments:

> When we discover there are several cultures instead of just one and consequently at the time when we acknowledge the end of a sort of cultural monopoly, be it illusory or real, we are threatened with the destruction of our own discovery. Suddenly it becomes possible that there are just others, that we ourselves are an 'other among 'others'.
>
> (Ricoeur, 1965:278)

As a counter to the perspective that globalisation equates to Westernisation, globalisation can be viewed as breaking the monopoly or hegemony of Western cultural dominance in the imaginary realm of cultural identity. In the cultural realm, globalisation needs to be understood as a fluid notion or process. This acts in contrast to notions of culture being inexorably associated with a fixed locality, as static or operating under the guide of boundaries and borders. The claim that nations are as old as humanity itself or that they are a natural characteristic of the human condition distinctly and neatly separated culturally and ethnically is disturbed by such a realisation of cultural globalisation.

What is undermined here is not only the hegemony of Western culture but also a sense of naturalised national distinctiveness, 'what has toppled our claims to sovereignty is actually the realisation that our culture is neither as homogenous nor as monolithic as we once believed it to be' (Owens, 1985:58). This can, therefore, engage with the apparent crisis of culture and identity associated with globalisation and its effects upon a perceived declining nation state such as Britain. The decline of the perceived hegemonic control of the West is also inextricably linked to the decline and demise of a perceived hegemonic notion of nation and national culture and identity. The realisation that 'our' culture is neither as homogenous or as monolithic as we once believed can lead into denial or an apparent retreat into a mythical imaginary world of nostalgia of an illusionary 'golden era'. The demise of national and cultural dominance and homogeneity is as much internally ideologically interpreted as externally perceived – it can be the very real consequences of globalisation, but also it can be a realisation that 'our' nation or culture was never such a homogenous entity as we have been led to believe.

When we analyse dominant discourse and notions of a supposed 'national' culture often, this does not incorporate the plurality of the very essence of culture, particularly when it is understood through an assumed and normalised conservative narrative. As pointed out by John Tomlinson, 'globalisation disturbs the way we conceptualise "culture". Culture has long had connotations tying it to the idea of a fixed locality' (Tomlinson, 2004:27). In relation to this, Jean Francois Lyotard (1979) comments that what the advent of postmodernity has constituted is the breakdown in a homogenous national discourse, as globalised culture has little in the way of a binding national narrative or motive legitimising functions. However, such a loss and dispersal can be seen to be exactly the elements required for a conservative nostalgic turn from the present; this then lends itself to conservative and traditionalist understandings and perceptions of culture in terms of globalisation.

Arguably, culture is created over a long historical period involving multidirectional global flows of interactiveness, interconnectedness and interdependence. Using casually determined concepts of territorially bounded or inherently distinct cultures in an era of accelerated globalisation is problematic as using such definitions become contradictory, irrational or can easily be transcended. Globalisation, in relation to culture, can be viewed as, 'paving the way the way for a more open conception of place and culture challenging the bounded spaces of nation-states' (Hopper, 2007:18). If the claim of modernity is that cultures are naturally national, then arguably postmodernism could claim that the context has now shifted to cultural globalisation which is transforming such a narrative and means through which national cultures are produced and reproduced.

## The Paradoxical Relationship Between Globalisation and National Identity

Globalisation, as already pointed out, is a problematic, contradictory and ambiguous concept. Theorising or applying this in conjunction with an equally problematical concept – national identity – is then ultimately going to provide theoretical and conceptual difficulties. Globalisation and national identity/nationalism can be viewed to have a paradoxical relationship in that it can be characterised by contradictions, ambiguities and discursive convenience. Ulrich Beck (2001) articulated such frustrations by stating that globalisation is one of the most rarely defined, the most nebulous and misunderstood, as well as the most politically effective terms in any language. It is difficult to contextualise a process that encapsulates our very existence, history or transcends boundaries as some sort of neat process yet as also an omnipresent theme. Even if it was possible to single out specific disciplines to be analysed, globalisation as a concept never neatly complies or dispenses with contradiction, 'if defined in terms of "the process by which the world becomes a single place", globalisation has also its ambiguities, irrespective of its silencing of economic, political or cultural parameters' (King, 1991:12).

The first aspect to consider when analysing such a potentially contradictory relationship between globalisation and national identity is not necessarily the political and ideological conflict but the discursive. Laclau (1989) comments that all identity is relational in character, and therefore, the ideal conditions of closure for such a system is never achieved as the social is groundless; all identity is therefore more or less a floating signifier. Without falling into the trap of cultural relativism, society can then be understood as a vast argumentative texture and narrative through which people construct their own reality; this is how a paradoxical relationship between concepts of national identity and globalisation operates and why dominant discursive content is so contested and contradictory.

Identity boundaries and definitions are nuanced, extremely flexible and ambiguous, so much so that it is doubtful whether any fixed answer can be attributed or found. Different functions, definitions, categories, criteria, goals and context through different specific interactions alter any workable meaning concerning identity. Indeed, 'national identity is constantly (re-)constructed through discourse, practices and everyday interactions' (Sindic, 2008:13). National identities and their definitions are narrational and rhetorical tools often used to mobilise people towards specific ideological and political goals or sustaining specific political and social projects. As Cameron and Palan (2004) point out, the most important lesson to be learned from the immense power of the narrative of globalisation is not that it is entirely theoretically and empirically secure, but that it is partial, fragmentary and fluid and that those who benefit most from it often have little or no idea of how it actually functions. As previously stated, national identities can be conceived as 'floating signifiers' (Laclau, 1989) and ambiguous in that they are unable to constitute themselves towards any closed and precise totality based upon a complete absence of socially objective consensus. Identities and signifiers based around specific social and political practices and sites of ideological conflict suffer systematic contradictions and ambiguities. This may provide some answer as to why in the case of globalisation such a paradoxical relationship exists.

Globalisation can be conceptualised as representing the ever-present threat to conservative or traditionalist notions of national identity as representing or bound up with concepts of flux, change and many aspects of modernity, such as immigration, supranational organisations, technological change, mass communication, cosmopolitanism and multiculturalism, even though globalisation is not exclusively a product of modernity at all. In this sense, a pejorative discursive characterisation can be viewed as 'the phenomenon of symbolic representation' (Laclau, 1989:81) where a particular signifier (globalisation) comes to represent a chain of equivalent signifieds.

A paradoxical relationship between conflicting signifiers poses problems for the maintenance and promotion of homogenous concepts of national identity, especially between the conflicting notions of globalisation and hyper-modernity on the one hand and notions of a conservative, traditional and nostalgic discourse of national identity on the other. As Gary Day highlights:

> There are many reasons for this anxiety: loss of empire, the spread of mass culture, the blurring of class boundaries, globalisation, immigration and devolution among them… another reason is the expansion and elevation of commercial values by which all others will be judged.
>
> (Day, 2011:253)

This anxiety and potential conflict exists beneath a paradoxical relationship; between free market individualism in an era of hyper-modernity on the one hand, and a village community-esq nostalgia of a mythical unchanging past and the political manifestation of a reterritorialised conservative politics of identity on the other.

Moreover, the rapid transformation of society through increased levels of globalisation can be seen to have an incommensurable relationship with more conservative notions of national identity, as Day (2011) suggests, England, Englishness and the economic transformation of Britain generally, and England in particular since the 1970s has generated a cultural identity that is slowly being replaced by a corporate one. In this sense, it can be said that the language of commerce determines public discourse. Cameron and Palan (2004) describe the paradoxical nature of the private economy of the nation state and some degree of traditionalist national identity as constituting a dilemma: it must reconcile the needs of the market with the often conflicting demands of a national society that continues to demand and expect social cohesion and economic prosperity. Social cohesion can be read as some degree of community, shared values and norms;

however, what the neoliberal market or economy demands is individualism. Arguably, the Conservative project of the 'big society', as an example, was created to bridge this chasm, yet it can be seen to be merely political and ideological tokenism which delivered nothing in real terms except rhetoric.

Ideological repackaging of cultural, historical, economic and political circumstance is key in fostering any sense of dominant national identity discourse in relation to globalisation. A contextualised discourse is positive in relation to business and individualism yet also positions itself towards a yearning for a village-community brand of social bonding. This can be viewed as historical and social cherry picking and amnesia – it is positive towards Thatcherite free market individualism that systematically destroyed cultural and community cohesion but also cultural conservatism and strong social bonds of an idealised rural idyll. It ignores or rather discursively airbrushes out aspects that do not fit into its mythical imagery of an idealised national identity, industrialism, mass politics, urban poor, mass migration, ethnic minorities or gender equality to name but a few.

Jurgen Habermas neatly highlights the underlying paradox within the relationship between globalisation and contemporary dominant discourses of English national identity in that:

> Neo-conservatism shifts onto cultural modernism the uncomfortable burdens of a more or less successful capitalist modernisation of the economy and society. The neoconservative doctrine blurs the relationship between the welcomed process of societal modernisation on the one hand, and the lamented cultural development on the other.
> (Habermas, 1985:7)

This national cultural domain is then saddled with the perceived negative attributes of cultural modernity: lack of social identification, hedonism, lack of obedience, narcissism, the withdrawal of status and achievement. Hence, all negative aspects through the socially conservative, traditionalist perspective are lumped on to the effects of cultural globalisation, while all the perceived positive aspects of economic globalisation are accepted, praised and are seen to be evidence of the success and triumph of neoliberalism/conservatism.

The nature of the state (within the context of a globalised world) has fundamentally changed in that, 'the nation state persists as an idea, but the content of that idea has fundamentally altered as different organising principles have come to the fore with the widespread acceptance and adoption of the narrative of globalisation' (Cameron and Palan, 2004:110). Politically and economically nation states have had to change to adapt to globalisation (this is often referred to in speeches about being 'competitive in a global marketplace', or adapting to 'global challenges' or providing a 'flexible workforce'), yet this can be seen to further create contradictory or antagonistic relationships with traditional or conservative notions of national identity.

In this regard, the idea of the state has fundamentally altered from a 'public' principle of universal inclusion to a 'private' principle of competitiveness; therefore, it can be seen that the state has become a private economy alongside the individualisation of social responsibility. A relationship based on these terms distinguishes between different populations across and within state boundaries according to their relationship to the norms of economic globalisation. This implies the idea that the nation state is no longer based on territorial, cultural, social, linguistic or any other form of identity associated with the confined boundaries or demography of the nation state, but instead on particular types of economic participation associated with the sovereignty of the 'competition state' (Cameron and Palan, 2004). Globalisation can be viewed as representing a zero-sum game since it is external and is able to transcend all national boundaries; nation states have no option but to accept and adapt to it. Narratives of openness, competitiveness and fluidity are therefore inbuilt to the national economic terrain and environment. Globalisation does not spell the end of the nation state, but it does pose difficulties and contradictions for national identities which are based on exclusivity, ethnic homogeneity and concepts of national social unity based upon nostalgic myth.

The fragmentation of conventional social practices associated with the nation state and a relationship of the private economy pose specific problems for national governments, especially those with a conservative political, social and cultural agenda. Established boundaries and frameworks are confronted with contradictions in that,

> The *histors* of the sovereign nation state are currently in the unenviable position of having to maintain a formal belief in the territorial state and faith in the security and coherence of its boundaries, while at the same time accommodating a *praxis* of sovereignty which is fractures, commercialised and partial.
>
> (Cameron and Palan, 2004:128)

In terms of this contradictory relationship between globalisation and national identity, the New Labour government arguably had much less trouble with bridging this ideological gap mainly due to the more modernist, progressive and inclusive character of British national identity which it sought to promote. This found very little contradictions with the nature of globalised market forces and economy as compared to Conservative/conservative notions of national identity.

The contradictions and paradoxical relationship between globalisation and contemporary English national identity can essentially be viewed as Britain, and in particular England being an intensely globalised space, one in which the dominant neoconservative free market political and economic discourse views globalisation as a positive process and an opportunity, yet on the other hand, the same dominant and prevailing conservative ideology views globalisation through a social and cultural discourse as a distinct threat and problem. In an historical, cultural and social context, Britain (and specifically England) has been an extremely globalised and globalising nation. In essence, England, or more generally Britain, is defined by globalisation – a long history of economically and politically generalising forms such as imperialism, colonialism and global trade and capitalism but also as a receiver of generalising cultural globalisation and successive waves of migration. Indeed, as Stuart Hall points out, 'it is almost impossible to think about the formation of English society or of the United Kingdom and all the things that gave it a kind of privileged place in the historical narratives of the world, outside of the process that we identify with globalisation' (Hall, 1997:173).

Conservative notions of Englishness are arguably built upon things that have disappeared or are in the process of rapidly fading into obscurity, mainly since an accelerated process of globalisation post-1945: economic global supremacy, large-scale industrial base, global military might and influence, direct and indirect imperial control and a stronger sense of union towards an internal and external national project. Contemporary reality presents a very different picture. Arguably, it can be observed that dominant discourse concerning Englishness has not moved with or kept pace with social, cultural, economic and political developments.

Crucially though, Britain does not have a monolithic relationship to globalisation (Martell, 2008). Scotland, Wales and Northern Ireland have distinctly different attitudes, histories and relationships with globalisation than England. The smaller, less politically, economically and culturally powerful UK nations tend to be generally more positive in their approach to globalisation in that they express a more positive approach to Europe and a less positive approach to Atlanticism and British global interventionism. Anglo-American, neoconservative and free-market capitalism involves a culture of individualism, which finds less traction in Scotland and Wales in particular. In general, Scotland and Wales are particularly more pro-Europe than England as they have more to gain politically and economically from a strong relationship with the European Union and are arguably more inclined to bypass the UK nation state (to which they have less an allegiance to and stake in) than the English. All of these themes will be addressed in detail in following chapters, yet at this juncture, a distinction has to be made between England and Britain in relation to globalisation.

As an entity and as a national culture, the United Kingdom rose with and is arguably declining with one of the successive epochs of globalisation, an era dominated by and defined by the economies and cultures of powerful nation states. In this sense, the past informs and frames our perception of the present, none more so than the relationship between processes of globalisation and English/British national identity. This can go some way to explain why an English national identity is so heavily indebted to concepts of nostalgia of a supposed 'golden era' and hostility or anxiety towards the present, as Krishan Kumar states, 'in whichever direction they look, the English find themselves called upon to reflect upon their identity and to rethink their position in the world. The protective walls that shielded them from these questions are all coming down' (Kumar, 2003:16). Arguably, when they try to resurrect those walls, such as the United Kingdom's exit from the European Union, it soon becomes apparent that the fantasy and myth does not live up to reality.

Any sense of English national identity is torn between the widely perceived glories of the past and anxiety towards the present and future. It must also be considered that the present and future places a sense of English national identity in a very ambiguous and conflicting position. Any sense of contemporary dominant English national identity is strongly related to the past; however, globalisation presents the problem of situating and contextualising this within the present, which is a significant departure from idealised notions of perceived former glories. As Martell (2008) points out, English national identity is more elusive than national identity for the Scots, Welsh or Irish and most of mainland Europe because as an imperialist nation, the English developed a sense of externally oriented missionary nationalism and less of an internal sense of national identity. The English have more trouble identifying themselves in the post-imperial era than other nations. For the English, the loss of empire calls for a new reassessment of identity, one in which it has yet to fully come to terms with both in an internal (the United Kingdom) and external (the European Union, global) sense.

## Reterritorialisation

Although it has been articulated and theorised that an accelerated process of globalisation is eroding the cultural, political, economic and social authority and relevance of the nation state and concepts of national identity, what is also occurring is a contradictory or contrasting process of reterritorialisation. As pointed out, it is often argued that the significance of national identities is on the decline due to increasing globalisation; however, national identities are still a key feature of our contemporary world and are likely to remain so despite the alleged fragmenting effect of globalisation and its associated processes (Sindic, 2008). Moreover, it can be argued that in relation to some of the key themes associated with a perceived threat to the nation state and national identity posed by an accelerated process of globalisation, reterritorialisation operates as a reassertion and reinsertion of nationally based identities in response to political, cultural, economic and social deterritorialisation. This functions much like a two-way disjunctive flow of globalisation but however through a nationalist cultural perspective – as much as globalisation can be viewed as a process of deterritorialisation creating alternate identities to the nation state, a process of reterritorialisation reinforces national identities bound to conservative notions of the nation and nation state.

While globalisation might be theorised as a ‘world of flows’ according to Appadurai (1996) and Castells (1996), Archer et al. (2007) argue that in fact these flows are not and cannot be deterritorialised as is often asserted. This notion suggests the lingering imaginary of the ‘fixed nation state/territory cultural nexus’ is now somehow transcended; instead, cultural relations are conversely being reterritorialised. It can be postulated then that we are witnesses to and participants in a massive two-fold process involving, as Roland Robertson points out, the interpenetration of the universalisation of particularism and the particularism of universalism (Robertson, 1992) or in other words, the explosion of social difference and a revival of boundaries along ethno-nationalist lines.

The paradoxical relationship between globalisation and national identity can be seen to contain a cultural element in that global forces seem to create and reinforce local cultures and identities (Pison, 2005) as well as undermine them. Instead of the prevailing view that national culture is a victim of globalisation, crucially globalisation can also be seen as the contemporary catalyst for nationalism or as Craig Calhoun states, 'globalisation can lead to renewed nationalism or strengthening of borders' (Calhoun, 2008:429). Indeed, globalisation can be seen to act to provoke a nationalist backlash through concepts of 'threat' and 'undermining' of the nation state and national identity. The creation or reinforcement of an ideological narrative through a discourse of national identity provides a framework of how to position oneself and one's nation within the contemporary context of globalisation.

It can be suggested here that the victory of the 'Leave' campaign in the 2016 European referendum was such an expression and articulation of a generally anti-globalisation (against the free movement of people across borders and the withdrawing from a widely perceived European superstate) reterritorialisation which projected a particular dominant national narrative and sense of identity. As Charles Leadbeater comments, the vote to leave could be viewed as being predicated on 'a sense of narrative' (Leadbeater, 2016:18) and not on practicality or rationale, particularly in relation to the economic arguments presented. An increasingly assertive sense of English nationalism 'may be the price that we have to pay for a sense of democratic control over our lives. This was a vote to reassert nation state democracy in a time of globalisation' (ibid).

Globalisation as a general process is often taken out of context and viewed as a specifically contemporary issue; however, in this sense, nationalism can be viewed as an articulation and manifestation of globalisation. What the concept of nations or nationalism can be seen to do is to create a sense of stability and security and positions itself as an historically embedded narrative linked to concepts of community and cultural identity and destiny. Nations or nationalism, therefore, provide a narrative of meaning and understanding, however one which often feeds off and results in a negative and defensive anxiety about such perceived threats or challenges.

In essence, this is why a process of reterritorialisation in terms of a discursive narrative concerning concepts of English national identity is essentially conservative, traditionalist and nostalgic in character. This response can be seen to be a form of resistance to a culturally deterritorialising process often characterised by a reactionary retreat into a defensive reimagined and bounded entity. However, as pointed out earlier, in terms of discourse concerning the nation and its relationship with globalisation, it is a contradictory and paradoxical relationship. It is openly welcomed and engaged with on one hand, yet on the other, it is often viewed quite differently. It is not necessarily a matter of being pro or anti-globalisation; it is the paradoxical character of this in terms of its relationship with identity and dominant discursive concepts of the nation.

## Englishness in the Contemporary Context of Globalisation

The relationship between globalisation and concepts of national identity has the potential to be dominated by a conservative backlash and a sense of longing for cultural belonging and boundaries in an age of fluidity. This can, therefore, lead to a deep sense of cultural anxiety, which can manifest itself through an ideological narrative of conservative tropes and dominant forms of discourse. A response of this kind can also be seen to actualise itself through the promotion and maintenance of borders and boundaries both tangibly but also discursively – politically, socially and culturally. A perceived neurotic reactionary need for boundaries and essentialised notions of culture and territory within the popular imagination can be seen to be fostered by dominant forms of discourse in the relationship between aspects of globalisation and national identity, where dominant forms of discourse can be fed by both top-down and bottom-up forms of self-perpetuating ideological narratives. In other words, for conservatives and those on the political right, globalisation affects a deep sense of national recoil.

Dominant discourses of Englishness (particularly social and cultural concepts) in relation to globalisation can be seen to be dominated and defined by a conservative, nostalgic, defensive and negative approach. However, from an ideological perspective, paradoxically the Conservative Party are both characterised by a culturally nostalgic and insular approach on one hand yet deeply economically globalised on the other. The basic rationale behind this approach, especially in relation to cultural globalisation, is that a process of globalisation represents key features that popular conservative notions of Englishness are not – modern, fluid, open to change, cosmopolitan and urban, to name but a few. Yet in an economic sense, the Conservatives are ideologically situated within an ongoing process of globalisation. Therefore, there exists an inherent tension between being culturally nostalgic, defensive and insular while being economically globalised.

This operates almost through a reactionary view of colonialism and imperialism, to occupy a space of global dominance and economic control while denying the freedom of movement and cultural melange that such interconnected and interdependence entails. These narratives are borne out time and again by the right; it expects to dominate, exploit and interact with a hyper-globalised world, yet metaphorically speaking, it doesn't want it in it's 'own backyard'.

Modern cultural heterogeneity (particularly within England) often stands diametrically opposed to conservative hegemonic notions of an imagined sense of English national identity. Debates and discussions of Englishness often lead into notions of a sense of loss of cultural unity or an erosion of national identity; yet combined with the very real and immediate perceived challenges posed by globalisation, any anxieties concerning such an ambiguous and contradictory identity can become much more heightened and frenzied.

A discursive interpretation of cultural formations and social processes that obsessively demand a holistic vision of society fixed upon historically arbitrary social and cultural boundaries will find a tension and perplexity in a narrative of living within the reality of modern global fluidity. A sense of loss or fear can be traced to what Archer et al. describe as living in 'the contemporary onslaught of neoliberal globalising forces and the concomitant transformation of nation-state functions upward and downward' (Archer et al., 2007:130). This can be viewed as signalling a rapidly growing context of destabilisation, threat and humiliation and a scramble to regroup 'based on what Cocks suggests is an 'impending sense of loss' of control over the processes most affecting individual and collective lives' (ibid). This has affected the English, a sense of English national identity and concepts of Englishness specifically. Arthur Aughey (2007) relates this to a double English tragedy. Since the sense of a world historical significance has been lost, the cultural inheritance of this legend has become a sense of 'crippling cultural absence' (Aughey, 2007:94). Dominant narratives of Englishness, therefore, can be viewed as running counter to prevailing trends and fundamentally impact a sense of identity.

Key to dominant notions of English national identity – world prestige, power, dominance and historical importance have become the very fountain of uncertainty and precarity, faded glory, ambiguity and irrelevance. The other side of being everything and being located historically turns out to being nothing. As key conservative thinker Roger Scruton (2000) observed, globalisation has been felt more keenly in England in the sense that they are really living nowhere. Englishness and insecurities concerning globalisation have become an inward looking crisis of identity looking for new patterns of belonging yet vacated of any meaning or relevance. The void of national and cultural anxiety is depicted quite aptly when Aughey comments, 'even though we're obsessed with leaving the country and talk nothing but holidays abroad, we react with xenophobic terror to the thought of losing our national identity. If only we had an identity to lose' (Aughey, 2007:95). Although concepts or notions of English national identity exist, the point is that these are mainly based upon things that are seemingly abstract and irrelevant in an era of globalised modernity and can be seen to be deeply unrepresentative or have any real relevance to modern society or cultural forms.

Within the conceptual context of reterritorialisation and a revived or responsive discourse, national identities can be seen within this context of insecurity and crisis as being episodic and highly significant, especially in an ideological sense. This is a key factor when considering contemporary notions of Englishness. Perceived threats, fears and insecurities feed into cultural anxieties concerning concepts of the nation (either real or imagined). Wider political, social or economic issues such as devolution, the European Union or more cultural and domestic topics such as immigration or multiculturalism set the current framing of the form dominant discourse takes and the debate over English national identity and directly pins down the main factors or issues where such ideological discourses are articulated. Areas of perceived 'ontological uncertainty' (Archer et al., 2007:122) and insecurity escalate cultural anxiety on one hand yet reinforce defensive conservative positioning's on the other.

If globalisation has not destroyed the nation state, one reason for this can be the resilience and emotive qualities of nationalism, especially in its ethno-nationalist form. This can be viewed through the ethno-nationalist metaphor of 'awakening' being inextricably linked to a 'people', 'since [forms of] ethno-nationalism regards itself as an organic expression of popular consciousness, it is regarded as rooted in nature as well as history' (Holton, 2005:117). This idea or notion lends itself very keenly to conservative or right-wing notions of English national identity, especially in relation to forms of cultural globalisation – this is then linked to ideological concepts of people, nature and history and notions based on narrow concepts of national inclusivity and citizenship.

Conservative concepts of Englishness are often characterised by a culturally defensive xenophobic position in relation to a process of cultural globalisation. Discussion of the limits of national cultural representation and homogenisation/heterogeneity perspectives indicates the complexity of relationships between the global, regional, national and local. As suggested by Holton, 'none of these is predominant in any simple senses while each retains a significance, albeit in some kind of inter-dependent relationship with the others' (Holton, 2005:117). Moreover, Arjun Appadurai's (2001) concept of globalisation operating as a cover term for a world of disjunctive flows can be viewed as quite aptly describing the discursively fluctuating concepts of globalisation, culture and identity and how they operate within particular ideological frameworks. The discursive presentation of globalisation representing a cultural or national threat is a very particular manipulation and distortion of such a process.

Attachment to the nation state and discursive concepts of national identity or forms of nationalism are a means to provide a narrative of meaning and understanding, yet often this results in a negative and defensive reaction and anxiety about such perceived challenges or threats. As John Hutchinson points out:

> Nations are dynamic entities that structure our response to the multiple and unpredictable processes we encounter. These insights are brought to bear on current debates about the future of nations, which are allegedly threatened by globalisation, regionalism, continentalism and religious resurgence
>
> (Hutchinson, 2005:5)

In this sense, the present is often contextualised and interpreted through a specific and narrow reading of the past, as noted by the historian E.H. Carr in 1964, what drives and characterises English national identity is the marriage between the present and the past.

Within the context of Englishness and globalisation, it can be postulated that a point of crisis has been reached. Although the nation state persists (and in many ways is reinvigorated), such are the challenges faced a perception of the erosion of the nation state, national economies and national cultural identities produces a very complex and dangerous moment. In fact, it can also be suggested that defensive concepts of nationalism 'goes into an even deeper trough of defensive exclusivism' (Hall, 2010:177). This is particularly pertinent in terms of decline and English national identity, one struggling to come to terms with relative national decline. Historically contextualised notions of decline coupled with perceived threats and challenges from an ongoing and accelerated process of cultural globalisation can indeed produce a defensive exclusivist response. Craig Calhoun

(2008) points out, unlike positive localist concepts of cultural globalised identity, growing global connections can become a source of fear and defensiveness rather than appreciation. In fact, 'globalisation can lead to renewed nationalism or strengthening of borders – as have often been the case since the 2001 terrorist attacks' (Calhoun, 2008:426). Moreover, this has become not just a Western or European issue but a global one.

The relationship between a process of globalisation and dominant notions of English national identity can be characterised by a deep sense of social and cultural anxiety, specifically in relation to discourse and concepts of a perceived threat and undermining of national sovereignty and cultural identity. Perceptions of cultural anxiety concerning a sense of loss or fear must be contextualised within a conceptual framework of deterritorialisation but also within a reactionary response through a counter process of reterritorialisation. Stuart Hall describes the contemporary situation in that, 'we have never been so close to an embattled defensiveness of a narrow, national definition of Englishness, of cultural anxiety' (Hall, 2010:177).

Anxieties concerning a perceived threat to national sovereignty, 'old certainties' such as grand narratives of stability and homogeneity and anxiety concerning future uncertainties and identity has helped foster what Aughey has termed, 'identity sickness' (Aughey, 2007:97). This suggests that past notions or conceptions of an identity built upon a conservative and traditionalist ideological perspective will inevitably conflict with modern reality. As Aughey claims, 'the mood is the message' (Aughey, 2007:99). That mood can be described as 'irritable growl syndrome' (ibid), a complaint of varying intensity against present conditions typified by a sense of anxiety. Such anxieties are intimately connected with contested and debated visions of the character of English national identity and have deep roots in the national imagination and conflicting discursive frameworks.

The strength of anti-European feelings, the reinforcement of a world divided into separate nations, even what we eat or how we pay for it is riddled with nationalist practice and assumed naturalness. The strength of such banal nationalism (Billig, 1995) resides precisely in it going largely unnoticed and can be viewed as operating as a form of low level antagonism towards an ongoing process of globalisation. It is maintained on a daily level and can surge in times of crisis, which those in positions of power seek to exploit. Politicians and moral entrepreneurs play an important role in the production and reproduction of nationalism and national hegemonic discourse, not because they are in any sense important, powerful or have commanding influence – indeed, many argue that their weight in key decision-making processes are declining partly as a result of globalisation. However, this can be a key theme to be exploited against a generally perceived negative process of globalisation. Indeed, key themes and characteristics of a hyper-globalised postmodern world have been specifically weaponised and put to extremely effective use by the right. Globalised media and in particular social media has turbocharged connectivity and wide ranging movements fuelled by unaccountable right-wing rhetoric and sweeping unsubstantiated claims that become taken as fact. Moreover, the postmodern post-fact world where experts are even explicitly excluded from debate plays into a fantasy world of rhetoric, myth and toxic national discourse.

Conservative notions of Englishness negate many of the things such a perspective would rather ignore – imperial loss, cultural hybridity and cosmopolitanism. Colin Wright terms this a 'myth of origin' as it is ever apparent that such an outlook of Englishness exercises a 'strategic amnesia' (Wright, 2007:162) concerning not only the hybridity of its early history but also the impact of imperialism on the racial makeup of its latter history. This is particularly relevant when considering the appearance and rise of extremist parties and groups which have in more recent forms pushed national debate and discourse further down the line of the imperilled, threatened and defensive nature.

Political, social and cultural commentary easily becomes rhetoric, outlining an ideological position or discursive parameter. It serves to reconstitute the symbolic particularity of nation and nationhood for their intended audiences but also for the increasing rhetorical force attached to the concept in this reflective-reconstitutive process. It is 'the Burkean concept of identification: the electorate/audience is made to feel that the speaker is "one of their own", and thus is qualified to represent them' (Wright, 2007:160), even if the speaker is manipulating and reconstituting a particular situation to serve their own political and ideological means. 'I am like you, and therefore I can speak for you' (ibid); this represents an unending process of rhetorical identification within a context of a nationally imagined community. The consequences of any particular identity content depend on how they are inserted in larger narratives, and in many cases such content can be used to justify hostility towards others or the discursive boundary construction of inclusivity and exclusivity.

Ideologically symbolic instances are keenly taken up by the mass media and social commentators through the dialectical positioning of 'we' and 'us'. This is framed as the concrete or naturalised foundation of the national narrative or positioning. The parameters of the debate and discourse on issues concerning cultural and national identity contextualised within a process of globalisation are firmly situated within a conservative and defensive narrative and framework. Right-realist issues such as immigration and Europe have become unquestioned and accepted terrain within political and cultural discourse concerning English national identity. It is 'a patriotism operating exclusively on the fuel of abjection – frothing at immigrants, "left-wing elites", [and Brexit] "traitors"' (Kennedy, 2018: 145). It is an 'irate Englishness' (ibid) defined by what it's not and committed dogmatically to a fantasy that it is oppressed. Again, these key symbolic issues dominate political wrangling over who can be more hardline or non-negotiable which is played out through public manifestations such as the mass media. In recent political circumstances, this can be seen in the relative success of the UK Independence Party (UKIP) – fiercely anti-European and anti-immigration combined with the usual so-called 'protest vote' against the mainstream political parties.

There is more to this traditionalist right-wing 'common sense' party and that is that they represent a growing accepted and mainstream right-wing reactionary position. This is articulated not only through the populist anti-Europe sentiments and the anti-immigration rhetoric but also through a racialised position on identity without the overt connotations of a BNP-esq approach, 'the success of UKIP rests on nostalgia for a brutal past shrouded in mythology, as well as fear of a future buffeted by neoliberal globalisation' (Younge, 2013). What UKIP and a sizeable chunk of the Conservative Party can be seen to represent is an ideological attachment to a specific political and cultural position against prevailing social and cultural trends. The two main platforms on which they have garnered so much support is actually indicative of a wider approach to social and cultural discourse – anti-Europe and anti-immigration rhetoric represents a clear defensive, threatened ideological boundary between 'them' and 'us' articulated through these flagship issues. Situated discourse has shifted all main political parties from clamouring for a supposed centre ground to a contemporary scramble to the right of political, cultural and social terrain, these positions represented as being non-negotiable.

As Gary Younge pointed out just after the local elections of May 2013, '[the] more successful and durable electorally have been the parties and tendencies that have sought not allies but isolation and not solutions but scapegoats' (Younge, 2013). This can be viewed as a continued trend across Europe where the far-right have become mainstream and normalised within a context of anti-immigration populism. From Greece (the rise of the neo-Nazi Golden Dawn Party to the election of centre-right New Democracy in 2023 and the rapid emergence of Spartans) to Norway (the anti-immigration Progress Party as part of a centre-right coalition), Austria (the far-right Freedom Party under Norbert Hofer and its 49% of the vote in recent presidential elections), France (Marie Le Pen achieving 41.6% in the 2022 presidential election), the Netherlands (Geert Wilders openly anti-Islam Freedom Party's second place in national elections), Italy (the election of Giorgia Meloni whose Brothers of Italy Party has neofascist roots), Spain (the far-right Vox Party recently doubling its regional and local vote), Finland (the far-right Finns Party in a new four-party coalition government), Germany (where the far-right AfD won a district council election for the first time in June 2023) and not to mention Hungary (far-right president Viktor Orban has been Prime Minister since 2010). This can also be viewed in a wider Western sense such as recent Australian and US national elections which have become dominated by the issue of immigration and have seen the rise of explicitly racist, sexist and homophobic contenders. What seems to dominate such discourse is a need to find solutions or to pitch blame over issues or problems which populations or nation states have little power to control. Anxieties over a perceived lack of control find political outlets, and uncertainty, exacerbated by the inability of many nation states to secure national economic sovereignty in the era of globalisation, can translate into a lack of tolerance of any sort of collective stranger. Globalisation can, therefore, be viewed as a force without a face and is difficult to tangibly blame or attack however visible minorities are. Perceptions of national and cultural decline can lead to very specific, narrow and exclusive forms of national identity driven by a hegemonic defensive and conservative discourse.

This is precisely the sort of effect concepts and interpretations of globalisation have had upon discourses of Englishness in the early 21st century – an embattled, defensive and narrow definition entirely grounded on mythical concepts of a past 'golden age' while existing within a negative and defensive position within modern reality. The important point here to consider is that 'when nation states begin to decline in the era of globalisation, they regress to a very defensive and highly dangerous form of national identity that is driven by a very aggressive form of racism' (Hall, 2010:178). Conservative and right-wing concepts of English national identity are dominated by a very narrow definition. This discursive account is bound up with traditionalist exceptionalism, yet this is arguably what makes it such a defensive socially and culturally anxiety riddled ideological position.

In particular, the theme of the 'outsider' is a constant historical oppositional tool used throughout the creation and management of dominant forms of national identity within England. Specific ideological management of the 'insider' 'outsider' boundary delineation is key for nationalists. Exclusionary codes of historical honour are drawn upon (be they grounded in pure myth or not) and used to contextualise perceived crises and threats of the present. Furthermore, boundary management not only specifically contextualises perceived crises and appropriates blame to or threats from 'outsiders', it also perpetuates an imagined existence of such groups and boundaries, as John Tomlinson notes, 'in modern societies we live our lives within structures that orchestrate existential experience according to well-policed boundaries' (Tomlinson, 2003:273).

Globalisation has not entirely offered a defensive narrative to dominant concepts and discourses of English national identity. Conservative ideological perspectives have attempted to use globalisation to turn the nation state into a competition state. This requires a reorientation of the state towards the norms of economic globality and domestic privatism (Cameron and Palan, 2004). Although this has caused much consternation regarding specific socio-economic reorientation and those still inextricably linked to an older state form and norm of economic participation, in regards to concepts of national identity this is significant. The exclusive individualist notion of Englishness plays very neatly along the lines of social and economic redrawing of the relationship between the state and the individual and discursive representations between a process of globalisation and national identity. The continued and accelerated erosion of the welfare state, welfare provision, education and health services, government services and provision represents the new order of the relationship between the state and the individual within the context of competitive individualism.

Cameron and Palan (2004) describe this particular discursive relationship as consisting of the 'included' as being those contributing to the private economy of the state and therefore able to reap the benefits of globalisation and the 'excluded' as those who fail for one reason or another to participate. Groups such as the working class or poor have become rebranded as the socially excluded not simply in a narrow political sense but in a discursive sense, 'the poor who were always with us have become the poor we can no longer support' (Cameron and Palan, 2004:134). The primary function of the competition state has become not the management of territory but the management of people, and this is carried out through the discursive realm therefore performing the social, cultural and political function of identity formation.

Within and through political and social rhetoric (which is symptomatic of dominant discourse on the subject), it is reinforced how 'taking responsibility' for one's own future, well-being or position is a moral choice – those who are poor or unemployed are no longer to be sufficiently helped or supported but are instead demonised and castigated for choosing their lot in life and it being up to them to change or improve their position. The debate and discourse concerning the nation state and the individual within the context of globalisation is so tightly bound up within such a particular narrative or set of ideological boundaries that for the most part, it is very difficult to even approach or conceptualise the topic in any other way. 'Within a series of evolving configural narratives, all of which have histories of their own, globalisation and social exclusion combine to form a meta-narrative about the contemporary state, producing a new distribution of socio-economic spaces and velocities' (Cameron and Palan, 2004:154). These narratives become self-fulfilling prophesies that are characterised by political, social and historically contextualised processes and discourses.

It is, therefore, no surprise that in 2020/2021, 13.4 million people were living in poverty in the United Kingdom (Rowntree Trust, 2023), meanwhile the richest 1% of Britons now hold more wealth than 70% of the population (Oxfam, 2023). This coincides with the dominance of a conservative neoliberal discourse which looks to position blame upon wider processes of globalisation meanwhile facilitating the systematic dismantling of the very fabric of society. It has been able to do this as it controls the discourse and narrative, regardless of reality.

When we look closer and analyse and explore concepts and perceptions of globalisation in relation to contemporary notions of English national identity, we can see a confused and contradictory picture. On the one hand, it can be argued that we are witnessing a process of deterritorialisation or the significant erosion of national boundaries and the undermining of the nation state and national distinctiveness. Yet on the other hand, a counter process of reterritorialisation or the reimagining and recreation of national identity and distinctiveness through a nationalist reaction or resurgence can be seen to be taking place. If globalisation is taken to generally constitute a complex and multidimensional process, then placing concepts of Englishness within this context can provide us with some of the effects this may have upon notions of self, others and nation within this wider process. Globalisation can be seen to have inherently affected all aspects of nation, identity and society. Its representation through a conservative and defensive ideological framework of contemporary English national identity provides a national narrative and collective imagining.

The representation of globalisation through concepts of English national identity is a deeply discursive ideological operation. It provides the expression and embodiment of meaning, purpose and place within a changing, confusing and highly fluid world. Arguably, the dominant discursive expression concerning the relationship between globalisation and English national identity or Englishness is one dominated by a conservative, nostalgic, defensive and negative position, however contradictory this might be. Globalisation within concepts of English national identity is viewed with a deep sense of cultural anxiety; indeed, concepts of English national identity can arguably be viewed as consisting of or being characterised by an essentialised backlash to a process of globalisation that can also consist of a deep sense of longing for cultural belonging and security in an age of fluidity and change.

The continual and often rapid process of globalisation has provided deep problems to a defensive ideological position. Dominant concepts of English national identity provide the ideological embodiment of discourse and power within society. Articulations of a national narrative within a multidirectional and ambiguous process provide purpose and meaning in an era of fluidity and flux but also a sense of familiarity. However, such narratives are often based on dogmatic and mythological representations that are often a subjective ideological embodiment of a social and cultural ideal but also offer at the same time a reflection of an opposite or another that we seek to be against. Globalisation arguably poses some of the biggest problems when searching for identity, especially within the context of Englishness, yet this also exposes some of the fault lines running through our society and some of the forces that are shaping it.

Chapter 3

# The Ideologically Constructed Myth of Englishness

This chapter will investigate dominant discourses of Englishness and their relationship to the creation and maintenance of ideological concepts of conservative and traditionalist notions of Englishness in the contemporary era. It will outline a 'traditionalist' approach and critically analyse conservative theoretical concepts of English national identity and their ideologically located articulations. This chapter will suggest that dominant forms of Englishness provide an ideological illusionary narrative through the essentialisation of culture and nostalgic historicisation.

It will explore how Englishness has been defined and constructed around a mythologised sense of what it isn't by the right, as being defined largely as suburban/rural, middle to upper class (although provides claims to represent the working class) and steeped in nostalgia. Although not explicitly racist, homophobic, transphobic, Islamaphobic et al., it is couched against political correctness or rather wokeness (although this will not be a narrative of so-called culture wars). What will be discussed here are discourses from the right which largely dominate political narratives and discourse within England through the media but within a wider contextual account.

## Ideology and Conservative Concepts of Englishness

Arguably, we have become prisoners in a very narrow and unreflective social and cultural understanding that dominates our interpretation of national and individual identity. In essence, this can equate to an illusionary and manipulated sense of common purpose that defines the boundaries within which concepts of who we are, national identity or social and cultural understandings are perceived. Sinfield suggests that, 'it is through such stories, or representations, that we develop understandings of the world and how we live in it. The contest between rival stories produces our notions of reality, and hence our beliefs about what we can and cannot do' (Sinfield, 1989:23). This directly affects how we conceptualise ourselves, others and who 'we' are or are not. Englishness, in this context, can be

**Constructing Realities, 51–82**
**Copyright © 2024 Stuart Cartland**
**Published under exclusive licence by Emerald Publishing Limited**
**doi:10.1108/978-1-83797-545-720231004**

viewed as a conceptualisation of purpose and identity within the contextualisation of time and circumstance. It provides an understanding and interpretation of our social world which perpetuates and legitimises a particular perspective or conceptual account.

Ideology can be viewed as the specific conscious or unconscious cultural and political outlook or interpretation of things, events and the world. According to Althusser (2012), ideology can be equated to a theory of ideas. This can then be interpreted as representing a system of ideas and representations which dominate the mind of a person or a social group. Ideology functions as a means to view ourselves, our communities, our society or nation and situates these formations as an ideological act. Ideology is 'a "representation" of the imaginary relationship of individuals to their real conditions of existence' (Althusser, 2012:123). It is an illusion that alludes to reality.

Ideology is not the representation and articulation of 'real' conditions of existence or the 'real' world. Ideology represents within itself and conveys to individuals a subjective relationship concerning conditions of existence. From this perspective, ideology is a creation and product of our position and interaction within our social worlds; it is the social, political and cultural creation of a framework of structural coherence. It is, as Terry Eagleton comments, 'the imaginary ways in which men [sic] experience the real world' (Eagleton, 1991:214).

Dominant narratives, or stories of understanding our social world, are subjective ideological interpretations of society; they are not an objective or natural perspective. However, to legitimise and create a dominant ideological discourse, it must be presented as the very opposite of this. It is the prioritisation of a certain viewpoint, perspective or understanding over others. Eagleton (1991) points out that the function of ideology is to legitimise definite forms of social consciousness (politically, socially and ethically) but also to legitimise the power relationship and situate power within our understanding of society and to naturalise it. A dominant sense of Englishness can, therefore, be viewed as a means to facilitate and legitimise ideological structures of unrepresentativeness, inequality and exclusivity. Ideology is concerned with specific interpretation and representation. It is about domination; it is not necessarily the content but its relationship to the subjective position implied by its own process of enunciation (Zizek, 2012).

Roland Barthes (1957) proposes that ideology represents the naturalisation of the symbolic order of things. This is the case of Englishness and its discursive relationship to the dominant conservative representation of it as a naturalised and reified symbolic order. Concepts of Englishness are so dominated by a conservative and traditionalist position and ideological representation that it is unquestioned and has become naturalised in its relationship to a hegemonic symbolic relationship, or as Zizek (2012) comments, it represents and is indicative of a battle for hegemony which takes place within discourse itself.

The privilege and monopoly of a sense of objectivity are fundamental for the dominance of an ideological perspective. It is within these carefully positioned boundaries that we operate in a wider sense of identity. This can be directly related to Grayson Perry's concept of 'Default man' (2014) as the ingrained and naturalised default mechanism of conceptualising the world through the gaze of the conservative, traditionalist perspective dominated by white, middle class, heterosexual male values and norms. It is so pervasive that it operates as an unquestioned default, common sense mechanism for viewing the world. It is not defined by a rational, representative or logical state of being – in fact it is quite the opposite; it is the casual and unquestioned acceptance of this ideological perspective and interpretation. As Perry (2014) describes it a great tribe, yet a small minority of our population whose numbers make up about 10% of the population (according to the 2011 national census and the 2013 social attitudes survey), 'they dominate the upper echelons of our society, imposing, unconsciously or otherwise, their values and preferences on the rest of the population' (Perry, 2014:25). As a social group, they make up an overwhelming majority in key positions in government, boardrooms and the media, 'they are, of course, white, middle class, heterosexual men, usually middle aged' (ibid).

Identity can be viewed as a process of reification as the construction and maintenance of a dominant conservative English national identity and narrative and is heavily reflective of the cultural, social, economic and political backgrounds of the brokers of power within society. For example, the government appointed Social Mobility and Child Poverty Commission Study (2014) stated that in regards to senior unelected brokers of power (those who have attended independent, private, fee-paying schools) as a national figure only make up 7% of the population. The report stated that those from this background make up 71% of senior judges, 62% of senior armed forces officers, 55% of permanent secretaries (or rather, senior civil servants), 53% of senior diplomats, 45% of chairmen of public bodies, 44% of the Sunday Times Rich List, 43% of newspaper columnists and 26% of BBC executives. The figures concerning the domination of power in the public sphere by Oxbridge graduates is even more damning. Although graduates from Oxford or Cambridge make up less than 1% of the population, they make up 75% of senior judges, 59% of the cabinet, 57% of permanent secretaries, 50% of diplomats, 47% of newspaper columnists, 38% of the House of Lords, 33% of the shadow cabinet and 24% of all MPs. This is in stark contrast to not only the 99% of the general population who did not attend these elite establishments but also the 62% who have not attended university at all. The report (the most extensive and in-depth to be carried out on this subject) rightly describes the figures as, 'elitism so stark that it could be called social engineering' (2014). Although these figures are from 2014, this cultural exclusivism has largely not changed. The 2019 general election intake saw 29% of MPs privately educated, indeed only '41% of Conservative MPs and 70% of Labour MPs attended comprehensive schools, whilst 16% of all MPs attended a grammar school, in comparison to 17% of MPs elected in 2017' (Sutton Trust, 2019), whereas 173 MPs went to fee-paying private schools, including 11 who went to Eton including Boris Johnson and Jacob Rees-Mogg.

When 'common sense' or 'the average person on the street' is referred to, for instance, it is a direct reference to Default man's perspective on things. When 'normality' is referred to, it is the image of Default man. Yet, Default man will never accept or admit to the advantages of his 'tribal belonging', instead posturing that society is a meritocratic level playing field in which they are unfairly judged in a 'PC gone-mad' world. The key issue with Default man and dominant ideological concepts of national identity are that:

> When we talk of identity, we often think of groups such as black, Muslim lesbians in wheelchairs. This is because identity only seems to become an issue when it is challenged or under threat. Our classic Default man is rarely under existential threat; consequently, his identity remains unexamined.
>
> (Perry, 2014:27)

It is so dominant that identity is only ever discussed when in reference to others outside of the Default man's realm, and even then when in pejorative, minority and exceptional terms.

The ideological Default man conceptualisation of our social world has such a monopoly over society and its framework of existence that only in times of crisis is Default man's position questioned. In this sense, the white, middle class, heterosexual, male perspective is rarely, if ever, discussed or recognised in the sense of a group or community (like other social groups) precisely because it is the default position and perspective. This position operates much like Laura Mulvey's (1975) concept of the male gaze in that, every other group is 'othered' and judged by it. As Perry states, 'Default man is the zero longitude of identities' (Perry, 2014:27). It is, therefore, the taken-for-granted and assumed 'normal' or 'natural' position or perspective.

Default man becomes an internalised sense of identity or values and attitudes. According to Bilkis Malek (2008), conservatives tend towards the position that perceived majority culture (personified by Default man) should enjoy a privileged status. In this regard, Default man is assumed to be rational, objective and the epitome of common sense; all else is a minority position, quirky, radical, extravagant or exotic. Default man is presented as the assumed empirical, objective view of the world, and consequentially, this is what generally dominates discourse concerning Englishness. Perry comments, 'the most pervasive aspect of the Default Man identity is that it masquerades very efficiently as "normal"- and "normal" along with "natural," is a very dangerous word, often at the root of hateful prejudice' (Perry, 2014:31).

Moreover, this inherently conservative and unrepresentative perspective is so naturalised that it is the default mechanism of normality, objectivity and common sense. This is what makes it such a dominant social, cultural and political discourse becoming apparent when concepts of Englishness are discussed or imagined. In a time of social and political uncertainty, dominant conservative or traditionalist discourses of identity are exaggerated to reinforce and maintain dominance in the face of possible challenge and change. Zizek (2012) comments that, the battle for hegemony takes place within discourse. If a specific ideological interpretation of the world achieves discursive dominance, inequalities can be passed off as natural, normal or go unquestioned.

The creation and belief in a form of Englishness as a means to conceptualise and contextualise community, history and people is a means to systematically rationalise and understand, in a self-serving form of coherence, what it means to identify as English. In a Gramscian sense, this can be used to contextualise dominance in an ideological field of conflict which produces, or at least tries to form, a hegemonic narrative of English national identity and purpose. This highlights the idea of 'social settlement' (Massey, 2014), where the hegemony of the current social order creates a dominant ideological framework and social narrative. Conservatism, traditionalism and neoliberalism therefore dominate, in an often assumed and taken-for-granted understanding of social and national discourse across all areas. Identity can become bound up with an intimate relationship with this ideological dominance framing our social and national existence and experience.

Political questions or perspectives are often disguised as social or cultural commentary when efforts towards achieving or maintaining dominant representations of identity are attempted. This operates as linguistic manipulation as it seeks to reframe issues within a specific ideological and political understanding. For example, in the case of immigration or the European Union, and the language and boundaries, these topics are couched within. Parallels can be drawn with how Stuart Hall (1983) theorised Thatcherism and the Conservative domination and exploitation of patriotism around the Falklands conflict. Politics, in this sense, is conflated with social or cultural questions or issues which produces a manipulated sense of purpose and disguises key issues towards a political or ideological end. The success of Thatcherite conservatism can thus be seen to derive its success from reinforcing patriotism and imperial nostalgia.

## Conservative and Traditionalist Approaches to Englishness

Conservatism and traditionalism form the ideological foundation of dominant contemporary conservative discourses of Englishness. While cultural conservatism relates to social attitudes and specific political positions, traditionalism is linked to a sense of historicisation and loss. Both frameworks share synonymous characteristics. Any framework, based on preserving or promoting customs, beliefs or values, operates within an interpretive conceptual framework and is inherently ideological. The traditionalist and conservative perspective favours specific values, social codes, and a socio-cultural-political approach. It can be viewed as a meta-ideological stance applicable to diverse social, cultural or political contexts.

## Conservatism

Conservatism can be understood by a series of what Oded Heilbronner (2012) calls fixed cultural signs, patterns of behaviours, institutions, representations and stereotypes. For instance, the concepts of an unchanging, timeless and reserved Englishness of a green and pleasant land – an England of a particular social order, or an England encapsulated by William Blake's *Jerusalem* (which symbolically is heard at one of the traditionalist bastions of England – Lord's Cricket Ground, before a test match). This ideological approach can be viewed as 'Tory nostalgia' which through Hobsbawn's and Ranger's critical analysis borrows much from an ideological invention of tradition to strengthen patriotism and to glorify a very specific view of heritage as a manifestation of a specific, narrow and exclusive conceptualisation of Englishness.

To understand conservative concepts of Englishness, Ben Wellings (2008) calls upon John Hutchinson who divides nationalism into two varieties: cultural and political. 'Cultural nationalists do not necessarily aim at the capture and exercise of state power, as political nationalists do, but instead seek to re-invigorate the national community through a critique of the present based on an idealised view of the past' (Wellings, 2008:399). Culture, therefore, becomes political as 'national culture' legitimises the existence of the nation and hence the nation state. In the case of Englishness and the Conservative Party, Wellings describes this as 'Rump Britain', or rather the Conservative Party's English nationalism as an antidote to 'Celtic nationalism' while also preserving a direct and overt link to the sovereignty of the Crown and Parliament. 'It was through an allegiance to Crown-in-Parliament sovereignty that English nationalism became identified with wider categories of belonging' (Wellings, 2008:402). These wider categories of belonging can include conservative attitudes towards Europe, race, the English countryside, the monarchy, political correctness, 'all served up in a historical narrative, represent the topography of Rump Britain' (Wellings, 2008:402). This can help explain why concepts of a conservative sense of Englishness are so culturally exclusive in character, politically and socially reactionary and defensive in nature and have in recent years been used to aggressively foster so-called 'Culture Wars' as a means to extinguish alternative or competing national narratives.

## Traditionalism

Both traditionalism and conservatism can be used interchangeably as they deeply impact and influence concepts of national identity and discourse. However, traditionalism can be viewed as the promotion and adherence to specific traditional values, beliefs, moral codes and approaches to cultural practices. Traditionalism is embedded within a perspective that is deeply informed by a highly selective view of the past to inform attitudes and perspectives of the present, for instance, a sense of timelessness heavily resistant to change or aspects of modernity, especially within the context of national identity.

Traditionalist concepts of Englishness draw heavily on carefully selected and cultivated historical construction of place, class, position and seeming superiority of the English ruling class as rightful rulers referred to by writers such as C.K Chesterton or Cyril McNeile as 'the Breed' who:

> Had been in the eleven at Eton, and was a scratch golfer. He had a fine seat on a horse and rode straight; he could play a passable game of polo, and was a good shot. . .He belonged, in fact, to the

> Breed; the Breed that has always existed in England, and will always exist to the world's end.
>
> (McNeile, 1953:155)

Tony Bennett (1982) comments that this myth of Englishness is constructed against the tide of history. It is related directly to a sense of a specific construction of history, and to a sense of loss or a yearning for a historical utopia. According to Heilbronner (2012) Wright and Hewison, ideologically motivated concepts of heritage characterise Englishness as the triumph of aristocratic and reactionary nostalgia. This nostalgic perspective draws deeply into a typically and purposefully white, rural, middle class and culturally conservative identity – a nostalgia for a 'green and pleasant land' England often defined by what it is not as much as what it is.

The interpreted meaning of a rehabilitated past informs and defines Englishness. A concept of traditionalism is drawn upon to deal with challenges thrown up by modernity, industrialisation, democracy, post-colonialism and globalisation let alone our postmodern existences of precarity and uncertainty. Traditionalism harks back to a sense of domination and stability and will always look to a glorified and idealised construction of the past in relation to the present. This can be viewed in relation to the nostalgia bombardment, prevalence and popularity of television shows such as Downton Abbey, Indian Summers, Poldark, Call the Midwife and Heart Beat et al. Cultural texts such as these provide a medium through which a crisis of identity (but also a contemporary economic crisis) is mediated. These attitudes are then reflected back upon 21st century English society through 'an immense construction of grotesque neo-Victorian snobbery – How Clean Is Your House, Benefits Street, Immigration Street, exercises in *Let's Laugh at Picturesque Prole Scum*' (Hatherley, 2017:24). It is also a manufactured nostalgia based around benevolent conservatism.

As Owen Hatherley comments, 'austerity nostalgia is in large degree a right-wing phenomenon. The background noise of television programmes like Downton Abbey or Call the Midwife promote a 1940s and 1950s where the working class was diligent and deferent' (Hatherley, 2017:44). It is the production and meaning of these texts within the given context that produces a dominant discursive understanding of Englishness as a traditional, familiar, old-fashioned and anti-egalitarian narrative. In this sense, we cannot escape the politicisation of language, as language is what is used to mediate our interaction with reality and form an understanding of it. Derrida (1967) stated, there is no getting outside of the text; text or language is not based on a neutral representation or understanding of the world, it is based on cultural and linguistic codes which affix meaning and understanding.

In an increasingly hybrid and cosmopolitanism era, England has come to represent a particular historicity, a social meaning and configuration of meaning and memories of what Britain may once have represented. These are explicit appeals to a historical past and specific cultural understanding. As suggested by Gikandi (1996), tradition derives its moral authority from its association with bourgeoisie civility. It produces legitimacy. An appeal to tradition is a defence against forces that threaten change, cultural liberalism or political and social revolution. It is an appeal to continuity and structure with the past.

## The Construction of Common Sense

Conservative and traditionalist approaches to nationalism are at the heart of discursive representations of Englishness and national identity. A very specific type of social order can be used as shorthand to characterise conservative and traditionalist approaches towards a particular conceptualisation of Englishness. Conservative discourses of Englishness represent power in a basic two-fold manner. It seeks to exert power over which discourse is used and seen as representative and legitimate; that conservative and traditionalist values should dominate how social order and relations are constructed. Dominant discourse is more than just a particular type of identity politics; it is the universalisation of a particular discursive account.

The conservative theorist and writer Roger Scruton (2013) articulates how core conservative values are influenced by the work of Edmund Burke. 'Conservatives believe, with Burke that the family is the core institution whereby societies reproduce themselves and pass moral knowledge to the young' (Scruton, 2013). For Scruton, and conservatives in general, this position underlies the theoretical perspective of an assumed 'moral knowledge' based on unquestioned, assumed and naturalised norms and lives structured, 'according to the unspoken norms of a shared way of life' (ibid). For Scruton, the word 'we' underlies the dominant conservative national narrative of a 'shared way of life'. It represents an assumed and constructed homogenous moral community, one that seeks to dominate any understanding of such.

Concepts of a particular type of national identity form the basis for conservative belief, an assumed and ideologically created 'common man', 'common sense', 'legitimate concerns' that share a fictitious universalisation and naturalisation of a conservative narrative or rather discursive account. Assumed accounts of 'common sense', from the tradition of Edmund Burke, underpin a universalised 'we' for conservatives like Scruton. However, this stands diametrically opposed to the distinctly contrasting political and ideological articulations of 'common sense' from Burke's contemporary, Thomas Paine and his publication *Common Sense* (1776). The contrast between Burke and Paine shows how such a basic yet assumed concept of 'common sense' is not only deeply subjective but also deeply political and ideological in nature. Historical selectivity forms the very character of conservatism; what can be seen as factual evidence does not necessarily matter, what matters is the articulations that claim a universalised 'we' and in turn forms the homogenisation of this account within wider discourse.

Universal claims are mediated and constructed illusions that naturalise social and historical narratives. Judith Butler comments that, 'universality is not speakable outside of a cultural language' (Butler, 2000:41). Butler's critical analysis can be viewed as what forms the framework of conservative discourse and a struggle to accomplish and maintain it within the context of contemporary debates and understandings of some form of English national identity or representativeness.

Symbolic meanings attached to social, cultural, ethnic and moral objects are highly managed and cultivated ideological signifiers. In this regard, meaning is relational and does not operate alone in a world of coincidence or neutrality. When conservatives discuss moral knowledge, 'we', 'us' or 'right' is the direct use of an ideologically mediated use of symbolic meaning and often works to veil power within society. Chantal Mouffe suggests that:

> In the domain of collective identifications, where what is in question is the creation of a 'we' by the delimitation of a 'them', the possibility always exists that this we/them relation will turn into a relation of the friend/enemy type; in other words, it can always become political.
>
> (Mouffe, 2005:2–3)

Therefore, when comment is made from the conservative perspective around the traditional family structure, or militarism and the use of the poppy, political rhetoric is loaded with very specific meaning drawing upon values, codes and accepted norms within a specific ideological perspective, which supports a conservative hegemonic discourse (arguably built upon an illusion and myth of 'normality'). This is presented as a non-ideological, 'common sense', 'ordinary' or 'normal' account. The interests or ideology of a conservative perspective is presented as being synonymous with the nation as a whole and therefore representative of such. This dominance acts to delegitimise any other challenging perspective, positioning itself as an assumed natural framework for understanding.

Conservative and traditionalist politicians, political theorists, political commentators and large sections of the national media on the right have long upheld particular nationalist and traditionalist models of social identity and community, based upon positions securing nationalism to conservatism and vice-versa. This is based on a specific premise of what England is or has been. England, contrary to the nationalist conservative model, has never been a homogeneous and unified whole. Homogeneity is a fantasy. There is no single cultural, social, historical or political whole which all people can be incorporated. Claims of homogeneity cannot be justified morally or ethically as it places sweeping value and normative judgements condemning anyone or group not accepting or fitting the ideological boundaries of this perspective. It is, however, this framework of homogeneity that conservative dominance of nationalism and representation sits. Linda Colley (2003) critically analyses this particular creation and building of national identity in relation to England and Britain. Within this context, ideological and political dominance is crucial to the character of national identity and is fully entwined with a historicised account of people, nation and purpose.

In an era of anti-essentialism, this discursive position assumes a defensive stance of essentialism. Conservative and traditionalist concepts of Englishness have emerged as the prevailing ideological perspective, establishing themselves as a 'naturalised' position. Traditionalism, as a universalising notion, perpetuates itself as a framework for understanding. It defensively upholds an essentialist position, reinforced by notions of threat, anxiety, against cultural diversity. The universality it claims is contingent on both what it includes and excludes. For instance, in 2012, when Communities Secretary Eric Pickles changed the law to prevent English parish councils from legal challenges for including prayers in public meetings, it symbolically affirmed a conservative, hegemonic understanding and dissemination of English national identity. This tapped into the cherished English bureaucratic web of local and parish council organisation, reinforcing an unchallengeable link between Christianity and the state while presenting the proposal as a common sense position. Pickles defended the move by asserting, 'heaven forbid, we're a Christian nation. We have an established church. Get over it. And don't impose your politically correct intolerance on others' (Guardian, 2014a). This statement reflects a specific ideological subjective position masked by the illusion of universality and a homogenised concept of community. It also flips political correctness into an imposed militant doctrine that threatens a sense of tradition and identity within an imagined community.

In a post-UKIP ideological terrain of social commentary, national discourse has hardened and become receptive to politics of thinly veiled hate, exclusion and the promotion of political incorrectness. The dominance of conservative discourse is bound up in social commentary represented through a normalised and naturalised 'common sense' rhetoric that influences our understanding of the world and our sense of national identity. A discursive conservative universalisation of identity is therefore rooted in particular values and frameworks of power through a process of social and cultural symbolism; as Zizek (2000) points out, universality is always rooted, like an umbilical cord, in a particular sense of hegemony, it is never empty of content or ideological meaning.

Alongside Burke's ideological concepts of 'common sense', the bedrock of a conservative perspective of traditional Englishness can be summed up in Stanley Baldwin's words:

> The sounds of England, the tinkle of the hammer on the anvil in the country smithy, the corncrake on a dewy morning, the sounds of the scythe against the whetstone, and the sight of a plough team coming over the brow of a hill, the sight that has been England since England was land... the one eternal sight of England.
>
> (Paxman, 1999:143)

This familiar evocative picture of a timeless 'eternal' sight and sound typifies the conservative English ideal, most importantly in its overt antiquated and historical basis of an illusionary land of traditional nostalgia. Its over emphasised and historically inaccurate claims not only idealise this position but also (by proxy) make other claim to Englishness illegitimate and false. This utopian conceptualisation of England is, based in what Colin Wright calls, 'visions of a prelapsarian, agrarian England that Powell points his counter-visions of urban decay, racial animus, and moral decline' (Wright, 2007:170).

The discursive content is defined in relation to what it contains as much as what it excludes. A basic adoption of a concept of binary opposites coupled with the ideological incorporation of 'exclusionary normativeness' (Zizek, 2009) normalises the ideological exclusion of people, groups, historical events, modern lived reality against an idealised yet illusionary homogeneous whole or experience. As Raymond Williams (1995) comments, the excluded area is clearly expressed by its very exclusion, since the dominant discourse has effectively seized the definition of the social or national understanding.

To legitimise an ideological position, especially one which draws heavily from a selective reading of historical accounts, it is easy to look to the past. As Eric Hobsbawm and Terence Ranger point out, 'for all invented traditions, so far as possible, use history as a legitimator of action and to cement group cohesion' (Hobsbawm and Ranger, 1983:12). Although Hobsbawm and Ranger largely treated the nationalist invention of tradition as a political movement based on a false consciousness (Calhoun, 1993), its real power and roots lie in the political economy which conceptually links a sense of historicisation, naturalisation and universalisation to a contemporary political, cultural and social identity based ideological project. Tradition thus equates to validity, regardless of whether it is based on a mythical representation of history, making it easy to link this to the popularity of ethno-nationalist understandings of nation and national identity.

The appeal to tradition in relation to concepts of national identity is not new. Those calling for a return to tradition argue that contemporary society has turned its back on national virtues or shared sense of moral norms and universalised values, resulting in a loss of discipline, respect and a collapse into self -indulgence and indifference. According to Nigel Whiteley, 'appeals to tradition imply either that something has been lost, or that it is under threat and in danger' (Whiteley, 2000:1). A perceived break with tradition is what can feed into social anxiety. Appeals to a sense of tradition, from a conservative perspective, are symbolic, emotive and politically charged. The perpetual presentation of traditional values being under threat is part of 'a modern set of categorical identities invoked by elites and other participants in political and social struggles' (Calhoun, 1993:211). Appeals play upon pre-existing frameworks of homogeneity and construct specific versions of identity around such frameworks.

A conceptualisation of a historicised sense of tradition and values can be viewed as the creation of an illusionary wall of language (Zizek, 2009), which places one value position in opposition to another, and then serves to sustain an ideological separation. This operates as the perpetuation of a conservative and traditionalist ideology of identity – a constant creation and reinforcement of the mirage of difference, threat and loss. Social and political movements often rely on identity claims, but identity itself is never fully constituted; this is how discourse operates at a level of power and dominance. The incompleteness of subject formation is one in which the subject in process is incomplete precisely because it is constituted through exclusions that are politically salient not structurally static (Butler, 2000).

Fundamental to notions of national identity is an incommensurability of hegemonic forms of representativeness; it can never represent the population it seeks to speak for, as every subject is constituted differently. One of the main problems concerning the construction and maintenance of conservative concepts of English national identity is the perception or general concept of a cohesive society with shared values, norms, experience and political consensus – this is clearly not the case and does not exist being only a mythical narrative. Regardless of the unrepresentativeness of the conservative 'us' or 'we', it is important how hegemony emphasises the ways in which power operates to form our everyday understanding of social relations, and to articulate the ways in which we consent to (and reproduce) those tacit and covert relations of power (Butler, 2000). These relations of power are created, reproduced and reinforced throughout everyday life, much like Michael Billig's (1995) notion of the banal. Discursively, 'it constitutes our tenuous sense of common sense' (Butler, 2000:14). It directs our understanding of the world through specific ideological perspectives and narratives. Dominant articulations and re-articulations don't need to be representative; to merely position and portray itself as populist is enough. To dominate the debate, it is the presentation as the only real or sensible choice or as 'common sense' that can triumph.

## Englishness as an Ideological Narrative

As identified, conservative and traditionalist identity politics are highly informed and shaped by appeals to nostalgia. At the heart of both concepts of Englishness is a sense of familiarity, or as Charlie Brooker sarcastically remarked, 'the cosy familiarity of a world in which you could walk down an English high street without your ears getting bunged up with foreign accents, unless someone was doing a hilarious Gunga Din voice in order to mock the waiter in a curry house' (Brooker, 2014:5). Familiarity is the cosy illusion of an ideologically created past, free from the contemptuous present of 'political correctness gone mad'.

Within this context, unsayable political and social commentary from the right becomes the sayable. It is repeated and reiterated across the media becoming familiarised as part of an established wider discourse. A cosy world of scrapbook images of pre-political correctness, traditional values and authority, social hierarchies and 'common sense' is a world many may want to return to, 'some because they feel financially or culturally threatened, others because they simply don't get along with our current reality full of lesbian retweeting and so on' (ibid). When traditionalist spokespersons on the right such as Jacob Rees-Mogg, Jeremy Clarkson or the general ideological stream of consciousness from the *Daily Mail*, *The Daily Telegraph* or the *Daily Express* evoke a highly idealised and sanitised image of the past, people applaud and desire the vague nostalgia regardless of the incoherence such a message may contain.

Althusser, Marx and Gramsci defined ideology as a body of norms and ideas that appear natural as a result of their continuous and mostly tacit promotion by the dominant forces in society (Herman and Vervaeck, 2007). Conservative and traditionalist concepts of English national identity operate in much the same way. Englishness, through various channels – from the banal to the overtly political – links ideological concepts to a narrative of tradition and a specific historicisation and subjective interpretation. Etienne Balibar (1991) defined this as an effective ideological form, in which the imaginary singularity of nation formations is constructed daily by moving from the present into the past. This feeds into an collective popular yet illusionary imagination of a shared sense of nostalgia with England represented as the country of class privilege, social inequality and Margret Thatcher, a white-washed selective and an ethno-nationalist sense of nation and citizenship, far removed from multiculturalism, (legal) sexual and racial equality, trans-rights, cosmopolitanism, urbanisation, urban decay, post-imperialism and a process of accelerated globalisation.

Dominant discursive accounts become situated as a naturalised position or rather they become 'natural narratives' (Herman and Vervaeck, 2007). Narrative becomes the main form of what Gramsci referred to as cultural production, which comes to embody values and norms and establishes a hegemony or monopolisation of a conceptual field within a wider consciousness. An established social order is historically presented as a 'way of doing things', and 'becomes naturalised and made into the way "things really are"' (Mouffe, 2009:5). 'Common sense' and 'rational' is then situated as synonymous with the conservative and traditionalist approach. Any deviation is presented as 'radical' or 'illegitimate'. This account is disseminated through ideologically compatible media, social and cultural outlets and can be viewed as operating as a quasi-tyrannical conceptual discursive majority, articulated through rhetorical hegemonic populism. A liberal democratic understanding is brushed aside in favour of a conservative and traditionalist hegemonic social and political approach and conceptualisation of the nation and national community couched within the language of defending 'British values'.

Conservative, right-wing, traditionalist nationalism normalises its particular narrow, cultural and historical interpretation of national identity and a national narrative. For example, *The Sun* (15 January 2023) proclaimed: 'Britains' No1 foe – the Empire of Woke'. This, it declares is the 'most pernicious threat to our freedom and the Western way of life, the screeching cult of woke authoritarianism' (Kavanagh, 2023). It positions Rishi Sunak as riding to the rescue of democracy and free speech by appointing a free speech watchdog, this being a very clear and overt strategy by the government to crack down on dissent or opposition to specific ideological representations or alternative accounts that challenge dominant conservative narratives, and pose (what it sees as) a moral and ideological threat.

A highly managed sense of cultural and historical continuity is essential when fostering a dominant account of Englishness, as McCrone and McPherson point out:

> National identity is not some essentialised badge which people carry around with them. It is the result of a complex interaction between historical memories, current social, political and cultural processes, and people's own predilection for self-identification. They are also part of what Bell has called 'mythscape': 'the temporarily and spatially extended discursive realm wherein the

> struggle for control of peoples memories and the formation of nationalist myths is debated, contested and subverted incessantly.
> (McCrone and McPherson, 2009:219)

The creation and maintenance of a dominant form of English national identity is not concerned with an objective representation of cultural and historical 'facts' or events; it is the specific ideological interpretation and re-articulation through a political prism of discerning 'facts' or events creating a mythical national history in relation to an illusionary national hegemonic community and social reality.

The conservative and traditionalist narrative of Englishness is bound up within a framework of a romantic dream, based upon a fantasy of greatness. This is an illusion trapped within its own historical creation irrevocably detached from reality. A romantic sense of greatness is also associated with a sense of uniqueness, purpose, entitlement and leadership. Figures from the right become mythologised demigods symbolising these attributes and are used to justify and legitimise claims to a natural symbiosis of ideology. The Churchillian and Thatcherite mythical characterisation embodies an ideological historicisation that largely dominates a socially, culturally and politically conservative sense of identity and purpose, used to form and perpetuate a sense of inevitability, normality, naturalness, homogeneity and moral order.

A process of dominating ideological narratives of the past, and 'the capacity of memorialisation to ring-fence a historical event against critique, to turn it into untouchable mythology' (Kennedy, 2018:113), is key to conservative discursive dominance. It has become instrumental for right-wing politics and discourses. Here, Joe Kennedy points to Angus Calder's seminal text 'Myth of the Blitz' (1991) in which a conflict is made the object of enforced deference precisely because it is used to authenticate political decisions taken in the present. In other words, it is the construction of prevailing historical narratives to dominate discourses of the present, 'an aesthetic warped by the intervention of forgetting' (Hatherley, 2017:31). It is the ideological weaponisation of the past, or rather, 'a' past constructed of an historicised national narrative built upon a reconstituted conservative social consensus that 'force a body of people to have memories that they do not actually possess' (Hatherley, 2017:19).

There is a sense, as Simon Gikandi (1996) suggests, that such 'imperialised knowledge' has its eyes or horizon set upon some kind of epistemic totality. England is perceived as a specific and historic destiny through symbolic representations of culture, tradition and class, 'at a time when the domestic space seems to be under threat from the forces of historical change' (Gikandi, 1996:88/89). A conservative perspective and discursive narrative seeks to explain the meaning of Englishness at a time of rapid historical, social and cultural change, one which has undermined the authority of tradition and place.

The past is an ideologically manipulated, mythologised, moralistic fetishisation and selective rendering, conjured up to reinforce conservative concepts of homogeneity and positive claims of a sense of traditionalism. This entails a repetitive returning to so-called 'past glories' such as the Empire, the Second World War, the 1966 World Cup and unifying values by way of an illusionary sense of uniqueness – all of which are selective social and historical constructs. As Stuart Hall states, 'a shared national identity depends on cultural meanings which bind each member individually into the large national story. . .The national heritage is a powerful source of such meanings. It follows that those who cannot see themselves reflected in the mirror cannot properly belong' (Hall, 2005:24). Politically and culturally specific constructions of national heritage, cultural meaning, relevance and identity purposely exclude those who do not fit in with traditionalist images of the nation and extinguishes any competing narratives. It enforces anti-egalitarian austerity while annexing cultural memory as a means of providing familiarity, security and continuity as an antidote to radical future possibilities of egalitarianism.

In their interpretation and reading of Kazuo Ishiguro's novel *Remains of the Day* (1989), Berberich and Aughey comment that, 'Ishiguro was critical of the way politicians, mainly but not only Conservatives, tried to manipulate the past to sell a wholesome picture of England domestically and internationally that did not necessarily reflect reality' (Aughey and Berberich, 2011:275). Arguably, this is still the case, the contested meaning of Englishness in an increasingly globalised world, with a nation trying to come to terms with devolution, its relationship with the European Union and large scale immigration. The England sold to the world (and more importantly – to itself) through a cultural hegemony and cultural obsession with tradition and nostalgia is reinforced through wistful sentimental paraphernalia such as calendars and tea towels, the cosy, comforting cultural security of the National Trust, Waitrose and farmers markets.

Cultural class deferentialism and conservative traditionalism encapsulated by Noel Coward, Merchant and Ivory, Julian Fellows and Andrew Lloyd Webber are now insidiously mainstream with TV programmes such as Downton Abbey, Victoria, Midsomer Murders, Heartbeat, the Great British Bake-off and Location, Location, Location. While movies such as *Four Weddings and a Funeral, The Iron Lady, Atonement, The King's Speech, the Queen et al.* represent an ever-present and social aesthetically pleasing England, one viewed through the gaze of the middle or upper classes, set in rural idyllic English locations and often located within ideologically triumphant historical 'golden eras'.

This sort of wistful nostalgia has become part of national narratives bound up with popular mass media entertainment, which entail a 're-imagining of an idealised Anglicised history and landscape' (Savage, Wright and Gayo-Cal, 2010:22). It also operates as a means to negotiate changed social, cultural and political conceptions of place and identity within a period of flux. It is an Englishness based upon a fantasy past reflecting a nostalgia for an imagined time and a dissatisfaction and unhappiness with a particular interpretation of a present. The exclusivity of Farrow and Ball pastel shades and a cosy smug utopia is fused with a 'narcissistic wallowing in fake poverty and barely coherent history as a way of avoiding any thought of how to drag ourselves out of our current, needless, and far less egalitarian version of austerity' (Hatherley, 2017:194).

It is suggested English cultural tastes have become even more conservative (Jones, 2012). Jones points out that political commentator Peter Oborne celebrated this cultural and social triumph in *The Daily Telegraph* by citing the popularity of David Hockney's exhibition at the Royal Academy as a sign of rejecting 'progressive pretensions' for 'conservative honesty'. Whatever Hockney's art might symbolise, Oborne interpreted landscape painting as being inherently conservative and symptomatic of a cultural turn. However, at the same time, Simon Schama (from a politically opposite perspective) wrote a stinging attack upon the successful country-house television drama Downton Abbey, where he savaged the, 'silvered tureen of snobbery' (Hough, 2012) based on an overtly right-wing novel by Evelyn Waugh that celebrates country houses, the upper class and a nostalgia for a world where 'people knew their bloody place' (Jones, 2012). He also commented that, 'nothing beats British television drama for servicing the instincts of cultural necrophilia' (Hough, 2012). These comments can be viewed as a critical and analytical reaction to the overwhelming amount of television based upon a cultural knee-jerk, reactionary dash to an imaginary sanctum of the certainties of a social and cultural world built upon rigid inequalities.

Examples such as these point towards a politically and culturally specific construction of nation and heritage, laden with cultural meaning and identity that purposely exclude those who do not fit the traditionalist images or values of the nation. It is a predominantly mythical representation that has no relevance to the majority of the population and one that most could never experience, yet it represents a well-established national, cultural and historical narrative, one that is cleansed of social and cultural relevance. 'The danger, as Ishiguro pointed out, lies not only in the fact that politicians would sell this image to their electorate but also that the electorate might buy it' (Aughey and Berberich, 2011:275).

Patrick Wright (1985) stresses the role of nostalgia, heritage and the potency for some of England as a place of rural heritage, cultural purity and traditional idyll through the concept of 'Deep England'.

> Deep England can indeed be deeply moving to those whose particular experience is most directly in line with its privileged imagination. {However}, just about anyone who, in the developing turmoil of modern society, has ever had cause to look back and wonder about old forms of security will surely be able to find meaning in Deep England.
>
> (Wright, 1985:85)

Even for those who experience the urban and unprivileged day-to-day, an attachment to this notion of 'Deep England' can be potent as it plays upon a nostalgic sense of loss, a loss felt not solely in terms of identity but also in terms of a particular mode of living, associated with place, class, lifestyle and values (Byrne, 2007).

A specific and narrow focus upon a sense of a shared experience can be viewed as the politicisation of heritage – similar to what Zizek (2009) terms the 'politicisation of culture'. Creating a sense of a naturalised or normalised order of things. This can be conceptualised as an illusionary sense of nostalgia, which serves to reinforce and legitimise a specific ideological national narrative. This narrative is perpetuated and reinforced through statements, speeches and rhetoric from the conservative and traditionalist right, and most notably through the banal.

## The Dominance of the Middle

The concept of 'middle England' has many parallel meanings to that of a 'deep England'; however, 'middle England' is a much more frequently used and ambiguous term, generally used to refer to the suburban and rural middle and upper middle classes. 'Middle England' is personified by the town of Tunbridge Wells in Kent (BBC, 1999) which embodies the privilege, and conservative, traditionalism that this much used concept has come to typify. It is also defined through dominant conservative and traditionalist discourse in relation to the perceived notion of being under attack from multiculturalism, environmental awareness, equality-imposing bureaucracy, political correctness, wokeism and health and safety obsessed contemporary society. The ideological conceptualisation of a threat operates in various ways. It signifies and reinforces a sense of binary oppositions between tradition and modernity, rural/suburban and urban, north and south, white and ethnic minorities, working class and middle class; indeed, it can be applied to an extensive range of 'in' or 'out' group signifiers around social, cultural or political topics of the day. It also operates as a means to articulate a sense of militant defensiveness to a way of life or certain values.

Although a discourse of Englishness might be read through a general and dominating narrative of 'middle England', it represents a default position in an era of general national identity crisis and anxiety. Concepts and proclamations of the middle classes under attack, wheeled out by the conservative right bemoaning economic policy that may be construed as taking from 'hard working normal families', are often a gross misrepresentation of economic social reality. The upper middle class are always included in this illusionary 'middle' yet the median income in Britain is £29,400 (Office for National Statistics, 2020). This normal or middle ground family is an illusionary concept used by the conservative right to rail against any perceived progressive economic policies and maintain the unfair economic advantage of the elite. It is presented as a homogenous populist position, whereas it is more representative of an elitist and exclusive minority, and can be viewed as essentially how dominant discourse operates. It presents its ideological position as being representative and populist, aspirational and normalised.

The origins of 'middle England' or 'little England' conservative traditionalism can be traced throughout English social and cultural history. Specific examples typify such a conceptualisation of a romantic and nostalgic Englishness which feeds into contemporary politicised (and often reimagined and manipulated) notions; Edmund Burke's 'Little Platoons' in his *Reflections on the Revolution in France* (1790) and the social and cultural reactionary conservatism not only in regards to the perceived threat of foreign political revolutionary fervour but the political and ideological anti-establishmentarianism contained within such a threat. Indeed, such reactions and ideological positions were present during the

Black Lives Matters movement in 2020. William Blake's *Jerusalem* (set to music by Parry in 1915) is a direct antithesis to the dark, gritty, industrialised cities of the Midlands and the north of England. Again, in the contemporary era, inner-city ex-council estates and their inhabitants provide the equivalent representations; for example, William Morris's notion of a future, rural utopia in *News from Nowhere* (1890), with the banishment of industrialised city living to the history books or Rudyard Kipling's idealised Sussex of *Puck of Pook's Hill* (1917) and the wider idea of a 'psychological retreat to the English countryside' (Marsden, 2000:26) to a rural England in contrast to the mechanised and industrialised warfare of the First and Second World Wars (Wellings, 2001). Again, contemporary examples of this can be encapsulated by the plethora of television shows such as 'Escape to the Country', Stanley Baldwin's (1924) 'long shadows on country grounds, warm beer, invincible green suburbs, dog lovers and pool fillers'. George Orwell's *Lion and the Unicorn* (1941) of 'old maids cycling to Holy Communion through the morning mist', and G. K Chesterton's famous lines, 'smile at us, pay us, pass us but do not quite forget. For we are the people of England, that never have spoken yet' (Chesterton, 1908).

Chesterton's words are the embodiment of English nationalism favoured by those opposed to political correctness and modernism, the fox-hunting elite and traditionalist militants, represented by the Countryside Alliance: as a rural population oppressed by urban values and a sense of a loss for (elitist) rural customs and practice. Chesterton's lines articulate and personify a defensive anxiety and a stance between the transformations of a modern globalised social reality, with a narrow, traditionalist, conservative sense of continuity and maintenance of a status quo. This sort of backlash suggests a more militant sense of defensive nationalism in the same way dominant forms of discursive articulations have come to dominate narratives over what it means to be English. It creates an ideological understanding of English values and positions them in a simplistic narrative of diametric opposites of good/bad, acceptable/unacceptable in which the dominant conservative discourse operates. 'It's a perspective that allows even the most well placed man of the world to imagine himself a member of an endangered aboriginal minority: a freedom fighter striking out against 'alien values and the infernal works of a usurping state' (Wright, 2007:68).

This representation of dominant articulation positions itself against a modernity that pays no heed to 'common sense' or traditional values, a contemporary period foisting 'alien' ideas as political correctness or multiculturalism, challenging 'our' sovereignty and ignoring the interests of the moral majority. It has formed the *raison-de-etre* to political campaigns and movements such as the Campaign for an English Parliament, the UK Independence Party (UKIP), the Tax Payers Alliance and the English Democrats while underpinning the lurch to the right of the Conservative Party held on a tight leash by its guardians of traditional values, the backbench 1922 Committee. Chesterton's words strike a chord with conservative traditionalists not because it draws upon an exhaustive list of characterisations but rather an attitude. Conservative, traditionalist rhetoric echoes to the sounds of Chesterton's 'secret people', whether in the right-wing media, through backbench Tory MPs and grass roots activists or other organisations and influential and well-resourced conservative think tanks and social and political commentators.

Chesterton's defensive definition of Englishness was formulated through a bitter awareness that the world was charging head-long in the opposite direction (Wright, 2007). It is a defensive narrative of retreat and denial. The England of Chesterton was a last ditch effort to defend against encroaching forces of modernity. This can be seen in the contemporary context by traditionalist concepts of Englishness against issues such as gay marriage, the banning of blood sports, environmental concerns, ethnic, gender and transsexual equality. As Wright notes, 'there is little doubt that, while Chesterton's version of "secret" England dates from nearly a hundred years ago, it expresses a way of thinking about identity and change that remains active to this day' (Wright, 2007:69).

However, dominant accounts of Englishness are not necessarily situated within an essentialised class position. In more recent years, politicians and commentators on the right have positioned ideological rhetoric to encompass 'legitimate concerns' of the 'ordinary person on the street' and to specifically legitimise narratives through appeals to the white working class. This is often couched within the familiar hyperbolic tropes of an identity that has become somehow banned, by so-called left-wing liberal elites intent on an aggressive agenda of woke cancel culture. For example, the right-wing outrage that Enid Blyton was going to be 'cancelled' in June 2021 provides a good example of such narratives.

Headlines such as 'Enid Blyton to be cancelled' represent two crucial elements of conservative right-wing populism, nostalgia and a sense of being under attack. Increasingly over recent years (but a common theme of the political right historically), there is a sense of social and cultural decay and a pining for times of past glory or 'the good old days'. Social or cultural elements that appeal to an older generation in terms of childhood are announced as being under attack by an updated PC police (or Wokerati according to Suella Braverman). This acts to enrage but also create a myth of how things were better back then, when you could say what you liked or thought, where everyone was white and spoke English. This also has wider links and connotations to a sense of national glory, dominance and empire. These are all ideologically created myths, presented as reality and as incontestable truth.

For example, 'Five gets cancelled! Enid Blyton's work "racist and "xenophobic," says English Heritage' (Harris in Daily Express, 2021), shows how ruling-class cultural hegemony works. According to English Heritage, Blyton's work is racist and xenophobic. Regardless that what it represents has no place in 21st century British society, right-wing commentators and mouthpieces use these stories to make sense of the present, to deny the racism, sexism and other catastrophic problems we face such as massive social and economic inequality and environmental disaster. The suggestion is that these problems are somehow foisted upon us, not that we have a responsibility to tackle them. Outlets like the *Daily Express* promote denial of these fundamental challenges, but also uses them as a tool to prove how the mythical 'ordinary person in the street' and common sense are under attack, that Great British culture and history is at risk of being cancelled by some sort of left-wing fifth column.

Within this very purposeful ideological reorganisation and oversimplification of the world, it is suggested that forces in the modern world have somehow undermined the possibility of greatness for the United Kingdom, that a triumphant and successful Brexit is threatened by traitors, but also that Brexit represents a triumph of common sense and a rejection of the forces of modernism. Such sensationalised and hyperbolic stories represent a two-fingers-up to those politicians and a wider society which is viewed as pandering to woke inclusivity. It follows the oft-repeated claims of left-wing bias in the media and particularly against the BBC, which are never substantiated with evidence. It crucially reinforces the familiar and well-worn narrative of left-wing bias, and a society that is dominated by a cosmopolitan, gay, Muslim, Black, disabled, trans, female agenda.

The symbolism from such portrayals in the media must not be overlooked; it represents an ideologically motivated attempt to dominate and reinforce public opinion with reactionary themes. These themes have also been articulated by a host of senior Conservative politicians, social and cultural commentators and rest on a pernicious mixture of utter incompetence and familiar, tired tropes powered by fantasy and blame.

## Landscape

Traditional conservative Englishness draws heavily from an emotive and evocative imagery based around landscape. It is an idealised England (and Englishness) which is viewed as both being under attack from and ignored by the marauding forces of modernity and alterity. It is typically rural, middle to upper-middle class and associated with the south – the basic formulation to understanding the conservative and right-wing position and perspective in regards to Englishness. As Wright elaborates:

> I believe it possible to argue that this version of a green and pleasant England persists in the Conservative psyche today. Indeed, the nearer one gets to the grassroots of contemporary Toryism in England, the nearer one gets to this puritanical discourse, and the defensiveness and paranoia that go with it (today, reactions to the very word 'Europe' serve as a reliable litmus test for this hypothesis).
>
> (Wright, 2007:171)

There is clearly nothing political or ideological about the English countryside per se. Indeed, it commands a critical sense of importance to many different and disparate political, social, historical and cultural movements and ideologies such as the Levellers and the Diggers, Orwell, Blake, Morris and the campaign for the right to roam typified by the mass trespass on Kinder Scout, all associated with the English left, radicalism and socialism. However, it is the hijacking and ideological manipulation of the subject matter, coupled with the constructed and constantly reinforced political and cultural subjective associated meaning that equates rural England to conservatism and traditionalism. It is also the attached and attributed symbolism that places a mythological idealised concept of rural England at the heart of conservative and traditional notions of Englishness, which has become synonymous with a sense of English national identity and what it represents. As Mark Perryman highlights, 'the temptation to retreat into an unchanging past, a theme park for an old country is strong, offering security versus global risk and the comfort blanket of the familiar' (Perryman, 2014).

Topographical representations are a highly contested and symbolically motivated topic area, one that is crucial to a sense of legitimised cultural understanding of identity. For instance, in the same week (March 2023) that BBC Match of the Day presenter Gary Lineker was hounded by both the right-wing press and government ministers for making comments on Twitter concerning government asylum policy (that breaks international law), the BBC were pressured into not broadcasting the final episode of its flagship David Attenborough documentary series 'Wild Isles'. In the tumult and embarrassment of the links between BBC Chairman Richard Sharp and financial support for Boris Johnson, the BBC decided not to broadcast the episode, 'because of fears its themes of destruction of nature would risk backlash from Tory politicians and the right-wing press' (Horton in *Guardian*, 2023). The power and fear of the right-wing lobby indicates the narratives and agenda setting so pervasive within the sociopolitical environment. It is also quite telling that to broadcast a fact-based and highly regarded nature documentary represents a threat to conservative and right-wing narratives based upon fantasy and paranoia, 'it would also uncover the vast scale of hypocrisy and double standards, let alone the feudal-esq land ownership system we have in the UK' (Cartland, 2023).

Cultural and ideological representations of topography are crucial to understanding a conservative discourse of Englishness. A timeless and enduring idolisation of place, culture, class and tradition is bound in a romanticised mythical scape or rather mythscape. However, this is one which is entirely ideologically man-made, contradictory and often barely legible. Idealised topographical representations articulate a moral national narrative in relation to and contextualised against the present. This draws upon national anxieties and contributes towards an illusionary sense of hegemony in an age of rapidly changing boundaries and realities.

Landscape can be viewed as the location of ideological clashes of fantasy, desire and anxiety. The conservative and traditionalist mythscape plays upon concepts of the north of England as symbolising the stereotypical working class, industrial city-scapes, while the south representing a middle and upper class idyll of English country gardens and cream teas. The timeless pastoral green dream of tranquility and social order, however, is an illusion often imposed to obscure what we actually see or encounter. As Robert MacFarlane (2015) describes it, this can be called 'landscape culture'. It is an idealised notion of 'dwelling', 'belonging' and 'heritage' that needs to be seen through the, 'turbulence of England in the era of late capitalism' (MacFarlane, 2015). It provides a fantasy of security and comfort in ideological constructions of myth.

The countryside has played an important part in the English imagination, particularly since the Industrial Revolution. As Ben Wellings (2008) points out, from Cobbett's 'rural rides' in the 1820s to the popularity of the National Trust after the Second World War, the English countryside has become synonymous with representations of conservationism which have led to a cultural conservatism. This has created a rural nostalgia culture industry of country dwellers clad in Barbour jackets and Hunter wellies driving Range Rovers, steeped in the cultural and political domain of the Cotswoldian elite rolling around in pastoral clichés. It is an England represented as a historicised rural idyll embodied by a sense of timeless and naturalised tradition and place, regardless of the reality or contradictions it throws up. Victorian poets and writers (Wordsworth and Coleridge), artists (Turner and Constable) and composers (Elgar, and latterly Britten) all employed to help perpetuate this ideologically evocative version of a decidedly green and pleasant land.

## Pain Free Politics of the Conservative Middle Ground

Englishness as a conservative and traditionalist narrative is a process of ideological imperial expansion. Arguably, cultural representation is part of how we view ourselves, others and the society and nation in which we live. The issue is that the dominance of a conservative, traditionalist concept of Englishness does not have any serious challenges to its self-imposed homogeneity; it has appropriated traditionally symbolic alternative representations of Englishness and does not need to seriously confront the question of difference.

This is evident in the way any real political alternative to the conservative, traditionalist position has capitulated and come to ape the neoliberal, conservative, hegemonic approach. As Chantal Mouffe points out:

> Neoliberal dogmas about the inviolable rights of property, the all encompassing virtues of the market and the dangers of interfering with its logics constitute nowadays the 'common sense' in liberal-democratic societies and they are having a profound impact on the left, as many left parties are moving to the right and euphemistically redefining themselves as 'centre left'.
>
> (Mouffe, 2009:7)

It is not just the systematic capitulation to the ideological market forces that has made the right the centre ground; this has happened hand-in-hand with the whole-scale adoption by the mainstream 'left' in England, of conservative economic policy and ideology evident in areas such as Europe, immigration and welfare and the exclusivist nature of politics, irrespective of how close Jeremy Corbyn's left-wing populism came to unseating the Conservatives in 2017.

This perspective is often framed, again, as being 'common sense' or 'pragmatic' as ideologically neutral, or an objective approach. However, it is a fictitious construction. What this signifies is the dominance of the conservative and traditionalist approach, which then informs all aspects of social and political ideology and identity politics. A banal, yet significant example of this, can be taken from 13 June 2014 when mainstream Westminster party leaders of the time, David Cameron, Ed Miliband and Nick Clegg, were individually pictured holding a special World Cup edition of *The Sun* newspaper which read, 'This is our England'. Although this can be interpreted as a harmless piece of pre-World Cup national unity and a cheap photo opportunity, its deeper significance is far more reaching. For a Labour leader especially, this is significant from an ideological and political standpoint, to the extent that Ed Miliband later apologised for the anger and hurt this may have caused, especially in regards to *The Sun*'s role in the Hillsborough tragedy. The capitulation to right-wing posturing and ideological approaches have become all too common for Labour leaders particularly since Tony Blair, with the exception of Jeremy Corbyn whose leadership (and defeat) ultimately purged the Party of any credible left-wing opposition.

What is symptomatic of contemporary mainstream politics, especially in England, is the domination of 'a pain free politics for middle England' (Coote in Mouffe, 2009:112). All three mainstream Westminster parties are typified by a middle class, middle ground politics, while superficially presenting themselves as representing 'hard working families' as a means to achieve some degree of legitimacy and authenticity. They all want no losers, 'especially among middle England voters. Moreover, it is led by a closed circle who enjoy power and do not want to give it up' (ibid). This mirrors the essence of government in Westminster since 2010 which can be viewed as dominated by the preoccupation of pain free politics for the comfortable sections of society while firmly holding the reigns of power within a very selective and narrow clique as the poorer sections of society shoulder the cost and moral responsibility of countless policies that have firmly redirected wealth and power to the privileged, powerful and economically well-off.

Just as Labour have sought to locate itself in the middle ground of British politics, the Conservatives have sought out such hallowed middle ground, only for rifts to appear between its political leadership positioning and its traditional ideological base. Although somewhat ameliorated since Brexit, this has emboldened the hard right within the party. This is how politics of anxiety and fear has become the common ground dominated by the Conservatives which has then become the centre ground. As Chantal Mouffe describes:

> When political frontiers become blurred, the dynamics of politics is obstructed and the constitution of distinctive political identities is hindered. Disaffection towards political parties sets in and it discourages participation in the political process. Alas, as we have begun to witness in many countries, the result is not a more mature, reconciled society without sharp divisions but the growth of other types of collective identities around religious, nationalist or ethnic forms of identification.
>
> (Mouffe, 2009:114)

A political environment such as this can breed contempt, distrust and isolation between the political class and its citizens and can also lead to unexpected and radical political departures, such as a rise of popularism depicted by 'straight talking' simplified rhetoric and political positions. Moreover, bland, homogenised political identifications open the door for more antagonistic and arrogant political messages carried by parties who feed off such disenchantment and promote xenophobia.

An obsession with centrist politics creates a democratic deficit, which is exploited by populist and dangerous right-wing parties evident from 2014's European election results (not to mention the EU referendum of 2016). This sort of political and identity politics allows parties from the right to appear as anti-establishment forces representing the will of the people, 'thanks to a clever popularist rhetoric, they are able to articulate many demands of the popular scorned as retrograde by the modernising elites and to present themselves as the only guarantors of the sovereignty of the people' (ibid). This can be used to describe the political and discursive success of UKIP and also the ideological shift within the Conservative Party against a so-called modernising leadership and towards the desires of its back benches and grassroots.

It should be mentioned here that meaning, message, motivation and reality do not match. What is important is the management of the political conversation regardless of intent. For instance, one of the key issues regarding Labour's political identity under Jeremy Corbyn is that it sought to provide an alternative to unrestrained free-market neoliberalism while addressing root causes of entrenched inequality. However, such an existential sociopolitical threat to power only served to create a huge right-wing backlash that positioned Corbynism as being the opposite, as representing an out-of-touch metropolitan elite. In a process of myth, fantasy and symbolic meaning, the Conservatives, on the other hand, sought to appropriate and manipulate symbolic messages otherwise not associated with themselves. They have gone from being ideologically opposed to the welfare state to identifying themselves as 'the party of the NHS', have sought to be 'the greenest government ever' (2010 Conservative Party manifesto) and after the budget of March 2014 proclaimed themselves the party that, 'helps hard working people do more of the things they enjoy'. However, all of these statements can be seen as outrageous attempts at political spin or simply, 'so patronising it looks like a crude attempts at satire' (Jones, 2014).

The contemporary hegemony of neoliberal discourse can be used to explain why the left (represented within the English mainstream politics by the Labour Party) is represented as having no credible project or purpose. If the Tories claim to be the party of the NHS and Labour apes Conservative neoliberalism and politics shadowing the Tories on immigration, and (to a certain extent) Europe or holding public utility companies to account, then it becomes apparent how conservative, traditionalist hegemony dominates English politics and national narrative. Importantly though, this cannot be said of Scotland where the SNP provides a populist, credible and wholesale alternative to the Conservatives in Westminster. Although the SNP are repeatedly couched within dominant discourse as being unreasonable, irresponsible and obsessed with equality and social welfare.

Although incrementally the left within Britain is viewed as being socially victorious, discursively, particularly at present within England, it is defeated. This is characterised by the language, rhetoric and ideology of the 'consensus at the centre'. 'Consensus at the centre' across all of the major English Westminster parties largely represents an exclusion of traditional working class concerns (although in terms of rhetoric, this is positioned as a key concern) and a normalisation of centre-right conservative politics. This forms the basis of a conservative, traditionalist, nationally dominant ideological discourse and frames the location of where pain will be felt socio/economically. As Ken Spours and Patrick Diamond (2016) comment, even following a largely surprise election victory in May 2015, having a slim parliamentary majority and suffering set-backs such as the loss of the EU referendum, the Conservatives enjoyed a process of consolidating their grip on the English political landscape. It retains the loyalty of the expanding retirees, the private business sector and is dominant in almost all English rural constituencies while making substantial gains in traditional Labour strongholds such as South Wales and the so-called 'Red-Wall'. Crucially however, 'they show an ability to summon and frame popular common sense through political "story telling" and the use of everyday analogies, in ways that continue to elude the left' (Spours and Diamond, 2016:16). Moreover, regardless of future electoral results, or even crushing defeats as in the 2023 local elections, the conservative, right-wing message remains dominant and discursively controls the agenda.

As Labour abandoned its traditional ideological base for the centre ground (roughly since 1994), English identity politics has become dominated and saturated by the middle class, middle England imperative. The dominant conservative perspective of Englishness is constructed within a rigid and narrow class, social and political framework. Subjective assumptions of class identity inform concepts of Englishness. It marginalises working class narratives instead representing them through stereotypes, while at the same time prioritising and naturalising middle and upper middle class narratives and discourses as being the authentic, representative and legitimate claim to Englishness. A distinct class-oriented narrative informs dominant conservative and traditionalist concepts of Englishness just as an ethnocentric and gender-based ideological normative narrative does.

An example of the dominance of such a perspective can be viewed in the way the financial crisis of 2008/09 was framed in British politics. Instead of the financial crisis providing the left with an ideological boon, it was used to further embed and consolidate a neoliberal attack against the welfare state (and any past Labour related economic policy) and to provide the articulation and contextualisation of constructed ideological enemies, such as welfare recipients or immigrants, further cementing a hegemonic binary oppositional narrative. At the same time, the Conservatives created the hypocritical myth-message of 'all in it together' with accompanying appeals to politically sanitised sentimentality of a 'Blitz spirit'. Labour failed to expose the real reasons for the economic crisis (speculative unsustainable capitalism, the banking sector and so on), instead generally followed the Conservative narrative. By the time Jeremy Corbyn became leader, the horse had bolted. Discourse, therefore, becomes a fundamental structure and means of understanding. It is a master signifier, which provides a consistent field of meaning (Mouffe, 2009).

## Discursive Boundaries and Borders

Nationalism fuses sociopolitical conservative elements and values into a dominant national narrative. This is typified by a neurotic attachment to ideological notions of oversimplified boundaries, fuelled by outpourings of anxiety and defensive posturing or, as Schlesinger (1987) describes it, the internal process of ideological boundary management. Traditional and conservative concepts of English national identity exist in a paradoxical world alongside a largely urban, multicultural and highly globalised reality where, 'the simplifications of identity politics are countered by the complexities of experience' (Hyland Eriksen, 2002: 160). As illogical as it may seem to assume that we can all experience and be represented by the same identity, in terms of national identity and dominant national discourses, this degree of simplification and creation of boundaries, stereotypes and normalisation of generalisations is *de rigueur*. Although 'all of us are composed of multiple social identities' (Hall, 1991:57), complexities and details are swept away and overlooked to fit in with the oversimplifications of socially, ideologically and politically motivated boundary management and maintenance of identity politics.

Homi Bhabha's dynamic model of cultural pluralism (1990) highlights the ever-changing and fluid boundaries of nationally imagined communities and the narratives that shape collective cultural discourses. However, the dominant discursive concepts of Englishness largely reject this perspective, instead favouring a stable and homogeneous sense of identity. These dominant forms of discourse construct a framework of displacement, attributing purpose, enemies and blame within an ideological context. They present themselves as the representative articulation of a populist and hegemonic 'us', disguising their positions as a 'common sense' approach. Owen Jones observes that 'most of the mainstream media is controlled by a very small number of politically motivated owners, whose grip on the media is one of the most devastatingly effective forms of political power and influence in modern Britain' (Jones, 2014:90). This is indicative of how conservative ideological discourses maintain dominance, regardless of their alignment with wider public opinion or concerns. The creation and sustenance of hegemonic political, social and cultural understanding take precedence in these discourses.

An example of the hegemonic use of 'us' can be seen in *The Daily Telegraph* (26/09/2013) in an article entitled, 'Why turn the other cheek to those who hate us'. This can be supplemented or replaced by any number of similar stories that appear daily in the right-wing press in the United Kingdom. This article (discussing Muslims) can be seen as an overt example of the discursive articulation of boundaries and borders, and as an expression and articulation of 'exclusionary normativeness' (Zizek, 2009). This represents a hegemonic position of an assumed, generalised and reinforced 'us' used against an assumed, generalised and reinforced 'them' who supposedly threaten 'us' and who 'we' shouldn't tolerate. The use and creation of 'them' is an ideologically framed opposite to 'us' as 'they' threaten the assumed, ideologically dominant and mythical hegemonic social order and power structure, articulated through 'us'. Framed in this way, diametric and ideologically opposed generalisations are created where the reader is forced to take a side – 'us', which then conceptually reinforces the differences and reasons why 'they' are both different and should be opposed.

Another key recurring theme in the right-wing press is to morally undermine and attack the Labour Party. For example, an article titled 'The man who hated Britain: Red Ed's pledge to bring back Socialism is a homage to his Marxist father. So what did Miliband Snr really believe in? The answer should disturb everyone who loves this country', provides a typical example of this. Here the *Daily Mail* articulates exclusionary themes prevalent in right-wing politics, immigrants, religious minorities and leftist intellectuals. While widely condemned at the time, this article exemplifies the ideological position of populist, right-wing, conservative and traditionalist discourse. Just on sales and readership alone, media outlets like the *Daily Mail*, *The Sun*, *The Daily Telegraph*, *The Times* and the *Daily Express* dominate information and commentary, perpetuating right-wing narratives on patriotism, identity and moral acceptability. Rather than acting as moral entrepreneurs, the media in this sense operate as moral stormtroopers enforcing a narrow national discourse, while systematically suppressing alternative viewpoints, and creating scapegoats through simplistic binary understandings.

It is not just right-wing mouth-pieces such as the *Daily Mail* articulating this ideology. The ideological representation of the left as unpatriotic or traitorous presents an oversimplified assumption that if you do not accept the dominant conservative position on nation and national identity, then you do not, and cannot, love your country. For example, former Labour MP Keith Vaz expressed such sentiments directly in a Commons Home Affairs Select Committee (03/12/2013). He repeatedly asked Alan Rusbridger (then editor of the Guardian) whether he loved his country, in relation to why he decided to publish the Edward Snowden files on spying by the security services. Vaz was making a symbolic statement that Rusbridger could not love his country if he wanted to expose illegal and unethical activities of the state security services. Vaz clearly implied that as Rusbridger did not subscribe to a conservative and reactionary perspective in regard to national identity, he could not love his country.

To expose wrong doing by government and the wider establishment towards the general population is unpatriotic as it attempts to undermine authority and trust. When Vaz implies that Rusbridger may not love his country because *The Guardian* newspaper leaked sensitive files, he is implying that to love your country is to hold a selective and ideologically bound perspective inherently situated within a conservative discourse that underpins a particular outlook on national identity. Vaz's statement cements the notion that this perspective is the assumed discursive position within mainstream Westminster politics and a wider dominant perspective. Rusbridger is unpatriotic because his intentions challenge the very notion of patriotism reinforced by Vaz. When Vaz asks, 'Do you love your country?' what he can be interpreted as asking is 'if you do not subscribe to the dominant idea of nation and values then you are a traitor'. This question represents the symbolic articulation of the dominance of a specific ideological approach to nation, national identity and the very terms in which it will be discussed and imagined.

According to Yuval-Davis and Anthias (1989), an imagined community divides the world between 'them' and 'us' maintained and systematically reproduced by what Armstrong (1982) calls 'symbolic border guards'. These tools of reinforcement of ideological dominant discursive articulations identify members or non-members by symbolic and specific cultural codes such as style of dress, behaviour, customs, lifestyle, beliefs, language et al. These border guards must not be viewed as exclusive producers of 'insider', 'outsider' delineation but within the debate and conflict over dominant forms of representations of the nation and national inclusivity/exclusivity.

From a macro viewpoint, identity politics of inclusion and exclusion operate as a philosophy of history, historicising people and identity ideologically. Here 'conspicuous forms of boundary maintenance become important when the boundaries are under pressure' (Hyland Eriksen, 2002:68). These constructed identities along specific lines embody a projected continuity with the past, which often functions to provide psychological reassurance and a form of comforting narrative. For its existence, such discourse depends on elements that it excludes, the homogenisation of the nation, for instance, can only be obtained in and through the construction of 'enemies of the nation', who are simultaneously outside and inside the nation (Torfing, 1999).

In a sociopolitical sense, ideologically conservative and traditionalist values are imposed which are, to varying extents, culturally, historically and ethnically specific. This is naturalised within the illusionary context of national identity and the homogenisation of a population through a discursive dominance. A right-wing, conservative nationalism attacks forms of anti-inequality from behind, by suggesting that political correctness or cultural tolerance in some way weakens the nation and threatens its cultural existence by being alien to a naturalised concept of Englishness. This is where concepts of 'common sense' are used as a coded meaning for exclusionary necessity; this is also linked to other forms of universalised discrimination.

The objective of conservative identity politics is to cultivate a sense of populism while referring to itself as the articulation and embodiment of an authentic and moral response. An obsessional quest for authenticity and legitimacy is personified within the conceptual domination of a universalist nature of the essence of Englishness; in other words, the only way to imagine the national character is through the universal illusionary domination of Englishness. It is an 'historical system of complementary exclusions and dominations which are mutually interconnected' (Balibar, 1991:49).

Recent trends concerning an upsurge in interest over what English national identity might mean, coupled with a sense of national soul searching for authenticity or expression of the security and comfort of tradition and nostalgia, can be viewed as a response to an increasing sense of unease felt in regard to identity within England (Skey, 2009). Skey points to interviews conducted concerning perspectives on English national identity. One respondent encapsulates a general sense of such anxieties, a convergence of dominant forms of conservative discourse by claiming, '40 years ago you wouldn't have to prove anything. This is England' (Skey, 2009:51). The allusion or implication here is immigration, multiculturalism and political correctness and their effects on what this respondent perceives in the national landscape.

Dominant forms of discourse seek to represent and purposely instruct. Categories, words and phrases such as 'this is England', 'we', 'us', and 'them' makes direct reference to ideological perspectives of exclusionary normativeness. Society is defined so as to automatically exclude certain categories of people (Schrover and Schinkel, 2013). This is how dominant forms of discourse operate in the public realm to conceptualise and create imagined ideals of society and concepts of culture. James Rhodes (2012) described this process as geographies of difference. This refers not just to imagined notions concerning race but also class and landscape dimensions. This can be defined as territorial stigmatisation, the constructed sociopolitical symbolisation of exclusion from an imagined and idealised sense of Englishness.

Skey concludes that a general picture emerged of English, British and white being used interchangeably to label the 'in group who were identified in opposition to a range of unnamed, though seemingly powerful, "others"' (Skey, 2009: 51). This clear identification to an ideological identity relates back to Zizek's (2009) concept of 'exclusionary normativeness', the ideological creation and reinforcement of group boundaries. A general theory of exclusion operates much as a theory of exclusionary normativeness, the conceptualisation of an imagined community and national space as a homogenised entity as defined by conservative and traditionalist values, the ideological 'out group' here being political correctness, this being repeatedly reinforced within a representative imagining of national identity, irrespective of how unrepresentative and manipulated this may be.

A reactionary response and engagement reinforces forms of exclusionary boundary enforcement, especially in regards and relation to a symbolic 'other', represented in relation to conservative conceptualisations of multiculturalism, cosmopolitanism and political correctness (as an internal threat) and by the European Union and immigration (as an external threat). A daily, reinforced, aggressively defensive and exclusionary position suggests that 'Englishness' is threatened by these elements. This position perpetuates a sense of 'threat' to further reinforce and consolidate an identity politics based on inclusion and exclusion. As pointed out, 'at particular times and under particular conditions, the sense of national identity is particularly threatened. In other words, the need to foster and assert the sense of identity may be stronger at some times than others' (Kong and Yeoh, 1997:214). Relating this to a perceived sense of unsettled, uncertain and threatened Englishness, the right easily manipulates and fuels such especially when casual and over generalised links to internal and external threats are made.

The imposition of limits and ideological boundaries through a conceptual subordination of 'others' is at the heart of a dominant framework that excludes but maintains the approach of an established conservative status quo. In other words, such objectivism and essentialism is dominant within western democratic theory. 'Any social objectivity is constituted through acts of power. This means that any social objectivity is ultimately political and has to show the traces of the acts of exclusion which governs its constitution' (Mouffe, 2009:21).

Western democracy requires first, homogeneity and second, if required the elimination of heterogeneity (Mouffe, 2009). Although this can be viewed as a broad symbolic statement, within the contemporary context, this relates to the boundaries of citizenship and belonging and associated dominant ideological frameworks. Democracy and identity are linked to the 'fundamental principle of the unity of the demos and the sovereignty of its will. But if the people are to rule, it is necessary to determine who belongs to the people' (Mouffe, 2009:43). However, such a generalisation can be viewed as populism not democracy. This is the problem when national identity is discussed. Identity politics often come down to representations of populism which, in turn, promote negative stereotypes, folk devils and political and social scapegoats. This can be conceptualised as 'tactical linkage' which clusters issues as 'areas of joint gain', such as the linkage of social cohesion, safety, criminality and terrorism, to migration (Schrover and Schinkel, 2013). This, therefore, controls how issues are dealt with and the context in which they are discussed.

Populism can be viewed as a self-serving and self-perpetuating ideological creation. The ideological manifestation and use of 'others' who threaten the 'national interest' only further reinforces conservative, right-wing dominance. This is then politically acted upon which, in turn, ramps up the rhetorical pressure. For example, the Bishop of Dudley and leading Anglican cleric, David Walker, commented that, 'public fear around immigration are like fears around crime. They bear little relationship to the actual reality' (Helm, 2013). This came as David Cameron announced in 2013 tough new measures to ensure that immigrants would have to wait for up to five years before they could access waiting lists for social housing. This compounds the negative exaggeration and demonisation of immigrants, which as Walker highlights, is 'wholly disproportionate' (ibid). Fuelling fears and threats creates a self-perpetuating political arms race of hardline anti-immigrant rhetoric, based largely upon an illusionary (yet ideological) problem. Policing these ideological borders of being tough on crime and immigration has been constant for any mainstream political party; however, for the Conservatives, these, especially immigration, have been the constant point of reference to reinforce their nationalist credentials, regardless of actual figures, impacts or effects any policy might or might not have. It has always been the symbolic message not the actual impact or results that matter in this regard.

Ideas concerning a sense of national consensus and identity coupled with expressions of an illusionary concept of hegemony are political and therefore should be contested.

> To deny the existence of such a moment of closure, or to present the frontier as dictated by rationality or morality, is to naturalise what should be perceived as a contingent and temporary hegemonic articulation of 'the people' through a particular regime of inclusion-exclusion.
>
> (Mouffe, 2009:49)

The foundation of liberal democracy being a forum for debate, contestation and heterogeneity of politics, beliefs and backgrounds has now been crushed by a hegemonic yet pseudo-democratic-representative ideology. Who is included or excluded from the notion of national identity explicitly indicates the political ideological boundaries contained in the dominant form of nationalism that defines and dominates debate over identity. Within a conservative and traditionalist conceptualisation of Englishness, difference can be celebrated as long as it is subsumed and does not force us to reflect critically on established national myths and ideological boundaries. Difference, in this regard, must still be viewed as fundamentally the 'other' and not be included as representative of a common narrative.

The fear preventing recognition of sameness is worse than the fear of difference as it critically undermines the carefully, socially, politically and ideologically created notions of difference. It would expose the deep social, political and cultural psychological investments created in how difference is currently understood (Naidoo, 2008). Moreover, it would undermine the internalised boundaries carefully cultivated and reinforced from a conservative and traditionalist perspective on community inclusion. Therefore, it comes as a refreshing surprise when the veil of ideological narratives is lifted and we see those portrayed as fundamentally different as being similar to ourselves, often in the most banal ways, such as a Muslim woman in a burka with a thick Brummie accent.

The fear of sameness – that we are all integral parts of and involved in this 'mongrel nation' – undermines dominant conservative discourse on Englishness. In this sense, tokenism is tolerated (or indeed required) as it emphasises difference and provides a claim to authenticity while not disturbing general ideological narratives around identity. Comfort with difference can only be found when difference is highlighted and reinforced as this, again, does not disturb dominant narratives on the nation as this does not alter fundamental relationships of power.

The 'mongrel nation' narrative of a historically hybridised population undermines conservative, right-wing concepts relating to immigration and asylum. The reinforcement of difference and 'otherness' used in this debate by the right encourages vicious ideological assaults on 'them', and for 'us' to lose 'our' humanity and compassion through an implied necessity. As Naidoo comments, 'the dehumanisation of them is so complete that even those whose backgrounds are recently migratory, and who thus could perhaps see similarities more clearly, can be just as vociferous in their dislike of these supposedly disruptive newcomers' (Naidoo, 2008:77). Recent examples of hardline Conservative Home Secretaries such as Suella Braverman and Priti Patel bear this out perfectly.

A narrative of sameness is, therefore, unsettling and dangerous to dominant discourses of Englishness. Issues such as asylum and immigration are dealt with in a strict, narrow and decontextualised manner. Rarely are historical similarities referred to and never are enlightened connections between 'them' and 'us' sought. Referring back to the example of individuals with a relatively recent migratory history, to become one of 'us' or assimilated is to decontextualise yourself from your own background and position yourself within a conservative ideological approach. Differences of ethnic others can be fitted into what makes the nation special, but taking us down the road of thinking about the ways in which we are all the same cannot help but cut through the arrogance, presumptions, distortions and half-truths upon which we build our national identity (Naidoo, 2008).

As pointed out by Mouffe (2009), we need to formulate a better understanding of liberal democracy – one which acknowledges its paradoxical nature but also comes to terms with the inclusion/exclusion dynamic which liberal democracy politics entails. Applying a contextual critical reflection to liberal democratic institutions, politics and forms of identity can be used to understand contemporary issues without forcing solutions that do not fit or are incompatible. Without such conceptual application, 'reason' or 'common sense' is trapped within the subjective confines of cultural ignorance or structural dogma.

What is needed is a new conceptual approach and shift in identity-based politics and a recognition that it is something that is constructed, not empirically given. In this sense, we are looking towards a radical shift from essentialised notions of national commonality to an ethical, heterogenous and inclusive bond among all participants of the political and social community, a community built on commonality of difference. This concept of an inclusive national identity opposes the right-wing, conservative and traditionalist concept based upon exclusion, division and defensiveness. As Stuart Hall points out, 'if we feel we have a unified identity…it is only because we construct a comforting story or "narrative of the self" about ourselves…The fully unified, completed, secure and coherent identity is a fantasy' (Hall, 1992:277). An anti-essentialist approach does not deny the existence of ethnicity, race, culture and nation as entities in the world but instead crucially questions the subjective, politically ideological boundary creation of such entities employed as immovable and unquestioned phenomena or 'facts'.

Chapter 4

# Racialised Discourses and Cosmopolitan Existences

This chapter will outline historicised and ideologically constructed identities that essentialise ethnicity and place and will investigate the suggestion that dominant discursive concepts of Englishness imply a specifically ethnic and racialised identity. Conservative and traditionalist concepts of Englishness provide a defensive and reactionary position from which they seek to find identity and meaning within the context of a contemporary, multicultural modern English society or reality. It will be argued and critically analysed that dominant conservative constructions of Englishness operate and exist within opposition to concepts of Britishness and how the New Labour Project has impacted upon concepts and discourses of Englishness.

This chapter will also explore theories around cultural amnesia concerning a long and positive history of immigration and myths concerning national ascendency, the general argument being that often dominant concepts around national identity are an ethnic fantasy and racialised myths of symbolic community and place. This chapter will not be an attempt to give an exhaustive and definitive account of race relations or the history of immigration to the United Kingdom or England. What will be discussed and investigated is the relationship of these processes and the wider debate, conflict and discursive narrative of a sense of English national identity.

## Englishness as an Historicised Ideological Narrative

Dominant conservative discourses concerning Englishness are, to varying degrees, ethnically, culturally and historically based. Colin Wright describes the inhabitants of England as a 'wonderfully mongrel people' (Wright, 2000:13). Dominant narratives of historical, political and cultural amnesia deny this ever being part of an inclusive, diverse and positive sense of Englishness and is excluded from idiosyncratic concepts such as 'quintessentially English'. What is most jarring and uncomfortable for those on the political, social and cultural right is how the present social reality experienced by the majority of the English population upsets

**Constructing Realities, 83–109**
**Copyright © 2024 Stuart Cartland**
**Published under exclusive licence by Emerald Publishing Limited**
**doi:10.1108/978-1-83797-545-720231005**

a myth of English ascendancy, most notably underpinned by what Graham Marsden (2000) characterises as a form of consolidated and centralised stability, stretching back to 1066 which laid the success and identity of the English. A myth of a sustaining self-image or fantasy has also formed the basis to the British and imperial projects over the last three centuries, yet both are either over (in relation to empire) or are directly challenged (in relation to the United Kingdom). 'The fiction of an England at ease with itself, little invaded or interfered with apart from the apocalyptic events of 1066, does not stand up to the scrutiny of the historical record' (Marsden, 2000:20). This illusion is twofold; it consists of believing that generations, which succeed one another over centuries on a reasonably stable territory, under a reasonably univocal designation, have handed down to each other an invariant substance. It also consists in believing that the process of development from which we select aspects retrospectively so as to see ourselves as the culmination of that process was the only one possible, that is, it represents a destiny (Balibar, 1991) and is, therefore, a 'natural' and legitimate entity.

To speak, or claim to be, English is to speak metaphorically as it is a socially, culturally and politically constructed concept. Yet, it is a concept deeply reduced to a form of natural and essential status. Identities are symbolic attachments to meaning, however they can become deeply exclusive and essentialist when linked to ethnicity, as Stuart Hall comments, 'we think of them as if they were parts of our essential natures' (Hall, 1995). Moreover, in terms of ethnicity, Englishness is deeply associated and assumed to be Anglo-Saxon (which paradoxically is based upon immigrant populations), not Celtic and not any of the subsequent waves of immigration and settlement since the Norman Conquest. This is largely an ethnic reductionist, historically narrow and culturally shallow representation and understanding that largely dominates discourses of Englishness and ethnicity.

These associations and meanings are the perpetuations of an ideological sense of a 'symbolic community' (Hall, 1995). This symbolic community is represented through discursive articulations. The English national imagination is dominated by discourse based upon heritage and nostalgia which is read through a conservative, traditionalist and right-wing ideology. It utilises concepts of '"race" and "heritage" which rely heavily on each other to deliver meaning but have to be kept separate so that the unpleasantness of 'race' doesn't impinge on the purity of "heritage"' (Naidoo, 2008:77). It is a largely negative ideology of loss, threat and anxiety towards a contemporary era, whereas Paul Gilroy (2005) states, we get transported into the frozen realm of mythic time that has been shaped around the master analogy of immigration as a form of conflict or warfare. That unhappy, archaic domain is populated by the timeless, iconic ciphers of post-colonial melancholia: criminals, spongers and their numberless alien offspring. Certain concepts or problematisations are created, maintained and used to sustain dominant ideological positions, such as (the need for) restrictions on immigrants which can be so dominant that it is hard to think outside them.

Problematising requires a process of legitimising. Appeals to consensus are constructed and required to deal with a 'problem' that affects 'us' and indeed that 'we' need to agree that there is such a unique contemporary problem. For example, discourse on immigration issues focuses almost exclusively on associated problems. The conservative and right-wing press emphasise the problems that immigrants are seen to create in housing, schooling, unemployment, crime and so on. The incessant negative repetition and framing through dominant discursive channels of these issues and relationships to different social and cultural groups solidifies known 'knowledge' or known 'facts' in the wider public realm where debate and rhetoric, therefore, becomes unquestioned common currency.

The ever-present image of immigrants trying to cross borders (the recent 'small boat crisis' being a case in point) and the focus upon immigration and asylum policies and political parties trying to out-do each other in their 'zero tolerance' approach are further discursive tools used to emulate exclusion into a wider public discourse and narrative. Border policing and immigration law enforcement produces 'a spectacle that enacts a scene of "exclusion"' (Schrover and Schinkel, 2013). These spectacles render migrant 'illegality' visible and help to generate a constellation of images and discursive formations, which supply migrant 'illegality' with the semblance of objective fact embedded within narratives of the nation.

Within a context of defensive nationalism and national anxiety, those (usually from a minority cultural background) who represent a challenge to or disrupt a traditionalist conservative, nostalgic national imagining are conceptually dealt with through a process of ethnic reductionism. As Geoffrey Hoskins points out, this is where 'ethnicity thus strengthens bonds of mutual trust within the ethos, but also often intensifies reciprocal distrust around its boundaries' (Hosking, 2016:213). Ethnicity provides a quasi-master status through which identity is shaped. This master status is located within a racialised and whitewashed sense of nation, national character and a very narrow historicised account of identity. Ethnic minorities are relegated to cameo and bit-part performances and are largely excluded from an assumed homogenised sense of inclusivity within an imagined community of Englishness.

Any imagined or perceived challenges to traditional roles and distribution of power are viewed as an imposed and alien onslaught of the forces of modernity. A defensive paranoia and an aching sense of loss are articulated through a constant theme of 'endangered whiteness' (Gilroy, 2005). For example, the *Daily Mail* front page from 15/07/2014(a) declared that the cabinet reshuffle was a deliberate clear out of white, middle-aged men, while at the same time declared the rise of women within the cabinet. However, the evidence to back this up is severely lacking – female representation in the cabinet went from a pre-reshuffle 3 to post-reshuffle 5 (out of 22), while Cameron actually appointed more men than women in his reshuffle, which represents an overwhelming majority of men. There were no appointees from an ethnic minority background (96% of the cabinet at the time of the reshuffle were white); while the median age of the cabinet remained at a very middle-aged 47.5 years (Guardian, 2014b).

The main point is that headlines from the *Daily Mail* (and other sections of the right-wing press) and those on the right only serve to reinforce a dominant conservative discourse of threat to the traditional status-quo by a deliberate, modernising politically correct agenda. Tokenistic gestures towards equality are treated as fundamental shifts of power, while an entitled aristocratic elite remain firmly in place. Englishness as an essentialised characteristic is portrayed as being fundamentally under threat by the forces of modernity. An exercise in anxiety inducing paranoia and claims of an attack on middle-aged, white men actually hides the evidence that quite the reverse is often true and often forms the pre-text to an aggressive and defensive rhetorical bombardment of discourse management.

## Exclusive Normativity

Calls or appeals to a right-wing concept of 'common sense' imply a homogenous and objective claim of shared norms which are harnessed into normative and naturalised discourse of Englishness. This often being articulated through dominant conservative, right-wing rhetoric and messages via political speeches, media commentary and in turn through everyday implied racism and negative stereotyping. This directly affects who is included or excluded within the national community and what constitutes national identity and national character. As Joe Kennedy highlights, 'the only way to imagine Englishness at all is as something that one isn't permitted to celebrate' (Kennedy, 2018:143). For example, objective expressions such as poppies, Spitfires but also allusions to, empire, exclusivism and expressions of chauvinism are used as cultural markers that are obstructed by some imagined metropolitan leftist elite and where 'the average person on the street' (code for white, heterosexual, male) are marginalised or forgotten.

For example, when Nigel Farage described parts of Britain 'like a foreign land' at the United Kingdom Independence Party (UKIP) spring conference in 2014 (Sparrow, 2014) he directly symbolised a strong and casual link between these themes. Such underlying themes form a simplified populist conservative narrative of modern urban society, ethnic minorities, race and diversity through an illusionary, defensive sense of alienation in 'one's own country' but also implies themes of decay, conflict and crime. It is a distinctly negative narrative and articulates modern, reactionary conservative and traditionalist ideology towards contemporary society. Repeated phrases such as 'Broken Britain' link a conceptualisation of an illusionary past free of these themes and present conservative or 'common sense' values as being under attack and besieged by a hostile present. Within this context, race, crime, ethnic minorities and modern society can therefore be seen as, 'a sort of prism through which the whole conjuncture could be "read" symptomatically' (Hall, 2007:148).

In this example, Farage is not just articulating his own personal prejudices and dislikes; he is carefully cultivating and tapping into populist right-wing discursive accounts while also reinforcing 'common sense' divisions between concepts of 'them' and 'us', 'then' and 'now' but also how the conservative right are benevolent crusaders for the working class. This perspective is not just limited to a conservative approach; the whole political debate and context has firmly shifted to taking on such 'concerns' or 'facts' as the basis for accepted grounds of discussion and debate. Stuart Hall (2007) points out, it is not just a political victory for the right but a profound change in political culture that the left has become centre-right in mainstream politics, especially in relation to topics such as immigration, multiculturalism and asylum. Therefore, such a seemingly off-the-cuff remark or claim is actually a seriously debated political point marking out the parameters of political, social and cultural discourse instead of being read as a very subjective, right-wing, conservative interpretation of contemporary English society.

As previously stated, a dominant discursive sense of Englishness can be read as a naturalised state of timeless belonging, or rather as Etienne Balibar states, 'the naturalisation of belonging and the sublimation of the ideal nation are two aspects of the same process' (Balibar, 1991:96). For example, a discursive proclamation of 'common values' are wholly framed and contextualised within a culturally and socially traditionalist identity including strong themes of Christianity and an implied homogenous white, ethnic cultural identity. Firmly rooted in 'traditional' values, this serves to frame national debate and discussion which is then located within a conservative and traditionalist sense of belonging, heritage and identity.

As Judith Butler (2000) notes, the Kantian presumption that when 'I' reason I participate in a rationality is then transposed and transpersonal and culminates in the claim that my reasoning presupposes a universalisation of such claims. This approach presupposes the priority and authenticity of such rationality much like the 'national values' rationality of the Conservative Party. It situates and universalises one's own values and to disseminate them as a 'norm' for an imagined hegemonic community. Nations, national identity and dominant discourse are specific ideological and political constructs often built upon mythical and assumed concepts of essentialism and hegemony.

Ethnic, racial, cultural and social divisions are not mutually exclusive categories within constructions of a national framework of a conservative, traditionalist narrative; they are interlinked in a complex historically and socially relative manner which are continuously undergoing revision and are a perpetual theme within conservative discourses. Moreover, as Roshi Naidoo points out, 'for people who understand British history on this binary of a white past/multicultural present it is not difference in its present guise which poses a threat, but the fact that it was always so' (Naidoo, 2008:74).

Interposed within these dominant conservative discourses of national identity, ethnic minority segregation 'is one of disconnection from the nation's cultural and political imagination' (Malek, 2008:23). Regardless of how well certain communities may outperform the national average in educational achievement, or how certain communities average crime rates may be below the national average, or how certain communities may have long historical and cultural roots in England, or how well integrated they might be into social life, community structures and employment, they are still excluded from an ideological imagining of a conservative and discursively dominant variety. This underpins and informs conservative, right-wing conceptualisations of Englishness as minority communities are excluded from a timeless essentialised vision of England.

Much like the largely stigmatised and demonised working classes, 'there is no attempt to understand the cultural resources of migrant communities beyond their in/compatibility with official discourses of the nation' (Malek, 2008:27). Understandings of racial and cultural boundaries are implicit and sometimes explicit in the political and social sphere when discussions of 'us' and 'them' or the included and excluded feature in debate concerning the nation or national identity. External frontiers and boundaries of the nation run parallel to 'internal frontiers' (Balibar, 1991). An imagined homogenised and exclusive community and identity, therefore, exists and is defined against such frontiers. These frontiers are articulated and re-emphasised constantly as a projection and defence of an internal ideological collective identity.

Within dominant concepts of Englishness, the past is mythologised as being untainted by political correctness, multiculturalism, globalisation, the European Union and political and social equality. This is an ideologically selective reading conjured up to reinforce concepts of homogeneity and to reinforce the 'insider', 'outsider' delineation. 'There is a fantasy of an all-white past of "proper heritage" which the mongrel nation narrative takes away from us' (ibid). Discursive insistence on imagined internal and external borders (and included and excluded peoples) are explicit sites of power struggles over legitimate forms of membership of the national character, national identity and national community, here 'discursive constructions and the practices through which they are effectuated are sites of symbolic power, and their study reveals the workings of power' (Schrover and Schinkel, 2013), but are also used to define difference and to reinforce a sense of naturalisation and legitimacy.

Dominant conservative discourse perpetuates, reproduces and relies upon the dualistic paring and binary opposites of the positive and negative representations in relation to race through language, presentation, choice of metaphors and analogies of Black/white, settler/native, legal/illegal, natural/unnatural and normal/deviant. To address and disrupt underlying racist and divisive discourse requires the destruction and repudiation of these simplistic and lazy stereotypical binary pairings. Conservative and right-wing concepts of Englishness invoke a parochial attachment to 'race' through the use of such symbolism. This often refers not only to biological or ethnic differentiation but, more importantly, social and cultural hierarchies situated within an historicised and essentialised mythology of colonial and imperial histories.

The relationship between mutually antagonistic imagined social groups of 'outsiders', 'aliens', 'them' and 'us' denies any possibility of a comforting resolution. This equates to a rationalised and legitimised moral and political economy of ruthless binary opposites operating as unquestioned common currency within a dominant conservative discursive field. What can be seen to feed regimented cultural segregation is a refusal to abolish the idea of defining a bounded community through 'race' regardless of well-intentioned, yet empty gestures that might suggest otherwise. In this regard, differentiation is the unintended consequence of making everybody the same but then rearranging them in an historical sequence that rationalises their differences in the context of race, history and culture.

## Victimology

Advocacy of the idea that there is a political or ethical obligation to deal with racism and its consequences has been dismissed as an endorsement of victimology, as special pleading or as an implicit rejection of universal and liberal standards of justice and governance (Gilroy, 2005). This stance can be often viewed as a strategy of being implicitly racist (or sexist, or homophobic) by the right-wing press, for instance. The claim is that racism does not exist, and that those who say it does (from an ethnic minority background) are pleading to be treated differently, deferentially or specially. Governmental or institutional concessions, programmes or policies that target racism (or any form of discrimination or inequality) are queried, criticised or rejected on the grounds that they are unfair, unjust or undemocratic and hegemonic claims of 'what about the rest of us' or 'perilisation of the white, male, Christian' are systematically wheeled out.

Right-wing responses to the Black Lives Matter (BLM) movement from 2020 being a case in point. The political moment provided the opportunity for platitudes and tepid words of comfort in response to the murder of George Floyd. However, it also demonstrated how shallow and insincere this was. For example, Prime Minister Boris Johnson commented on how racism has no place within society, while in a 2002 column in *The Daily Telegraph*, he described Africans as 'flag waving piccaninnies with watermelon smiles' (Forrest, 2019). The BLM movement also delivered an entirely expected response to concerns and criticisms raised around issues of institutional and structural racism within the United Kingdom, particularly around the legacy and impact of colonialism and empire. What was offered was empty words and limp gestures by the government while being entirely unapologetic around the role the United Kingdom had in the transatlantic slave trade and the extensive catalog of colonial atrocities and abuses, at the same time defending the institutionally and systematically racist police force in the United Kingdom, particularly the Metropolitan Police.

The BLM protests provided an existential threat to dominant discursive representations of history, identity and structures of power within contemporary society. When protesters threw a statue of notorious slave trader Edward Colston into Bristol Harbour in June 2020, this challenged a dominant or accepted understanding of the past and of structures of power and acceptability in the present. This was seen by the right as an affront to an acceptable ideological worldview, or rather, woke revisionist madness and extremism. It also fed into the creation of a so-called 'culture war' by the right where 'cancel culture' (or rather the challenging of institutional inequality) represents an attack on the very fabric of history, culture, society and nationhood. However, the point being that to recognise a statue of a slave trader in a prominent public place is the symbolic representation of an entirely constructed concept of the past that legitimises the structures of power, place and identity of the present. The Colston Statue is just one example, however the point is that to take down such a very public symbol would be at least to recognise social, cultural and political inequality, this being something that was not (and is still not) acceptable.

Another example of the compartmentalising of racist inequality and the defence of structural inequality can be gleaned from the resignation from government of Sayeeda Warsi on Tuesday 5 August 2014. Warsi cannot be viewed as a conservative moderate (she voted against gay marriage and offered no objection to key divisive Conservative policies such as 'the bedroom tax'), however it is what she symbolically represents in terms of access and proximity to power and concepts of Englishness that made her position so uncomfortable and unique but also why she inevitably tendered her resignation. Warsi resigned over the 'morally indefensible' government position and policy over Gaza. In his response, David Cameron symbolically (and tellingly) indicated that issues regarding the killing and suppression of Muslims can only be close to her heart because she is a Muslim herself. This can be detected in his letter of acceptance to Sayeeda Warsi's resignation letter when he stated that, 'I understand your strength of feeling on the current crisis in the Middle East – the situation is intolerable' (BBC Politics, 2014a). Indeed, Warsi was the first Muslim woman to sit in the cabinet (as a Conservative Party co-chair).

The resignation of Lady Warsi represents further advances of the dominant back bench right-wing of the party who always rejected the appointment of Warsi into senior governmental positions, 'from the beginning, Warsi's rise was viewed with suspicion by some in the party's grassroots and the right-wing press, who regarded her as tokenistic' (Guardian, 2014c). For traditionalist Conservatives, Warsi was an uncomfortable fit for front bench politics – being a female Muslim from the north of England who attended a state comprehensive school. This distinctly un-Conservative background made her the focus of much negative and critical attention but also fundamentally led to her incompatibility with the party and its ideological direction. Warsi increasingly criticised government direction and policy decisions – she 'irritated party bosses in March [2014] by holding up a sign on ITV suggesting there should be an end to the "Eton Mess" at the heart of Downing Street' (Guardian, 2014c). Her sidelining by the party and resignation only served to further solidify the homogenous and exclusive make-up of the Conservative Party, their image, appeal and message. Lady Warsi's resignation (particularly over such an emotive and sensitive issue) is symptomatic of the ideological exclusivity of the Conservative approach and outlook and the incompatibility of such a position with the flux and diversity of modern English cultural experience. Moreover, even though in 2023 the two most senior political jobs in the country are held by two people of colour and descendants from immigrants from the Indian subcontinent Rishi Sunak and Suella Braverman, the institutional approach towards identity, ethnicity and inclusion has not change – indeed, with Braverman, it has become ever more toxic and divisive. The point being that the personnel might change but the ideological approach and dominant narrative stays the same.

## Cultural Amnesia

What underlies the conservative position towards national identity and 'race' is the inability to come to terms with contemporary English society. That inability and denial is intertwined with the gradual break-up of the United Kingdom, successive political and economic crises, the arrival of substantial numbers of post-colonial citizen-migrants, and the shock and anxiety that followed from a loss of any sense that the national collective was bound by a coherent and distinctive culture. Feelings of loss, anxiety and threat have been turned inwards towards a sense of failure, crisis and blame. This is also turned inwards towards those that are living reminders of empire are treated and how they are discursively dealt with, 'the error of imagining that postcolonial people are only unwanted alien intruders without any substantive historical, political, or cultural connections to the collective life of their fellow subjects' (Gilroy, 2005:90). The unwitting bearers of an imperial and colonial past, they project and reflect the anxiety, fear and loss back towards their neighbours.

Conceptual and ideological discursive manipulations and convenient cultural and political amnesia is termed by Gilroy aptly as 'postcolonial melancholia' (Gilroy, 2005). This description of a pathological state of guilt, loathing, denial and depression can be seen to characterise the xenophobic response from the conservative, right-wing traditionalist conceptualisation of Englishness to the 'aliens' or 'strangers' that have intruded or trespassed in recent decades. This response or discursive representation is not new. Xenophobic popularism whipped up through discursive representations is characteristic of countless instances throughout English history, for example, the passage of the 1905 Aliens Act and accompanying feverish cultural anxiety towards Eastern European Jews being a case in point. Themes of immigration are a constant within English history and identity, so too the discursive xenophobia towards such immigrants, the irony being that England itself is a nation of successive waves of immigrants. Politically incited and manipulated hatred can therefore be viewed as national self-flagellation, an incoherent and irrational hatred of difference, for the ever-evolving and changing self.

No truly inclusive or positive national identity is possible without coming to terms with the complex and negative implications of imperial and colonial history. A mature, psychological and cultural approach to diversity, plurality and differentiation is the only way out of the defensive and negative xenophobic corner of dominant national discourse. Also necessary would be the recognition of everyday encounters with difference (in all aspects), and a renunciation of the pursuit of global superiority instead of a pathological traditionalist pursuit of mythical homogeneity.

Within this plethora of emotive cultural histories and contested meanings, a racialised identification endures and becomes a generalised means to codify an understanding of place and historical culturalised contextualisation. Enoch Powell's infamous speeches on immigration (and power) played with these powerful feelings of aggression, guilt and fear and articulated them as outwardly racist policies. Intensified feelings of resentment and rejection are, and have been widely stoked up, manipulated and discursively articulated wherever a perceived threat to the existing order may develop or where reasonable requests for equality, fairness and representation are called for.

Two distinct speeds of accommodation and inclusion can be seen to be in operation – on the one hand, there is the continually unfolding and evolving social and cultural development of the heterogeneous nation. On the other hand, there is the dominant discourse of a national collective imaginary – the former changing and developing very slowly and bound up with an illusion of an unchanging homogeneity that is distinctly out of step and out-of-touch with the later. 'Race' becomes a means of symbolically anchoring a sense of nation and identity. It is welcomed for its apparent certainties and is, therefore, exploited as an essential means to keep bearings in a world experienced as increasingly confusing. In this sense, English identity is casually and implicitly conflated with race and can be seen as being symptomatic of the ethnic and racial exclusivity and ambiguity which constitutes much of conservative, right-wing and traditionalist narrative.

Attitudes and public debate towards race, nationalism, aggressive rhetoric towards the European Union, assertive 'common sense', right-wing politics of the anti-PC, anti-woke variety and a wider sense of disquiet over a political system that is perceived as being out-of-touch with the 'common man' are the consequence of what Mark Perryman (2009) calls the right-wing popularism of the 'post-political consensus', or as Slavoj Zizek (2009) describes it, 'post-political bio-politics'. This can be viewed as the result of the lack of an effective democratic debate about possible alternatives that has led (in many countries in Europe alongside the United Kingdom) to the success of right-wing political parties who claim to be 'the voice of the people' or the disenfranchised and neglected, indigenous majority.

Discursive dominance by right-wing populism and rhetoric fuelled by the economic crisis of 2008 onwards 'has been framed, fundamentally, by a version of nationalism that defines itself against outsiders, immigration (and latterly Muslims in particular), Europe, and a form of social democracy it thinks of as un-English' (Perryman, 2009:38). As Eric Hobsbawn pointed out in relation to the nationalist fall-out from the Falklands War, the appeal of such nationalist discourse 'acts as a sort of compensation for the feelings of decline, demoralisation and inferiority. This is intensified by economic crisis' (Hobsbawm, 1983:19) This is precisely the type of assertive nationalism displayed, for instance, at the Lindsey Oil Refinery in early 2009, alongside union banners, Union Jacks and 'British Jobs for British Workers' placards were waved (Perryman, 2009). Here, emotive and reactionary sentiments mix with localism and racism where a populist right-wing narrative acts to simplify the key underlying issues and divert blame and solutions.

Simplified nationalist messages and narratives are both reinforced and ratcheted up by the response and reaction of political parties whereby it becomes almost obsessional to blame and attack Europe, welfare and immigration within the context of political/economic crisis'. The conservative, right-wing stance, particularly on immigration, has hardened to such an extent that Gordon Brown (in Carrell, 2013) in his first major speech since leaving office, labelled the

Conservative Party as Powellite in their approach to, and rhetoric on, this topic. Indeed, under Prime Minister Rishi Sunak and Home Secretary Suella Braverman, the Illegal Migration Bill was approved by the House of Commons in April 2023, meaning that anyone arriving on a small boat crossing the English Channel will be prevented from claiming asylum in the United Kingdom and will either be deported to their homeland or sent to Rwanda, a clear breach of the International Refugee Convention, thus further demonising refugees and asylum seekers and pandering to right-wing populism.

Often discussions or debate concerning the 'state of the nation' fall into an aggressive, assertive and melancholic tone concerning national history, direction, race and national identity. Responsibility for any perceived national crisis is laid directly at the door of twentieth century post-colonial immigrants, Eastern European welfare tourists, small boat arrivals and a perceived moral decay and corruption of an equality obsessed modernising agenda.

Roger Scruton's *England: An Elegy* (2000), Peter Ackroyd's *Albion: The Origins of the English Imagination* (2002) and 'freedom of speech' anti-intersectional polemics such as Douglas Murray's *The Madness of Crowds: Gender, Race and Identity* (2019) or right wing historians such as David Starkey have all lined up to provide a quasi-moral defence that supports simplified rhetoric, discourse and national narrative evident throughout mainstream media. Right-wing conservative discourse on immigration can be viewed as part of a wider process of casualisation of ethnic compartmentalism in relation to the national narrative and concepts of Englishness. Powellite right-wing themes on immigration become normalised through repetition and then become part of mainstream narrative. Sensational rhetorical claims such as David Cameron describing a 'swarm of people coming across the Mediterranean' (Grierson, 2021) or Victoria Ayling proclaiming, 'I just wanna send the lot back' (BBC, 2013a), to GB News proclaiming; 'The UK's offering shelter to terrorists. It's time to put Briton's interests first... you guessed it! Soft touch Britain cannot deport them thanks partially to human rights legislation' (Grimes, 2023). Moreover, Home Secretary Priti Patel in 2021 refused to even use the terms asylum seekers or refugees to describe people crossing the channel in small boats, insisting on labelling them as 'economic migrants' claiming that 70% of people who come to the United Kingdom via small boats are 'single men who are effectively economic migrants' and 'not genuine asylum seekers' (Grierson, 2021). A point the Refugee Council stated was misleading and inaccurate, that in fact the opposite being true, that nearly two-thirds being genuine refugees.

The point being that aggressive anti-immigration and anti-PC rhetoric becomes more or less acceptable political commentary. These inflammatory claims become part of the dominant narrative and taken as fact. In other words, the message stays the same regardless of the semantics; moreover, it can be seen to symbolically represent the prevailing 'common sense' dominant right-wing conservative discourse on immigration and political correctness, however articulated.

A steady stream of UKIP and Conservative elected officials and members have been caught voicing racist, sexist, misogynistic or homophobic comments. While UKIP as a domestic political force has dwindled since Brexit, during the 2015 general election, they pulled the Conservative Party (and to a lesser extent Labour) further to the right on issues such as immigration, Europe, welfare and equality which has largely remained. However, it is not just the Conservatives that followed UKIP with such a right-wing ideological approach. Labour's own rhetoric on immigration (and to a lesser extent, Europe) can be interpreted (in this context) as a catch-up position with the Conservatives who were in turn trying to catch up with UKIP over a hardline approach which plays to the created popular fear and anxieties created over such emotive issues.

Labour's former shadow chancellor, Ed Balls, in his speech at the 2014 Labour Party conference took a decidedly Conservative tack on Labour's position on immigration, offering apologies for its immigration policy on Eastern European migrants while in government in 2004 and promising a tougher line in the run-up to the 2015 election. Apologetically peddling myths and half-truths about the effects of immigration, 'by moving to the right on immigration, Labour is acquiescing in shifting the whole political discourse on immigration to the right. Ultimately, this only benefits UKIP' (Wigmore, 2014). This highlights how both issues are central to national discourse (and the perceptions of the public in the run up to the 2015 election) and also how far to the right Labour have shifted by publicly apologising for previous immigration policy. Indeed, Nigel Farage even proclaimed that 'Labour are now to the right of the Tories on immigration' (Allegretti in *the Guardian* (2022)) after Keir Starmer vowed to wean businesses off their 'immigration dependency' at a speech to the CBI in 2022.

The point to consider is that, when it comes to the politically discursive, hardline and increasingly contentious topic of immigration, a hostile, right-wing rhetorical landscape has become the framework in which discourse is constructed and in which a popular narrative is set. Whether it's UKIP officials, Conservative MPs, a barrage of right-wing rhetoric and fear-mongering from the media or television personalities, the intentional pejorative use of thinly veiled racialised language creates a normalised regressive environment of toxicity and division. The intentional creation and manipulation of a climate of fear and hatred makes such a position increasingly acceptable, legitimate and creates the parameters of the debate and discussion of what it means to be English or accepted within the national imagination.

Politically contested and emotive issues such as immigration are highly symbolically important in the wider conceptualisation of identity and nation. Regardless of a lack of an informed, mature and rational debate and discussion over such an issue, it is a 'contested discursive zone over meaning' (Lewis and Neal, 2005). It underlies the political and cultural ambiguity over constructed meaning and the discursive contestation over normative codes and legitimised ideology. Englishness is largely read through the prism of race and cultural exclusivity, which is indicative of dominant narratives and discourses on such a carefully socially constructed identity.

If recent discussions and debates concerning immigration, for example, are critically analysed, although the subjects under discussion might not necessarily be Black, the underpinning of that discussion, the 'alien wedge' (Shire, 2008) notion is still there. The notion of being 'invaded' by 'hordes' of people 'coming over here' to 'rip us off' and 'swamp us' is repeatedly used. This is met with an ideological defensive anxiety and a fearful yet assertive form of nationalism couched within the frame of 'common sense'. Although the linkage concerning skin colour is not as overt as in the heyday of Powellist nationalism, such a link returns quietly and is implied and alluded to as a return to Powellism in the English cultural and social landscape 'but with a twist' (Shire, 2008:11). In this sense, Englishness operates as a supra-language of metaphor and meaning, Englishness as whiteness, but also as a particular cultural whiteness, for example, white but not Eastern European, white but Christian, white but not homosexual or trans. It is not a simplistic dichotomy of white-included, Black-excluded; it is a nuanced cultural and social exclusivity concerned with power, legitimacy and concepts of authenticity expressed in a normative manner.

Hylland Eriksen points out, 'ethnic identity becomes crucially important the moment it is perceived as being under threat' (Hylland Eriksen, 2002:76). Within this context, 'race' denotes a particular way in which threat and individual and communal differences are read and come to be constructed. 'Race', or rather, ethnicity does not always exclusively equate to ideological exclusion; this can operate alongside or secondary to other social factors such as class, gender, sexuality or religion. Within a constructed sense of Englishness, this must be contextualised within the boundary construction of those who can or can't belong to a particular interpretation and articulation of English national identity. Boundaries within concepts of national identity are ideological creations and are open to struggle, contestation, negotiation and change, 'ethnic resources (such as language, culture, religion, gender relations) can be used in interplay with the class and political resources and positionings of the group' (Anthias and Yuval-Davis, 1993:4). Therefore, such processes are often manipulated to serve political and ideological ends.

## Englishness and Concepts of Britishness

In the contemporary context, Englishness is a resurgent emotive, political and cultural identity, whereas British national identity has increasingly become to be abandoned in populist terms (events surrounding the monarchy aside). In an IPRR poll in 2013, 35% of respondents saw themselves as predominantly English rather than British, which represented more than twice the number who considered themselves predominantly British (Moore, 2014). Moreover, Britain as a political national project and overarching identity has become increasingly fragile and in very real danger of becoming obsolete. In other words, it is wielded and 'celebrated' at certain times (particularly around traditional institutions such as the monarchy) but is increasingly becoming less relevant as a primary source of identity attachment. As highlighted by John Denham, if asked to choose one identity, more people in England will choose English rather than British. Englishness is the most widely shared national identity and in particular 'people emphasis their Englishness rather than their Britishness' (Denham, 2018). Indeed, as for the political salience of identity, 'just under 70% of the English not British voted Leave; over 70% of the British not English voted Remain' (ibid). Although not a scientifically proven deduction, these figures indicate the ideological polarisation between identification choices.

The salience of both Englishness and conservatism must be recognised as the key relationship when discussing narratives around identity and belonging within England. According to a YouGov poll (2016) as opposed to attitudes in Scotland, English voters overwhelmingly think that empire was a good thing; also support for the monarchy is far stronger in England. Indeed, 'during the 2012 Queen's Jubilee, there were 9,500 street parties in England and Wales, but only 60 in Scotland, mostly organised by the Orange Order' (Ramsay, 2020). Both of these issues are icons of an Anglo-centric nationalism which the Conservatives embody. Issues such as monarchy and empire are inherently and implicitly tied to ideas around class and race; here the Tories dominate an anti-introspectional understanding and narrative around these topics while tapping in to reactionary and conservative discourses around history and identity. Moreover, the Conservatives are viewed as the party of the status-quo and ruling class, 'this is why David Cameron and Boris Johnson were considered "prime ministerial"' (ibid) whereas Gordon Brown, Ed Miliband and unequivocally Jeremy Corbyn were not.

Regardless of the outcome of the Scottish independence referendum of 2014, politically and culturally a sense of impending Englishness has gained momentum, currency and strength from the increasing fragility of Britishness or even a largely Anglo-centric Britishness. A defensive, traditionalist and conservative Englishness can be viewed as a defensive fall-back position in a time of such perceived uncertainty and anxiety and provides simplistic responses to complex social, cultural and historical issues such as the legacy of colonialism and empire. A national narrative and discourse has gone from an arguably progressive and largely inclusive Britishness under New Labour (in rhetoric at least), to a regressive and largely exclusive Englishness in more recent times.

For the English, there is the question: which nationality are they and which community do they belong? Officialdom and international sporting events aside, this suggests confusion and ambiguity in the imagination and narration of the nation. As opposed to a more established sense of Scottish or Welsh identity, a lack of a developed and entrenched English national identity can be viewed as being historically and officially sacrificed in the service of a unification of the British nation state and the project of imperialism. Britain was best served by emphasising an imperial, or at best British identity, rather than an English one (Byrne, 2007). In this respect the English did not so much as celebrate themselves as identify with the projects or mission that defined them and which they felt providentially called upon to carry out in the world. The English could not see themselves as just another nation in a world of nations (Crick, 1991). Pressing issues that had not been seriously dealt with (such as the end of a global leadership role, cultural and political devolution and aspects of globalisation such as deteritorialisation) has forced the English to consider and contemplate where they fit into the reconfiguration of Britain, and to a further extent, the world.

In many respects, the 19th and 20th centuries can be viewed as the British era where certain distinctions were overlooked or forgotten. During much of the

19th and 20th centuries, English identity would be expressed through the ideology of 'Britishness'; 'often, this imperial-based ideology was expressed through the language of "national character", which itself was a means of integrating diverse interests and cultures within an overarching British national identity' (Wellings, 2001:100). Englishness, or a distinct sense of English national identity, was simply not necessary. To be English also implied British to a large extent, and the two terms could be viewed as synonymous and interchangeable. Britain was also the agency of the empire with the Scottish, Welsh and Irish participating alongside the English.

Concomitantly, the 21st century can be viewed on the other hand as the post-British century for the English. In a general sense, Britain offered the English a national purpose, a conflated, interchangeable macro identity. It also generally offered a model of stable representative government (and to some extent identity), yet it is now clear that perhaps such a concept of Britain is a historically contingent and relative experience. As Tony Wright and Gamble (2009) points out, the deliberate forging of Britons is the story of a historical construct. Vital to this is also the clear political, social and cultural construct, which was served through war, empire, monarchy, but also through institutions such as the BBC and the NHS. From this perspective, it can be claimed that 'the mid-century of Blitz and Beveridge as the high tide of Britishness' (ibid).

What is important to remember (and also helps to contextualise the political terrain) is that grand narratives of thought and a background environment such as imperialism, liberalism and socialism have largely disintegrated. The imperialist school of thought and national mission faded by the beginning of the Second World War, Liberal constitutionalism by the early 1970s and a wide national appeal of socialism by the early 1980s through Thatcherism and the collapse of Communism. As Clark commented in 1990, now that the old overarching ideologies have been deconstructed, it seems likely that all cultural images will look as if they are regionally and culturally specific (Clark, 1990). This represents a distinctive alteration in public understanding. If everything becomes regionally and culturally specific, then the one universal thing remaining is identity. Within the context of devolution, Brexit, political and economic crisis and a general all-encompassing process of hyper globalisation, old (and relied upon) certainties are increasingly few and far between. This only seems to serve to generate confusion and anxieties about what it means to be English in the contemporary era where even concepts of nation and region have become subsumed by the increasing pervasive and interdisciplinary effects of globalisation.

As previously illustrated, conservative and traditionalist concepts of Englishness represent an exclusivist retreat into a defensive form of ethnic, social and cultural nationalism. However, this is in contrast (and often in opposition) to a more specifically multiethnic, multicultural and multinational concept of Britishness. This concept of a more inclusive British identity can be viewed as being somewhat defunct, largely through a combination of a diminished position of global power, a toxic association to the New Labour Project and a crumbling of the union through a process of ongoing devolution. Although much of the symbolism of a traditional sense of Englishness is inherently bound up with a 'golden era' of Britishness (empire, global power, outward projection of nationalist identity), conservative discourses of Englishness shed the rebounding consequences of these past projects – colonialism, imperialism, globalisation and deterritorialisation. In this sense, Britishness is largely abandoned by the conservative, traditionalist discourse of identity, and a distinctly anti-British and exclusive Englishness has instead become dominant currency.

## New Labour and Discourse of Englishness

The New Labour Project sought to re-energise and reclaim Britishness as a distinctly inclusive, multicultural and outwardly looking sense of modern identity, far away from the stuffy and implicitly racist nationalist dogma of Thatcherite Conservatism. By the end of the New Labour administration in 2010, such an ideology and identity had become distinctly outmoded and obsolete through an increasing discursive dominance of the conservative and traditionalist position, particularly in relation (and as a response) to immigration, globalisation and the European Union, set within a context of ongoing devolution, economic crisis and uncertainty and contemporary socio-geo-political conflict associated with 'the war on terror'.

The conservative trope of fear, and an imperilled nation fatally, undermined a bedraggled sense of New Labour's quasi-inclusive and cosmopolitan ideology of Britishness. From the mid-1990s, New Labour worked a positive spin on a more modern notion of British national identity to their advantage by identifying a stuffy, traditional and elitist brand of national identity to the Conservative Party. In a distinctly ideological sense, New Labour also set about creating a recognisable identity of modern Britishness which incorporated a pro-European, pro-globalisation, cosmopolitan stance that was distinctly urban and far less southern upper/middle class English in character. The New Labour government (especially in its first term) emphasised what Tariq Modood (2005) highlights as the plural and complex character of British culture and society by referring to it as 'a young country' (Tony Blair), a 'mongrel nation' (Gordon Brown) and as a 'chicken tikka masala eating nation' (Robin Cook). The New Labour agenda also specifically pushed for greater devolution as a form of political and cultural freedom that would never have been possible under a Conservative government.

To escape the negative notions and connotations concerning nationalism, New Labour consistently re-enforced a Burkean and Powellite identification of England's colonial past with the Conservative Party, while at the same time ceaselessly appealing to concepts of modernity and modernisation. New Labour inverted the classic conservative grievances and exclusions and sought to distance itself from the 'xenophobic nationalism of Powell and his successors' (Wright, 2007:173). Indeed, Robin Cook stated in his infamous 'Chicken Tikka Masala speech' in 2001 that, 'the British are not a race but a gathering of countless different races and communities'...'and it is not their purity which makes the British unique, but the sheer pluralism of their ancestry' (Cook, 2001). New Labour used what the Conservatives wished to ignore as their greatest assets to forge a modern and inclusive sense of Britishness. Cook, for instance, turned conservative, traditionalist Powellism on its head and instead, in its most basic essence, expressed an ideology of national identity consisting of plurality where the Conservative's conceived of it as purity. As Colin Wright states:

> New Labour have extrapolated not an ahistorical but an anti-historical outlook. This would cause the oblique separating the past/ future couplet to perform also as the oblique separating both the Conservative/ Labour and imperialism/ cosmopolitanism couplets. To state this crudely: the Conservatives cling tenaciously to (albeit a very partial) History, but, with Powell, deny the role of the colonies in the formation of Englishness; New Labour enthusiastically embraces the ex-inhabitants of the colonies and their descendants, placing them, with Cook, at the very fulcrum of national identity, yet deny History the possibility of an entry visa into its carefully policed ideological borders.
>
> (Wright, 2007:176)

New Labour inverted traditional notions of Britishness, rejecting the rule-by-elite, top-down, imperialist nature to a more, 'cozy, collective contract agreed, horizontally as it were, among friends who speak the same language' (Wright, 2007: 175). In other words, all the negative, nasty elements and connotations positioned as belonging to them (the Conservatives), not to us, or you the electorate if you vote for us. What this creates is a simple, easy to relate to and arguably highly successful precursor/successor relationship between New Labour and the Conservative Party. Indeed, a 2002 Ipsos MORI poll found that 86% of Britons disagreed with the statement that to be truly British, you have to be white (Shackle, 2011), suggesting that most make the distinction between 'British' and 'English', the former being considered as more inclusive and less tied to ethnicity. At a very base ideologically symbolic level, New Labour suggested a new approach, a new relationship and a jettisoning of tradition and radicalised identities.

The sanitisation of cultural hybridity by New Labour into a utopian 'melting pot' of racial harmony should not blind us to the concrete reality of its unceasingly difficult nature. This over emphasis of a modern, cosmopolitan, urban and open co-existence specifically targeted at a younger, more liberal audience can be viewed as to why New Labour's rhetoric could not shift engrained, traditional notions around nation, and why conservative themes and elements fled to notions of a timeless, more exclusive and unspoiled England as opposed to a distinct sense of a multiracial and multicultural 'Cool Britannia'. A projection of this mythology could indeed serve as the 'paradigmatic site of its re-inscription of the Conservative tropology of national identity: the passage from an authoritarian, patriarchal, and indelibly imperial "Rule Britannia", to an approachable, hip, and post-colonial "Cool Britannia" is the fundamental tropological shift which New Labour have enacted' (Wright, 2007:174–175). In light of a post- 9/11, 7/7, economic crisis, global reality, this tropological shift by New Labour to a progressive, liberal, cosmopolitan and inclusive form of Britishness can be seen as a key element to the discursive dominance of a distinctly, conservative, nostalgic and defensive Englishness as a response.

There are huge problems when placing complex political positions, especially concerning relationships and dynamics of colonialism/post-colonialism within identity. Much of New Labour's rhetoric was so metropolitan in character that it can be viewed as ghettoising Britishness to the large urban areas of London, the Midlands and the north-west of England and therefore failing to be persuasive the moment it steps out of these areas, an issue which further signals the partial universality of its claimed cosmopolitanism. It is also arguable that New Labour's positive reconfiguration of an unproblematic multiculturalism equates to the de-politicisation of a multiracial society under the catch-all term of cosmopolitanism which in turn feeds perceptions of a disenfranchised and abandoned white working class rump. Tariq Modood's concept of state multiculturalism as deployed by New Labour certainly has some relevance here. In essence, a liberal (and often government sanctioned) championing of multiculturalism can obscure actual empirical racism and inequality. Using highly selected contemporary metaphors and rhetoric of cultural hybridity does not make up for a distinctly one sided form of cultural hybridity, nor does it achieve much in the way of creating a concrete and lasting equal and inclusive identity or society. In terms of a contemporary sense of English national identity, it has arguably cleansed the concept of Englishness of any hope of an inclusive, pluralist or progressive accommodation of cultural hybridity or cosmopolitanism.

## Englishness as a Racialised Concept

All forms of nationalism are to varying degrees racialised; however, according to Bridget Byrne (2007), Englishness is racialised in a way that is different from Britishness. Englishness is retained as an ethnically homogenous category as opposed to concepts of Britishness. The crisis of identity within a context of post-empire, urban modernity plurality is most likely to be felt by the English than the Scots, Welsh or British ethnic minorities in that:

> The striking contradiction is that we now seem to know far less about the racialised identities of the ethnic majority (notably English whites) and who they are in the present post-imperial moment. The 'burden of representation' endured by visible minorities has unwittingly implied that they have an ethnicity or a culture whilst others, in particular the white English have not. This has led to an over-racialisation of visible minorities at the expense of a de-racialisation of ethnic majorities.
>
> (Nayak, 2003:139)

White individuals in England are far less likely to be asked throughout their life, 'and where do you come from?' What is at play here is a process of identifiable boundaries where controversial debates around issues such as immigration and control tend to focus on the problem of 'too many' and the identity of particular marked groups whose presence is seen to be problematic (Skey, 2010).

What lies at the heart of conservative, right-wing, traditionalist concepts of Englishness is an identity that acts as a response to an underlying feeling and narrative of threat, but also as a means for representation and identification for those who may also not be considered part of the metropolitan clique, or as Suella Braverman stated in Parliament on the 18 October 2022 'the Guardian-reading, tofu-eating wokerati'. A framework of control is at the centre of these national debates and discourse, where, not only the 'other' acts as the 'threat', the presence of the 'other' also functions as necessity to contextualise the identity of the conceptualised 'in-group'. Membership and symbolic ownership of the national space therefore must be controlled; this sense of control is often articulated through rhetoric over key issues such as immigration. This issue of loss of control could also be contextualised in terms of wider contemporary issues such as globalisation and the global economic crisis or a fractious relationship with the European Union.

The conceptualisation of nations being bounded and homogeneous cultural entities dominates discourse concerning national identity within England; this can also be seen to be achieved by drawing a distinction between the categories of English and British, with the former characterised as indigenous, stable and closed (Condor, 2006). Englishness can be defined as being racialised, equating to an ethnic white identity, while ethnic minorities are more closely associated with the British prefix and its associated colonial and imperial history. The racialisation of Englishness and its enduring ability can be read symbolically from the seeming dissonance of the phrase 'Black English' as opposed to the politically struggled for identity of 'Black British' (Byrne, 2007). The term 'Black British' is commonly referred to and utilised through officialdom; however, the term 'Black English' is remarkably and symbolically absent. Moreover, as Graham Macklin (2008) observes, prefixes such as Black and Asian British make Britishness synonymous with multicultural Britain and Englishness, or according to ex-BNP Deputy Treasurer David Hannam, as the refuge for the racially aware voter equating it to a more exclusive identity. Racialisation of the two identities of Englishness and Britishness acts, as Bridget Byrne (2007) describes, as a modality through which British people, and particularly white English people, talk about race. This represents a specifically English complex, as Mark Perryman points out, 'to a much greater extent than arguments over Scottish, Welsh or Northern Irish identity, debates about Englishness are dominated by the question of race' (Perryman, 2014).

It is not inevitable that Englishness equates to a more overwhelmingly white and conservative identity and Britishness as a more multiethnic and open identity; however, identities must be viewed within the context and social/cultural history of empire and post-colonialism. Indeed, it is telling that in the 2021 Census, there was no option for Black English. Only Black, Black British, Caribbean or African were available, whereas the Welsh Census allows respondents to identify as Black Welsh and Black British. The Census 'doesn't just gather information, it carries a message about the assumption that the state makes about us. One of these seems to be that no one can be Black and English, or Asian and English' (Denham, 2021). As Bill Schwarz (1996) comments, the elusive and displaced notion of Englishness, insular and self-contained, cannot be grasped or understood without seeing its intimate and complex connections to the wider imperial world and its historic connections between England and its colonial empire. At the same time, the separate but overlapping relations between the white English population and its ethnic, cultural and racial 'others' lie at the very heart of the matter of identity, especially when it remains unspoken.

According to Etienne Balibar (1991), the relationship and connection between nationalism and racism is a question of historical articulation. This relationship is necessary to sustain nationalism and operates as a historical system of complementary exclusions and dominations which are mutually interconnected. To a large extent, a dominant conservative ideology of national homogeneity operates as a 'presence of the past' (Balibar, 1991), which seeks to codify and legitimise an ideological understanding and narrative, fusing the past and present in an imagined and yet narrow discursive field.

Discussions, debates and rhetoric about national identity, especially in perceived times of 'crisis', have the dangerous potential to become racialised and exclusionary, particularly when right-wing conservative and traditionalist parties such as UKIP have made significant symbolic political gains and impact in recent years. Current conversations about Englishness have also been triggered by mainstream political and media discourses questioning the national identity and loyalty of non-white (particularly English) citizens at a very basic level. The wider point is that regardless of the waxing and waning of formal political party's such as UKIP, the wider and ongoing dispersal of a dominant conservative discourse clearly indicates a relationship between perceptions of nationalism and identity and political populism. The constant barrage of articles by papers such as *The Daily Mail* (2012) calling figures such as Mo Farah a 'plastic Brit' who 'insults our games' (which can be also viewed as an attack on the multicultural representation of Britain at the 2012 London Olympics) clearly reinforces the discursive point raised of a perpetuation of the ideological and racial origin to dominant discursive representations of identity. In this regard, Englishness is more often than not represented as a racial or ethnic understanding. Conversations concerning Englishness or English national identity are largely focused on race rather than belonging to place and a multiethnic space. In other words, anyone can become a 'Brit' but English is far more ideologically, ethnically and culturally exclusive.

The conservative right has a long tradition laying suspicions around loyalty and race. This being infamously whipped up by Norman Tebbit in April 1990 when he suggested that immigrants and their children could not show loyalty until they supported the England cricket team. The problem here is that England, and particularly within the conservative context of test cricket, is largely racially exclusive to ethnic minorities, whereas Britishness being far less exclusive with four out of every five people from the Black Caribbean community living in Britain describing themselves as British, and three-quarters of the Indian, Pakistani and Bangladeshi communities identifying themselves in the same way (Carvel, 2004).

What is at play here from the likes of Norman Tebbit are thinly veiled racist evocations of traditional leather-against-willow conservatism which clearly spell out an identity politics of exclusion. Indeed, the Independent Commission for Equality in Cricket (2023) found cricket within England to be systematically and institutionally racist, sexist and deeply elitist. The number of ethnic minorities representing England have plummeted in the last 30 years, while the percentage of ethnic minorities experiencing racism and practices of exclusion have rocketed 'a staggering 87% of respondents of Pakistani and Bangladeshi heritage, 82% with Indian heritage and 75% of all black respondents reported encountering discrimination in the game' (Liew, 2023). Meanwhile, the percentage of England male cricketers who were privately educated was 58% in 2021, compared to 7% in the population at large, whereas the England women's team have never played at Lords, while the Eton Vs Harrow match is an annual event there, as too is the Oxford Vs Cambridge University match.

Dominant conservative and right-wing discourses of English national identity and Englishness seem to hinge around a rejection of non-white ethnic minorities or perceived 'foreigners' as being part of such an identity. As Paul Thomas points out, 'despite positive evidence to the contrary, some white people do not accept ethnic minorities as "English". This may seem surprising, given the extent of ethnic diversity in England' (Thomas, 2011:91). As indicated by the Office for National Statistics (2011), the areas in England with the highest percentages of the population identifying as English as a national identity are those which correlate with the highest percentages of white as an ethnicity. On the other hand, areas with a higher percentage of ethnic diversity, such as inner boroughs of London, have the highest percentage of the population who identify as British.

The social reality of urban England is now so intimately bound up with that of its long-standing ethnic minority population that it is hard to imagine it otherwise. The 2021 Census found that 19% of the population of England is considered as being from an ethnic minority, whereas the figure for both Wales and Scotland is 4.5% (the Scottish figures being from Audit Scotland, its annual diversity report 2022). The vast majority of the United Kingdom's ethnic minorities reside in England. The English racial landscape on a day-to-day basis is inherently multiracial. London's population is roughly comprised just over one-third ethnic minority. Alongside Birmingham, Manchester, Bristol, Leeds, Bradford, Liverpool and Leicester all share over 90% of England's ethnic minority population and such lived day-to-day experiences. This proves to be one of the great contradictions and paradoxes within a seemingly exclusive and traditionalist discourse of identity – Englishness is overwhelmingly constructed as a racially constituted ethnic identity; however, it is a particularly ethnically heterogeneous population.

The ever-growing split identity between country and city is managed by the discourse of an imperilled Englishness threatened by negative concepts of urban modernity and a timeless rural idyll of tradition and place. This operates alongside the presentation of Englishness as represented through an ideologically acceptable and sanitised prism of middle England. The result of discursive outpourings will not be the lack of an English identity, but a culturally narrow and ethnically exclusive identity and a racist, monochrome and melancholic Englishness that denies the reality of its own land (Gilroy, 2004a).

A conservative representation of Englishness is situated within a dichotomy that experiences multiculturalism and a multiethnic society within modern day England as being uneven, with big cities being highly diverse places, whereas many suburban and rural areas remaining largely monocultural. This is a key factor when reaching an understanding of an illusionary sense of dominant forms of discursive Englishness. When Nigel Farage (Guardian, 2014a) commented that his commute on a suburban rail line into London was like being in a 'different country', he consciously projected his very own narrow and culturally specific background on to the everyday experience of one of the world's most diverse and multicultural cities in a very negative way, also using this anecdote to justify divisive and hardline immigration policy. Thus, when conservative, right-wing traditionalists such as Nigel Farage discuss identity, belonging and everyday experiences, strong and yet casual links to a 'common sense' approach frame these key issues in a very simplistic yet binary opposite manner which many people can find simple to understand and relate to, even if this is a very decontextualised and selective ideological interpretation and framing of such an experience.

Linking rhetoric to experience (either lived or imagined) and manipulating this towards an ideological end is the strength of dominant conservative discourse, and yet, arguably it has no serious and sustained mainstream political challenge. The Labour Party in particular has fundamentally bought into the conservative narrative, especially on issues such as immigration, further entrenching right-wing conservative approaches as taken-for-granted mainstream terrain.

Misplaced intolerance can stem from a commonly held and perpetuated belief that prior to the labour shortages of the late 1940s that drove the first waves of post-colonial immigration, Britain was an unchanging, homogenous country with a clear sense of its own identity. This is an historical, cultural, social and ideological illusion and myth. The reality of immigration and accompanying hostility towards new arrivals has been a continual thread throughout the history of these islands (Winder, 2004). A mythology of nation, history and its people underpins the false and misleading dominant discourse on a contemporary sense of Englishness and English national identity. 'At any specific time, there may be a dominant view of what characterises the essential character, needs or interest of an ethnic group' (Anthias and Yuval-Davis, 1993:8). Widening this out further, when relayed through a dominant group, this can then be related to nation and be used to provide a dominant national, exclusionary narrative and belonging. Contemporary issues or topics can, therefore, be ideologically interpreted and used for political ends or as a means of boundary management.

A specific social, historical and political reading or interpretation can be legitimised through the creation of a national narrative dichotomy of 'us' (the majority) as opposed to 'them' (the 'outsider' minority). This can very easily lead down the path of ethnocentrism and xenophobia and can ultimately lead to racism and a radicalised understanding of identity. A conservative and right-wing tradition of referring to a sense of cultural and moral community directly refers to an essentialist category construction based on race, ethnicity and cultural background. Hylland Eriksen (2002) points out, the ethnic group is defined through its relationship to others, highlighted through the construction and maintenance of the boundary, and the boundary itself is a social product which has variable importance and which changes through time. Social, historical and cultural classification expresses power disparities, discursive dominance and contextualisation of boundary construction and maintenance. The complex social and cultural world and experience is reduced to a simple exercise in power relations – just as Nigel Farage demonstrated with his comments. Hierarchies of power, culture and ethnic background can be seen as a means and a way of creating a simplified order of power and preference in the social and cultural world, and generally speaking, social identity becomes most important the moment it seems threatened.

This represents an ongoing theme within notions of national identity and inclusivity/exclusivity. Those deemed from an 'alien', 'outsider' or 'incompatible' background are excluded from incorporation into dominant cultural or ethnic discourse of national community. This becomes a de facto and implicitly racist ideological framework that frames discursive representations of inclusivity. For example, citizens from a post-colonial background even after two or three generations of settlement are largely excluded from dominant conservative and right-wing discourse of national identity and inclusivity, irrespective of where they are born, even their children and grandchildren are viewed as never really belonging. This is not the case for all immigrants. It can be seen to be limited to those who provide a constant reminder to the national psyche of a once 'glorious past' and notions of superiority. White, (largely) English speaking, immigrants from Western nations are often incorporated almost immediately without constant reference of national or cultural background, for example, Irish, German and American immigrants register within the top 10 locations of origin of immigrants to the United Kingdom (Guardian, 2013b); however, these groups are almost entirely absent from any negative discussion concerning immigration.

There are clearly key factors which point to why Englishness or English national identity is disputed, contested and confused in a largely socio-politico-cultural sense. In wide ranging and in-depth interviews conducted by Bridget Byrne (2007) concerning the racialisation of the politics of English and British national identity, a theme which emerged throughout was a distinct sense of narrowness and emptiness (Byrne, 2007). Classic renditions of a quintessential 'green and pleasant land' and historical and emotive concepts of village greens and country pubs are clearly referenced within a racialised discourse of national and imperial superiority. Clear juxtapositions are echoed of a discourse between England and 'others', where upon, Englishness equates to a white, middle class and rural identity as opposed to the, 'threat posed by dirty others (such as gypsies or Muslims selling Halal meat)' (Byrne, 2007:154). However, there is a clear insecurity over the basis of Englishness, which is disturbed and disrupted by modern, urban life, by the presence of different ethnic subjects and by a blurring of class divisions. An illusionary and mythical sense of a 'deep England' also related to an inflexible and stubborn concept, which makes it hard to sustain in the everyday reality, 'some of this tension was expressed in the difference between the image of a nostalgic "deep England" and multicultural and multiracial Britain' (ibid).

This is an important and ongoing theme for a conservative and traditionalist conceptualisation of Englishness – its relevance and meaning operates as an opposite to constructed notions of Britishness. According to Harris (2014), people see British identity encompassing a huge range of people, as against an Englishness that is too often exclusive and xenophobic. In the census of 2011 (the first to ask people to tick boxes for their national identity), a majority (60%) of people in England described themselves as English only, but there were important and symbolic variations. Most interestingly, in England, 38% of people from an ethnic minority background said they were exclusively British, as against only 14% of white English respondents, and the ethnic groups in England most likely to say they were British were Bangladeshi, Pakistani and people who trace their background to the Indian subcontinent. It's not difficult to interpret those differences; for many people, Britain is an inclusive outward-looking place and identity, but England and Englishness represents something much more problematic. As Dreda Say Mitchell (2011) comments, one of the great advantages of being 'British' is that it has never been an ethnic definition, so it is therefore an easier identity for different ethnicities to assume. In this sense, being British has always meant being part of a multicultural society long before the term was even thought of.

As Byrne (2007) confirmed, being British or claiming Britishness is viewed as being 'PC' and inclusive; however, being 'quintessentially' English equates to being southern, middle class and white. 'Englishness is something that is not "politically correct" with which to identify. But at the same time, Britishness does not have the same purchase on the emotions or identity' (Byrne, 2007:149). As an example of the responses, Byrne interviews a Black woman on the racialised politics surrounding national identity in Britain and England:

> I see myself as British, um because, even though I was born here, society has shown me, has led me to believe that I'm British. Not that I'm English, that I'm British. The way that I look at it, just because of what I've seen, just through working, going to school and working in, you know, in England, you are British, you're not English. English people are white, that's how we see English people, they're white.
>
> (Byrne, 2007:140)

As another example, a white woman in her late 20s living in Peckham describes Englishness as being about myths of history, civility and honour. For this respondent, her England was rooted in the past, tradition and nostalgia and, in particular in class and gender roles and relations. Her imagined sense of Englishness was also very much related to a sense of loss and presented the streets in which she lived as 'alien' and 'foreign' to be contrasted to the 'quaintness of a village shop'. This juxtaposition between these two interviewees underlines the distinct imagined ethnic and cultural boundaries of established concepts of both Britishness and Englishness.

To further illustrate this inscribed and normalised specific difference between Englishness and Britishness, Paul Thomas (2011) confirms that surveys among adults suggest that there is strong support for Britishness rather than Englishness among resident ethnic minorities; 'the emphasis of young Asian people on "British" rather than "English" contrasted to the views of young white English people, who clearly favoured "English" identity' (Thomas, 2011:83). He specifically found that for young Asian people, Britishness is more positive than Englishness, for instance, in one of the responses to the study carried out in Rochdale and Oldham, one respondent was quoted as saying: 'I suppose because British is more inclusive, that's how people can relate to that more than the St George flag' (Thomas, 2011:84). This perspective and association was common throughout the extensive study on attitudes and perceptions of national identity, 'British means you can be multi-cultured yet keep your identity' (ibid), 'English people are the opposite of us. English people are white people' (Thomas, 2011:85), which also echoes the response from the Black female respondent by Byrne in her 2007 study. Crucially though, these responses also echo the characteristics implied through dominant discursive representations of a conservative sense of Englishness.

Thomas points out, 'this focus on Englishness amongst young white people may well reflect the challenges to past notions of Britishness posed by devolution, European integration and inward migration, all of which has made it harder to hold on to unexamined, "taken for granted" notions of Englishness' (ibid). This can be used to explain why notions of Britishness prove to be so problematic and why increasingly notions of Englishness are seen to be a more simplistic ethnic and cultural category. At the same time, symbolic representation of ethnic and cultural 'others' has taken place and has been reinforced through a conservative and traditionalist, right-wing narrative. For example, non-Muslim communities have understood international political events through a 'white' political and media discourse, which attributes and reinforces associated projected feelings and prejudices about the Muslim community. The discursive narrative projected is of identified and associated religious markers such as, headscarves, beards, traditional dress, strong religious observance of the Qur'an and common references to radicalism, terrorism and illegal immigration enflamed and normalised by the right-wing press.

Although minority communities such as the Muslim community are often portrayed as 'alien', un-loyal and as distinct ethnic and cultural outsiders, research carried out by the Open Society Institute (2009) suggests that British Muslims are, in general, far more patriotic than co-religionists in any other western European country – 78% of Muslims in the United Kingdom consider themselves to be British, compared to 49% of French Muslims considering themselves to be predominantly French, and 23% of German Muslims considering themselves to be predominantly German (Rahman, 2009). These attitudes can be attributed to many varied factors; however, the key difference with British Muslim respondents could be ascribed to the inclusive multicultural association of concepts of Britishness as opposed to possibly more exclusive notions of French or German identity and a positive British Islamic identity gradually developed through a long-term process of multiculturalism. The key word here however is 'British' as opposed to 'English'.

Data such as this suggest clear support for a more inclusive and multicultural British identity for immigrant and non-white ethnic minorities. This is further confirmed by an Ipsos MORI survey (2007) of young people, which found that ethnic minority youth, '[Do] not identify themselves as being English and consider Englishness to be exclusively [for] people who are white or come from white parentage and lineage' (Ipsos Mori, 2007:41). Both of these surveys also found that in Scotland and Wales, a very different picture emerges where non-white ethnic minorities are significantly happier to identify themselves as either Scottish or Welsh. Although both Scotland and Wales have significantly smaller non-white ethnic minority populations, what this does suggest is that both nations have been much more successful in developing inclusive national identities focused specifically on place and not race. This shows the way forward towards an inclusive Englishness that allows people of all ethnic backgrounds to 'belong', one that is focused on place not race and which positively celebrates England's historic engagement with the world and the world with England.

Contemporary, dominant forms of a conservative English national identity can be viewed as a 'reactive identity' (Modood, 2010:52). The 'otherness' or 'groupness' that is appealed to and that is developed through conservative and traditional concepts of Englishness are connected to cultural and racial 'otherness'. In this sense, 'Muslim' represents a racial and cultural concept and identity presented as incompatible and mutually exclusive to a sense of Englishness. However, 'Muslim' is not a putative biological category in the way that 'Black' or 'South East Asian' or 'Chinese' is but neither was 'Jew'. What is at work here is a long, non-linear history of racialisation of faith and cultural groups into 'race'. This generally and briefly describes the ideological and historical process involved in essentialising 'others' into quasi-racial groupings. What drives such incoherent 'racial groupings' is a discursive, ideological and narrational reinforcement of role performance, driven by events, manipulated, exaggerated and whipped up by a feverish media and moral entrepreneurs. As Michael Skey (2009) points out, in the case of England, there seems to be some evidence that the undermining of a previously taken-for-granted and largely settled sense of identity and place among the dominant English in Britain may be generating a concomitant desire to re-assert their position as the symbolic owners of the national space through active embodiment and coordinated displays, such as a defensive, reactive and traditionalist exclusivity.

The English have to seriously consider a future identity outside and apart from past certainties and a taken-for-granted position in the world. Unlike the Welsh and Scots, the dominant form of English national identity is one that is assumed and based on a default mechanism of defensiveness from modern, globalised realities of contemporary society. As Tony Wright observes, 'to respond to the remaking of Britain, and to a decentralising moment, with a mean-spirited nationalism would be a victory for the worst kind of Englishness over the best kind' (Wright, 2000:16). The renegotiation of Britain has proved to be an opportunity for Conservatives and the right to play the nationalist card in England which has solidified their dominant discursive position. Wright (2000) justifiably claims that the version of Englishness 'peddled' by the right has to be countered and resisted; however, as a dominant concept of Englishness becomes so dominated by a conservative and traditionalist reactionary position, this only pushes liberals and those on the left to identify with Britishness even more, which in turn then only serves to further concede Englishness to worst excesses of the right.

Englishness has become the identity for those willing to escape from what Britishness is viewed as or to stand for in a pejorative sense. The dominant, conservative approach and conceptualisation of Englishness is so bound-up with notions of preservation and exclusion that it fundamentally cannot incorporate or represent an identity that is not home-county or southern English bound, white, middle class and traditionalist. Englishness should not be an exclusionary or an ethnic or cultural separatist identity. For it to have any relevance or representativeness in the contemporary era, it is essential that it is an inclusive identity that celebrates difference, is plural in nature and is outward looking.

Chapter 5

# Discourses of Englishness and Multiculturalism

The relationship between concepts of multiculturalism and dominant conservative discourses of Englishness is an integral part to understanding contemporary notions of English national identity. It will be argued that conservative discourse in relation to concepts of Englishness is in essence anti-multiculturalist and regressive in terms of inclusivity, and that such discourse is the dominant and common political, social and ideological framework in which concepts of multiculturalism are viewed. The symbolism and implications of both David Cameron's 'end of state multiculturalism' speech and Trevor Phillips's 'sleepwalking into segregation' will be explored and examined as two specific yet important examples. The crux of the argument is that the term 'multiculturalism' has become an easy and lazy social, political and cultural byword for division, disunity and inequality and has in itself become the figure of blame. It has become associated (largely through the dominance of a right-wing conservative discursive dominance) with an ideologically constructed self-fulfilling prophesy of failure concerning ethnic and cultural minorities to integrate within an illusionary homogeneous identity. However, multiculturalism as a social reality (not loose political or social policy) must be recognised and included within contemporary concepts of Englishness if there is any hope of achieving a representative and reflective sense of English national identity.

## Anti-multiculturalist Discourses of Englishness

Discourse (especially in relation to concepts of identity and nationalism) can be viewed as operating as a mirror, reflecting back from constructed and imagined concepts of nation and society what we see in ourselves, our backgrounds and our ideological beliefs. From this theoretical perspective, it operates as a process of reification, or rather, a process of legitimising concepts of identity. Therefore, from a conservative and traditionalist perspective, this is how concepts of a multicultural and multiethnic society are either ignored, rejected or considered illegitimate as they do not fit in with narrow cultural, social, historical and often implicitly ethnically based concepts of Englishness.

**Constructing Realities, 111–134**
**Copyright © 2024 Stuart Cartland**
**Published under exclusive licence by Emerald Publishing Limited**
**doi:10.1108/978-1-83797-545-720231006**

What is employed here is the use of a cultural and political language between image and understanding. As conservative discourses of Englishness are an attempt to reassert 'traditional values' that multiculturalism is seen to have eroded or undermined, the political and social conservative language of the state and dominant concepts of 'common sense' are therefore inherently anti-multiculturalist. Multiculturalism is represented as a failed project, as a modernist folly. The danger of the normalisation of such rhetoric and narrative is that, (a) it is not seriously challenged in mainstream (predominantly English) politics, (b) it leads to cultural chauvinism and the increasing acceptance of more extreme right-wing rhetoric and positioning, (c) it becomes a self-perpetuating and self-legitimising fact through anecdotal evidence presented through discursive outlets such as the predominantly conservative media which creates a discursive feedback loop relating back to both previously discussed points.

If identity is a process of reification, then the construction of a dominant conservative English national identity and discourse is heavily reflective of the cultural, social, economic and political backgrounds of the brokers of power within British (yet more specifically English) society. It is no coincidence that prevailing discourses of Englishness are dominated by conservative, right-wing and traditionalist concepts of national identity. Power within the United Kingdom is held by a very small and narrow social elite from very similar and privileged backgrounds. If concepts of identity and society are reflective of our own backgrounds, experiences and expectations, then it is no surprise that dominant conservative discourses of identity are so far removed and unrepresentative of modern social reality, even when through populist politics and rhetoric they purport to represent and understand the concerns of the general populace.

If power within society is so inherently bound up with a very small and elite section of the population with very similar backgrounds, it is then no coincidence that the dominating ideology concerning national identity will be so heavily weighted to their very specific backgrounds and experiences and thus conservative, monocultural and deeply lacking in diversity. In the Social Mobility and Child Poverty Commission Study conducted by the government and published on 28/08/2014, found that indeed, such a narrow and exclusive concentration of power within British society 'risks narrowing the conduct of public life to a very small few who are very familiar with each other but far less familiar with the day-to-day challenges facing ordinary people in the country', and that 'it is not a recipe for a healthy democratic society' (2014). Instead, it is in fact the making of a very elite and concentrated social and culturally one-dimensional society where political representation becomes increasingly disconnected from the general population.

Rhetoric emanating from the Conservative government about a meritocratic society, where talent and hard work, not socio-economic status, background or nepotism, determines your place in society, is therefore clearly an illusion and a smokescreen of disinformation. A culturally very narrow elite and concentrated power status quo clearly rules, not just economically, politically or socially but also crucially ideologically. What is still apparent and implied through conservative and right-wing discourse is an underlying belief and assumption that the elite should rule, and that a conservative and traditionalist ideology is the only 'natural' prescribed ideology of such order. As Etinne Balibar (1991) highlights, it is a perceived 'historic mission', and a fictive expression of a naturalised order that can be viewed as being present in the state. Even when figures such as Rishi Sunak are elevated to become prime minister (the first person of colour and non-Christian in the United Kingdom), this exclusivism does not change, regardless of the platitudes that some on the right suggest this represents. Sunak is a multimillionaire; indeed, Rishi Sunak and his wife Akshata Murty have a combined net worth of around £730 million according to the Sunday Times Rich List. Sunak also attended the exclusive Winchester College, Oxford University and Stanford University (Neate Rupert, 2022).

Although it is possible to imagine old centres of power and influence away through various theories such as disjunctive flows, scapes, deterritorialisation, the end of history et al., nationalism in its many incarnations will not go away (Chowdhury, 2002). Traditional notions of legitimised order and stability hold particular sway in times of perceived crisis and anxiety. Regardless of political gesturing or rhetoric, nationalism, 'order', 'stability' and strategically placing blame retain an emotive pull and provide meaning and motive, especially when placed within a defensive nationalist rhetoric. A dominant narrative of crisis and anxiety is reflected back through right-wing populism such as, 'Government ministers publicly criticising the England football team for taking a knee [Priti Patel in 2020] in support of the BLM campaign, to the *Daily Mail* [2021] publishing an article on "no-go areas" for white citizens, it is clear that despite empty platitudes of anti-racism and inclusivity, narratives of race, ethnicity and politics of inclusion are closely controlled by the right' (Cartland, 2021).

In this sense, dominant concepts of national identity, nationalism and social order are intellectually appropriated (Fanon, 1963) or become expressions of 'bourgeois nationalism'. This can be viewed as evident within contemporary concepts of Englishness, especially in relation to the monopolisation of power and influence highlighted by the Social Mobility and Child Poverty Commission Study (2014). This would, therefore, indicate the existence and dominance not only of conservative, traditionalist and right-wing discourse but also a very particular type of an exclusivist national narrative. A conservative dominance of discourse concerning national identity is a moral imperative and a systematic claim to privilege. It is, and operates as, the maintenance of systematic imbalance, one that is continually positioned as being under threat and therefore positioned as being a defender of 'common sense', 'order' or some degree of rightful socio-political balance. In recent years, this has come in the guise of being the defender against either by political correctness, socialism under the leadership of the Labour Party under Jeremy Corbyn or wokeism.

Nations, as an imagined cultural and collective space, are deeply contested in an ideological sense. The severe cuts or 'austerity' programme imposed by the Conservative-led government from 2010, especially to publicly funded and accessed bodies such as the NHS, libraries, social services, benefits and legal aid, delegitimise those that depend upon it and give them less of a stake or claim to national space or the imagined ideological national community. In other words, whole groups of people are alienated as well as excluded. They are discursively alienated and are situated outside of the boundaries of the national collective. Anne McClintock points out, 'nations are contested systems of cultural representation that limit and legitimise peoples' access to the resources of the nation-state' (McClintock, 1997:89). For those that depend upon the state for support and assistance (except for some groups such as pensioners) are represented outside of the ideological boundaries of a homogenised and idealised national community, regardless of contradictory political rhetoric suggesting otherwise. In this regard, the national space has arguably become a privatised space, 'the entire notion of cultural identity and nationalism, then, has been put into crisis in this age of global capital' (Chowdhury, 2002). Although the endlessly performative postmodern openness of a globalised modern reality may have spelled the end to boundaries regarding trade and flows of finance, it has also revived old boundaries regarding social, cultural and ethnic inclusion and exclusion. This is the paradoxical world of late global capitalism – open borders (for some things) yet closed and defensive dominant ideologies. This has melded boundary disintegration of globalised economies within the closed social and cultural imagination of the nation.

## Pejorative Understandings of Multiculturalism

Due to a conservative, right-wing discursive dominance within the contested terrain of contemporary English national identity, multiculturalism has come to be understood through a pejorative reading of the concept. The term 'multiculturalism' is often the subject of political and media commentary, vilification and criticism, yet it is often unclear what precisely is being criticised (Uberoi and Modood, 2013). The vague and unclear notions of what the term means often lead to crass oversimplifications. 'Multiculturalism is often said to denote a culturally diverse citizenry, or what may be called a "multicultural society"' (Uberoi and Modood, 2013:129). Yet it has become symbolically loaded and associated with a right-wing narrative of a 'paralysis of political correctness', 'the nanny state' and as an affront to conservative ideological concepts of 'common sense' which is couched within a narrative as making the nation weaker, susceptible to terrorist attacks (particularly in relation to 'home grown' or domestic attacks) and destroying any sense of social and cultural unity or continuity. Politically, the involvement of British Muslim citizens in the battlefields of Afghanistan, Syria or the London transport network of July 2005 becomes a retroactive indictment of the United Kingdom's supposedly overly lax immigration control, nationality and so-called failed attempt at multiculturalism and integration (Cartland, 2021).

Cultural and social questions disguised within political commentary can be detected in the aftermath of the terrorist attacks in Paris in January 2015. Here Nigel Farage and other far-right European politicians blamed the shootings on a 'really rather gross policy of multiculturalism' (Farage in Watt, 2015). Although condemned by mainstream politicians, Farage's simplistic message was an opportunistic attempt to manipulate and blame the incident on decades of European multiculturalist policies while seeking (in the same speech) to link the Rochdale child abuse scandal to multiculturalism. The key point is that Farage does not blame individuals but rather politically and symbolically conflates issues to promote narrow, incoherent ideas about cultural constitutions. For example, Farage states that, 'what I mean is that we've encouraged people from other cultures to remain within those cultures and not integrate fully within our communities' (Watt and Mason, 2015).

The ideologically motivated assumption here is that a stable hegemonic culture existed before multiculturalism (using an assumed historical teleological positioning of such a process), and that people who practise minority cultural lifestyles are equated to a fifth column. Both of these ideological assumptions are misguided and only serve to further a right-wing anti-immigration agenda through the creation of an illusionary hegemonic national character, identity and ethnicity. As pointed out by George Eaton, 'rather than offering a simple expression of sympathy for the victim's families, and a defence of free speech, Farage could not resist grandstanding against multiculturalism' (Eaton, 2015). For a high profile figure to make overt blame claims equating multiculturalism with terrorism further legitimises social inequality, division and prejudice.

Although condemned and representing a minority opinion in relation to the Charlie Hebdo attacks, the key point is that Farage casually links the ideological myth that multiculturalism is both a) a recent instituted phenomenon and b) something that can be stopped. Multiculturalism has a long and complex history within English culture and society and is constitutive of England as an entity itself (from language to people, for example). The position that multiculturalism is somehow to blame for society's ills or that we can blame a particular faith (within a wider remit of multiculturalism) is naive, illogical and dangerous. However, this sentiment is used to justify inequality and the promotion and perpetuation of a particular political narrative.

To further reiterate the point, Rupert Murdoch stated on 10 January 2015 (just after the Paris attacks) that all Muslims must be held responsible for the French terror attacks, 'most Moslems[sic] – even if peaceful – must be held responsible for the religion's growing jihadist cancer' (Guardian, 2015). Murdoch followed up this tweet by claiming that 'political correctness makes for denial and hypocrisy' (ibid). This misinformation is based upon the ideological belief that the actions of three individuals can represent over 1.5 billion people, that Islam is inherently dangerous and promotes violence and that if three people act violently in the name of a belief, all who share their faith are culpable. It also makes the sweeping judgement that multiculturalism made such an act possible, and that to quibble this view is hypocritical and a denial of reality. The conflation of multiculturalism, Islam and political correctness is situated as a catch-all representation of a symbolic otherness against conservative, right-wing conceptualisations and ideological imaginings of a quasi-hegemonic social, cultural and national identity.

In forming and promoting a crude binary opposite understanding of good versus evil, or Islam versus the West Gary Younge (2015) points out, only serves to corral us into crude camps where there are no dilemmas only declarations and what lacks in complexity is made up for in polemical clarity and the provision of a clear and distinguishable enemy. This echoes the rhetoric and narrative of 'you're either with us or against us'. This is producing a reductive narrative devoid of nuance and ideological rational discussion, debate or clear evidence.

The issue is that Islam, 'Remainers', 'champagne socialists', 'the liberal elite' et al. are reduced to a synonym representing anti-democratic, anti-common sense and anti-Englishness. Conservative reductionism and determinism in relation to discourses of nation, identity and simple categorisations are in essence essentialist constructions. What can be viewed to be at work here is not a coincidental focus on certain issues from a standpoint but a concerted and dominant ideological discursive account. The repeated focusing upon and targeting of issues such as immigration, multiculturalism or a close relationship with Europe is presented as a 'denaturing' (Balibar, 2002) of supposed and constructed national identities. Negative and targeted stereotyping and narratives are often carried out in a banal sense, often reinforced by politicians or major media outlets; this is often articulated or represented through mutually incompatible mythical narratives (Balibar, 2002).

It is no coincidence that the message communicated by Murdoch in the aftermath of the Paris attacks mirrors the general narrative presented in his influential and domineering (ideologically conservative) media empire. Symbolic manipulation and intended division shows the intent of not only Murdoch and Farage but other influential right-wing opportunists, seeking to blame multiculturalism (in its most general form) for the woes and dangers to society while also providing a dangerous and malign narrative of understanding. This conceptualisation and commentary is precisely what David Cameron alluded to or was interpreted as when he referred to the failure of state multiculturalism in 2011. The comments of Farage et al. in this context can only be viewed as a less tactful expression of the same sentiment which directly shapes the context in which multiculturalism and national identity is discussed and imagined.

However, we all live in multicultural environments. Our social spaces are inherently multicultural; therefore, as Zygmunt Bauman (2016) states, talk of policies of multiculturalism does not make much sense. Although we live in highly multicultural environments, we create and entertain a world largely insular and cut-off from strangers and others from different backgrounds. In other words, we filter out those unlike ourselves. The issue though, according to Bauman, is that there is not a developed cosmopolitan consciousness developing the interactions between us that can withstand the simplistic populist messages of conservative and right-wing nationalism. Where uncertainty has become omnipresent and we seek answers to fears and anxieties, this helps to formulate and drive dominant national narratives and discourses unconstrained by political correctness and instead embodies fear.

Multiculturalism as a simplistically understood concept is bogged down with a constrictive and restrictive government and state policy field that has ultimately failed in creating an inclusive, equal and unified sense of national community. This has blurred into a general discourse of an overgeneralised sense that multicultural society coupled together with national identity is not possible – the two being distinctly different yet have become inseparable and conflated within official rhetoric and subjective interpretation. The sense of a cosmopolitan and multicultural, pluralist identity is at distinct odds with imagined notions of a conservative ideological national discourse. Discourses of this perspective only serve to separate, essentialise and create binary opposites within an imagined national narrative. One of the fundamental problems when discussing culture, nation, national identity and conceptualisations of communities is the assumed constructed existence of compartmentalised, homogenous, social and cultural groupings, whether that be a majority dominant group or the existence of a range of minority groups. These conceptual constructs do not have space for the power conflicts, individualised heterogeneous qualities present in any social grouping including, interest difference, conflicts along the lines of class or gender, political orientation and cultural background in either a majority or minority context. As Yuval-Davis and Anthias highlight, 'the whole notion of multi-culturalism assumes definite, static, ahistorical and essentialist units of "culture" with fixed boundaries and with no space for growth and change' (Yuval-Davis and Anthias, 1993:38). Imagined deterministic and essentialist units of cultural separation provide legitimisation for an ideological undermining of a general concept and process of multiculturalism.

Highly diverse, multicultural, multi-ethnic, largely urban areas challenge, contradict and undermine mythical conservative, traditionalist and right-wing concepts of a contemporary Englishness. Ethnicity and cultural difference can be viewed as a political and ideological tool when discussing concepts of belonging, as Gerd Baumann (1996) points out, reification, homogenisation and essentialism are characteristic of official approaches to political discourse concerning multiculturalism. The whole paradox that exists within dominant conservative discourses of Englishness or national identity is that racism is dismissed as being intolerable and to be rejected, yet people are compartmentalised into different racial and ethnic groups, which are then loaded with cultural and social assumptions. The same can also be applied to (to varying degrees) gender and class. In this sense, Englishness or English national identity operates as an abstract concept. Conservative concepts of Englishness are represented as being mutually incompatible with a general process of multiculturalism, yet England exists as a highly multicultural community.

As Uberoi and Modood (2013) point out, when the state uses the language, norms and sensibilities of the cultural majority in its political institutions, or establishes only 'their' religion in them, or teaches only 'their' history in schools, cultural minorities are excluded and are treated unequally, despite being citizens who are entitled to equal treatment. Official rhetoric points to an equal, just and tolerant society yet what is enforced are the ideological values and norms of a conceptualised homogenous (conservative and traditionalist) majority hidden behind the language of 'national values' or 'common morals'. Yet the moment that minority cultures or marginalised groups are recognised or official efforts are made to incorporate them they are often met with howls of right-wing indignation or outrage.

The fears and anxieties perpetually maintained within the public imagination about the threat from outside and the threat from within are bred by the dominant discursive depictions of culture and difference, yet difference is all around us and between all of us, yet it is often not recognised as it does not fit in with prescribed pejorative recognition of difference. Difference, it seems, only terrifies us when it is articulated and associated with some degree of threat. The recurring immigration issue with its associated essentialist discursive articulations and ideological framework of diametric binary opposites and exclusivism perpetuates such a conservative and traditionalist concept of 'threat' to Englishness, which is forever trapped from the realities of the lived experience of the vast majority of the English population.

For example, the recurring theme of an invasion of small boats across the Channel represents this threat while maintaining a degree of order in how community, nation and inclusion or exclusion is imagined. Although those crossing the English Channel number around 45,000 for 2022, the overall number of net migration was around 600,000 to the United Kingdom. Clearly, this number is a tiny fraction in terms of migration, yet it is what this small group represents and how it is ideologically positioned which is important. They are positioned outside of the imagined community, as an alien threat and as being 'out of control' unless radial steps are taken. Even when radical steps are then taken such as the controversial plan to send asylum seekers to Rwanda for processing, the narrative and threat continues. Even when the United Kingdom leaves the European Union, largely on the back of a whipped-up narrative of 'taking back control' of borders and immigration policy, the narrative and threat remains and continues, the point being is what this group represents, not the actual numbers, to take this ideologically motivated narrative around migration one step further.

Many in these small boats are refugees. Indeed, the term refugee has been symbolically loaded by the right in the United Kingdom with concepts of threat, invasion and many other pejorative and xenophobic ideas, regardless of the plight of the people under discussion, such as those fleeing the worst instances of conflict, persecution and desperation in the world from locations such as Syria, Afghanistan or Yemen. However, the same moral entrepreneurs on the right (the government and media to name the most prominent) welcomed the huge number of Ukranian refugees from the conflict that began in Feb 2022 with not only open arms but as a moral duty to do so.

The point being that it is not whether those seeking to enter the United Kingdom can speak English, or if they need assistance, where they originate from, the number of them or if they are ethnically or culturally different in any way, the point is what they are positioned as representing and how that is used to maintain dominant understandings or narratives around place, identity and order regardless of how contradictory, confusing or nonsensical this may prove to be.

Conservative discourse on race and ethnicity has been centred around what Paul Gilroy terms 'Post-colonial melancholia'. This concept as previously highlighted is used as a means to articulate the ideological representation of issues such as immigration and the maintenance of a conservative sense of national identity, 'this unstable mixture identified the social and political problems embodied in the invasive presence of immigrants and their kin as an intrusion, an alien wedge cutting in to the body of the unsuspecting nation' (Gilroy, 2005:121). This analysis can be viewed as an accurate means to articulate and embody the ideological framework, which underpins the discursive position on the topic of 'race', immigration and national identity, particularly within the context of an historicised perspective on empire. What Gilroy is suggesting here is that an ideological articulation and conceptualisation of immigration and immigrants has turned post-colonial settlers actively recruited and welcomed in the immediate post-war period into perpetual outsiders. This interpretation can be viewed as dominating all talk of refugees and asylum seekers as being illegal or illegitimate invaders using tacit insinuation and coded discussion of racial exclusivity. To take this even further, Home Secretary Suella Braverman in April 2023 labelled Pakistani males' culture values totally at odds with British values. As former Chair of the Conservative Party Lady Sayeeda Warsi commented 'these sweeping statements branding British – Pakistani men, without nuance or caveats, as child sex abusers' (Warsi, 2023) represents a Government indulging in racist rhetoric while pandering to those who cry 'free-speech'. This defensive and openly hostile discourse has 'neatly dovetailed with the new mood that fixes the interpretation of September 2001s horrors (and their ongoing aftermath) as a clash of contending civilisations with mutually incompatible cultural systems' (Gilroy, 2005:122).

> Multiculturalism as an historical account of an ethnocentric reading of society is firmly positioned within a modern context and is deeply embedded within a post-war narrative. However England has always been a multicultural and multiethnic society, from early history right up to the modern day. Multiculturalism is couched within an historical reading and is presented as something 'new', 'modern', 'alien' and out-of-step with tradition- this could be no further from the truth or so contradictory from historical record and experience. As highlighted by Byung Chul Han, "the insight that culture is hybrid or impure is nothing new. According to Herder [. . .] European culture is 'a plant sprung from Roman, Greek, and Arabic feed'. It is a bastard culture."
>
> (Han, 2023:19)

Social commentators expressing dissatisfaction about immigration, ethnic and cultural mixing and grumbling about feeling like a foreigner in their own land is also nothing new, as The Chronicle of Richard of Devizes (c. 1190) illuminates:

> I do not like that city [London] at all. All sorts of men crowd together there from every country under the heavens. Each race brings its own vices and its own customs to the city. No one lives in it without falling into some sort of crimes. . .whatever evil or malicious thing that can be found in any part of the world, you will find it in that one city.
>
> (Sturgis, Brunton-Smith, Kuha and Jackson, 2013)

Even from this medieval extract from almost 900 years ago, the urban inner city signifies the antithesis to imagined notions of national homogeneity and timelessness.

Within the contemporary context of a 'crisis of English national identity', xenophobia and conservative nationalism seem to be thriving. 'Difficulties arising from what is now seen as the unrealistic or unwelcome obligation to dwell peacefully with aliens and strangers somehow confirm the justice of these sorry developments' (Gilroy, 2005:2). The themes of cultural diversity seem to be incompatible with a sense of national identity, one which may in fact (in rhetoric) pride itself on tolerance yet has now become the subject to derision and ridicule. Moreover, the master signifier of identifying as or with English has become a refuge for an implicit ethnically exclusive status.

The paradoxical position is that one look at present day English society will confirm that multicultural society has not died, in fact it cannot die. The only thing that can die or has been extinguished through the dominance of conservative, right-wing discourse is a conceptual inclusivity of multicultural society within imagined notions of English national identity. The almost triumphant proclamation of its death is itself a political gesture and a dangerous symbolic ideological position. It is also an articulation of the end of any ambition towards such a possibility. It is the delegitimisation of the positive notion of a multicultural society backed by the state. It also links diversity towards negative connotations, such as a failed project. Homogeneity is insinuated as the safe and stable regime of the future by being linked to mythical concepts of it in the past.

Revisionist accounts of British (and English) social and cultural history have come to dominate this terrain over recent years; however, 'this popular, revisionist output is misleading and dangerous' (Gilroy, 2005:2). Tied into the social, cultural and political connotations of the death of multiculturalism is an implied separation of contemporary social and cultural reality from imperialist and colonialist history. This is very dangerous as it takes multiculturalism out of context and seeks to isolate and relocate its legacy as an inconvenient problem. We need to begin to consider the role of ethnic absolutism in securing the modes of inclusive exclusion that betray a distinct ordering of power which also invoke a sense of incommensurable 'otherness'. From a conservative and right-wing perspective on national identity, multiculturalism is laid out as an essentialist understanding of ethnicity and a sense of natural hierarchy within society. It becomes a self-evident force, which legitimises analogies of history, social division and cultural separation.

## The 'Death of Multiculturalism'

Multiculturalism, as a progressive, inclusive and politically correct general process of official, state-backed policy and direction and being actively encouraged (in rhetoric at least) by the New Labour Government, arguably came to a turning point in 2001. In rapid succession over a few months, David Blunkett became

Home Secretary; there were riots in some northern English cities and the attacks of 9/11 took place.

> These events, especially the riots and the global 'arrival' of a certain kind of armed, messianic jihadism- which, some feel, too many Muslims in Britain (secretly) support- have led to not just to a governmental reversal, but to a new wave of criticism of multiculturalism from the centre- left, including from some of its erstwhile supporters.
>
> (Modood, 2013:62)

Although there had always been some critics of multiculturalism from the left when it was ridiculed in the 1970s and 1980s as 'saris, samosas and steel bands' when, at the turn of the 21st century, it lost its centre-left support, as a political and cultural concept and process it was left to be savaged.

The New Labour Government's White Paper of February 2002 *Secure Borders, Safe Haven* reflected the prominence of the combination of political and policy anxieties over asylum, multicultural citizenship, terror threat and immigration. It called for highly 'managed' migration, as Lewis and Neil (2005) point out, this recognition was conducted and obscured at the same time by the wider public's focus on asylum, 'a focus that often verged on the hysterical and xenophobic as the public mood seemingly became increasingly hostile to the presence of people seeking asylum in the UK' (Lewis and Neil, 2005). Post-9/11 and after the events in London on 7/7, the New Labour Government took a relatively hardline approach to immigration and surrounding issues while still promoting what many saw as a contradictory stance towards identity. Responding to profound and widespread anxieties and consternation (in a large part whipped up by the political and media right-wing), this mood of fear was reflected with the controversial imposition of citizenship testing and the passing of the Nationality, Immigration and Asylum Act (2002).

Although the birth of New Labour arguably spelt the end of a mainstream political party based upon egalitarian values, a political and rhetorical swing to the right took place wholesale at the start of the 21st century. Political tolerance, inclusion, understanding and equality all became fatally undermined by the reaction to the events of both 9/11 and 7/7, which concomitantly have been used as justification for such a divisive response. As Tariq Modood points out, 'it is astonishing how the general thesis that "multiculturalism is dead and was killed by 9/11 and/or 7/7" has become part of the inter(national) common sense without any reference to the work of any key multiculturalist theorist or text' (Modood, 2010:106).

The events of 9/11 and 7/7 have been used by the political right to seize the moment of public anxiety and fear and firmly established its ideological approach as the dominant national discourse, as the 'right', 'common sense' and 'robust' approach to the perceived and alleged corrosive effects of multiculturalism. It has become widespread common currency that in many western European countries (not just the United Kingdom) that multiculturalism, as a quasi-official programme for giving recognition to ethno-religious minorities and their cultures has failed and instead, as Heath and Demireva (2014) point out, led to the entrenchment of separate communities with corrosive consequences for trust and solidarity.

Most infamously, this ongoing argument has been forcibly expressed by senior politicians. On 5 February 2011 at the Munich Security Conference, Prime Minister David Cameron (echoing remarks made by German Chancellor Angela Merkel) stated that:

> Under the doctrine of state multiculturalism, we have encouraged different cultures to live separate lives, apart from each other and apart from the mainstream...We've even tolerated these segregated communities behaving in ways that run completely counter to our values... This hands-off approach tolerance has only served to reinforce the sense that not enough is shared. And this all leaves some young Muslims feeling rootless. And the search for something to belong to and something to believe in can lead... [to]... a process of radicalisation.
>
> (Cameron, 2011 in Heath and Demireva, 2014)

Within this speech, David Cameron also declared the failure of 'state multiculturalism' in Britain today. Whether he is referring to specific legislation, policy or programmes or not, declarations and denunciations by European leaders such as Cameron and Merkel concerning a 'failed experiment' are actually referring to the failure of Western Europe's response to immigration, not the failure of multiculturalism in itself (Watson and Saha, 2013). What politicians have endeavoured here is to blame a long, largely unplanned process of increasingly diverse and visible social and cultural heterogeneity for failings of the political class itself. When Cameron declared, 'we have failed to provide a vision of society to which they feel they want to belong' (Cameron in BBC News, 2011), he is highlighting the increased racialisation and exclusivity of a sense of national identity, not created by minority groups but by the very conservative, traditionalist and right-wing holders of power such as himself. This dominant discourse on the topic has been referred to by Arun Kundnani (2007) as the end of tolerance. Rhetoric and narrative concerning failure of 'the multicultural project' suggests that it was a temporary project, one that was planned, and one where the tolerance of the ethnic majority is the litmus test of a subjective reading of 'success' or 'failure'.

Although the language employed by Cameron in his speech is very subjective and claims to be speaking for a moral majority, he also strongly links multiculturalism to other linked systematic failings of the state. He makes the very strong link between the apparent failure of multiculturalism and Islamic radicalisation, that multiculturalism fosters and breeds separate and parallel communities and social lives and hence leads to hostility and distrust between majority and minority groups. 'Perhaps the most pernicious aspect of Cameron's speech was the way he associated multiculturalism not just with segregation and separateness, but with extremism and terrorism' (Hasan, 2011). This is a critical element to the vindictive misinterpretation of the Muslim community in the contemporary period. London suffered at the hands of fundamentalist Islamic terrorists on 7/7 and other subsequent terrorist plots have been uncovered and averted, yet the Muslim community and the actions of individual Muslims are read through discursive interpretations entirely through their faith alone. It has become entirely normalised for British Muslim communities to be viewed exclusively through the prism of security and counterterrorism. Problems of integration and community cohesion have become wrapped up in the discourse of the 'war on terror' (Hasan, 2011). It frames how communities and individuals are viewed and represented, much like the way the Black community can be seen to have been treated in the 1970s and 1980s in relation to urban disturbances and crime.

Assumptions between apparent failings of multiculturalism and the Muslim community are easy and lazy right-wing stereotypes that have become taken-for-granted social fact. Negative stereotyping constructs a depiction of the Muslim community as being an insular, radical and alien presence; however, only a cursory look finds very contradictory evidence; 92% of Pakistani respondents agreed with the statement 'minorities should mix and integrate', and 67% of respondents agreed with the statement that they 'feel equally or more British than black/Asian' (Uberoi and Modood, 2013). Much of the anxiety concerning the alleged lack of Muslim integration is misplaced and misinformed and tends to be driven by alarmist, right-wing, often Islamophobic press coverage and misrepresentation. As Mehdi Hasan comments:

> Contrary to popular opinion, most Muslims in this country are patriotic, loyal and integrated, by most definitions of these contested terms. According to a Gallup poll published in May 2009 [just 6 years after the UK's involvement in the illegal invasion if Iraq], British Muslims are more likely than non-Muslim Britons to say they identify strongly with the United Kingdom (77 per cent for the former, compared to 50 per cent with the latter). British Muslims are also more likely than non-Muslim Britons to want to live in mixed areas, among people of different backgrounds (67 per cent, against 58 per cent).
>
> (Hasan, 2011)

Although the issue of a British identity as opposed to an English identity being more inclusive and multicultural in character may account (in some part) for the first questions response, nevertheless such figures clearly undermine populist reactionary claims.

The sustained assault and derision towards multiculturalism, the open hostility, enflamed rhetoric, fear and anxiety is no longer the preserve of the far-right but common government policy espoused from the political and media elite. For example, when Cameron claimed in his Munich speech, 'frankly, we need a lot less of the passive tolerance of recent years and much more active, muscular liberalism' (Cameron, in Hasan, 2011), he is not suggesting a discussion but instead a hardline imposition of conservative, right-wing values, norms and state policy irrespective of the real causes of social division. Comments and claims by senior Conservatives in Government of 'straight talking' are not isolated or unique. In a 2018 column for *The Daily Telegraph*, former Prime Minster Boris Johnson labelled Muslim women as letterboxes when discussing a proposed burqa ban. Cameron's speech in Munich and Johnson's racist comments must however be seen in context. A conservative ideological position towards immigration and its association to terrorism is not exclusive or monopolised by the Conservative Party. Mainstream centre ground Westminster politics has become dominated by this position and has normalised right-wing rhetoric (Johnson, 2018).

For a decade prior to David Cameron's Munich speech, this position had dominated Westminster politics, government rhetoric and policy under Blair and Brown, especially within the context of New Labour, eager to show its centre ground populist credentials of being tough on crime and immigration. This must also be viewed in response to the 9/11 and 7/7 terrorist attacks and the reactionary response that they generated. Instead of a conciliatory search for understanding, dialogue and a fundamental desire for a unified, inclusivist reaction government policy and rhetoric (influenced to a large extent by fear and anxiety whipped up by the right-wing press and political and social elite), at least since 9/11, has been focused upon assimilation, punishment, exclusionary normativeness, infringement of civil liberties and individual rights and a general demonisation of not only the Muslim community and immigration but multiculturalism as a whole.

Leading public figures have queued up to deliver the last rites of multiculturalism, the criticism and condemnation transcending political and party lines. Trevor Phillips, the then head of the Commission for Racial Equality warned in a report (published in 2005), commissioned by the government following the riots of 2001 that the United Kingdom was 'sleepwalking into segregation'. The report highlighted the dangers that a divided and unequal society will face and was deeply critical of government failure to promote, address and create a fairer and more inclusive society. Phillips stated that, 'the fact is that we are a society which – almost without noticing it – is becoming more divided by race and religion' (Guardian, 2005). However, instead of criticising the real root of the problem and why a general process of multiculturalism has been allowed to fail, 'sleepwalking into segregation' has been used to provide a general narrative of multiculturalism as a cause within itself to blame. Mehdi Hasan comments, 'in truth, over the years, Cameron, Blair, Brown, Phillips and the rest have constructed a mythical version of multiculturalism – a "cardboard cut-out," to use Clegg's phrase – and held it responsible for a raft of sins, from segregation and separateness to extremism and terrorism' (Hasan, 2011).

The very lack of a defined, unambiguous and accepted definition of 'multiculturalism' has both meant its manipulation and reinterpretation along ideological lines and its normalised and reductionist conceptualisation by the right to generally equate it to ethnic minorities and political correctness. Labour MP Jon Cruddas suggests, 'its very elusiveness allows people to reinterpret the whole idea in a shrill and sour language' (Hasan, 2011). 'Sleepwalking into segregation' can be viewed as an appropriation of *laize faire* attitudes of promoting social justice, equality and inclusivity. It blames the victims not the institutional perpetrators.

Multiculturalism, as a half-hearted and ambiguous policy programme, is blamed for the systematic failure of a widespread inclusive and pluralist identity and social and cultural policy, whereas the real problematisation lies at institutionalised and systemic locations of long established exclusive power, located within inherent conservative social and cultural exclusivism. A championing of a so-called death of multiculturalism and the domination of conservative, traditionalist discourse will only serve to create, foster and perpetuate alienation, division, disillusionment and disempowerment specifically from those who are already relatively under-represented and excluded from any notions or conceptions of a sense of national identity.

The critical point to make here though is that an attack on multiculturalism is an attack on the very real, lived, diversity of the nation. That is what makes statements and comments from Cameron, Johnson, Braverman et al. so dangerous. It strongly suggests, and can easily be read as, a negative commentary of the diverse societies in which we live. What is also apparent is that, such leaders are deflecting blame and failure away from hegemonic structures of power and inequality and on to the oppressed themselves. Watson and Saha highlight, 'discourses of multicultural failure when applied to questions of migration, identity and belonging are simply a way of avoiding talking about issues of race and power' (Watson and Saha, 2013:2020). The simplified message that is interpreted and read from anti-multiculturalist commentary and rhetoric is that diversity is a failure; it has led to a negative impact upon society, culture and the nation and it is 'their' fault, not 'ours'. However, this is certainly no coincidence; it is a key aspect of a conservative, right-wing national discourse. When such commentary is surrounding issues regarding integration for instance, what is really implied or meant is assimilation.

The paradox of the conservative position is staggering and the claim bold. A conservative, right-wing understanding and representation of multiculturalism is precisely the very opposite of what a multiculturalist society can actually accurately be defined as. A general and central aim or goal of a multicultural society is to break down division, yet from the conservative discursive position, it apparently promotes this. As Uberoi and Modood (2013) point out, this understanding of multiculturalism becomes a caricature and functions like a stereotype as it is intuitively appealing and thus widely believed; it is also pejorative and an inaccurate depiction of what it claims to relate to. The more leading politicians and others assert this understanding, the more they help to normalise the climate of opinion it reflects and shapes. In his 2011 speech, Cameron claimed and advocated 'a national identity that is open to everyone' (Uberoi and Modood, 2013: 136); however, this is precisely the sort of identity he is denying when he systematically attacks multiculturalism and confines it to the dustbin of history. Cameron is promoting a divisive and exclusive national identity, one that is based on homogeneity and assimilation not diversity and heterogeneity. He is promoting and protecting power interests not encouraging equality, representation and inclusivity. What Cameron and the conservative discursive position can be seen to be playing to is a general anxiety about identity, particularly within England and within a wider context of globalisation and the fear that England may have lost a sense of distinctiveness. Again, this can be seen to relate back to a resurgence and support of traditionalist notions of Englishness and why conservative, nostalgic and lamentable narratives provide a potent and emotive message.

Although the message seems to be from all sides of the mainstream political spectrum of inclusivity, how this is communicated and what is seen to be required is the crucial element. What is also widely shared within mainstream political policy proposals from all sides is the belief that there are systemic flaws in the United Kingdom's official management of immigration. Immigration is inherently linked via conservative, right-wing discourse to negative social, cultural and economic qualities and effects. According to Sturgis et al. (2013), this pessimistic view of the effect of immigration on the social fabric finds high-profile articulation and expression in David Cameron's pronouncement that 'multiculturalism has failed'. Within this link can be seen a common underlying theme and belief that racial and ethnic heterogeneity is problematic for healthy community and national life. Through a conservative discursive dominance, this has become a largely unquestioned populist narrative. Calls for sending the navy to stop small boats crossing the English Channel or sending asylum seekers to Rwanda are direct consequences of narratives around a 'more muscular liberalism' and only further promotes and normalises homogeneity and social and cultural exclusion, 'similarly, there is also an implicit assumption that segregation or assimilation are the only possibilities' (Heath and Demireva, 2013:163). Symbolic and systematic misinterpretation and manipulation of 'multiculturalism' not only serves to bolster a conservative, anti-PC, anti-woke discourse; it can also be viewed as helping to open the door to more casual use of xenophobic rhetoric as it symbolically sends out signals (and is interpreted) as heralding the end of a multicultural and multiethnic society instead of spelling out the failings of an ambiguous and *laize faire* state multiculturalist programme.

The view from many public commentators on multiculturalism is that it is now commonplace that the cultural separatism and self-imposed segregation of the Muslim community (which is also conflated with asylum and immigration in general) is a challenge to national identity, and that a politically correct multiculturalism has fostered fragmentation rather than integration. Regardless of the intended finer meaning of statements made by David Cameron or Trevor Phillips, the key issue is that such debate, commentary and rhetoric has certainly become simplified and high-jacked by the political right to infer that multicultural society does not work and cannot work. As Tariq Modood (2013) points out, the argument becomes one about the public/private distinction, and the question of what is 'normal' or acceptable within society – and why some groups are thought to be and are considered abnormal, different and unacceptable, hence why Ukrainian refugees are welcomed while Syrian or Afghan refugees are not. Moreover, 'normal' is judged along very specific and prescriptive subjective social, cultural and ideological lines. Plurality or heterogeneity (which can be viewed as an inherent part of a multicultural society) falls outside of these constructed and constrictive boundaries.

## Multiculturalism as an Inescapable Social Reality

Although multiculturalism has become a politically and culturally tarnished concept, the general notion of what it stands for needs to be understood as an essential narrative and framework of inclusivity and heterogeneity. Multiculturalism as a lived social reality, as a bottom-up, everyday experience that has long social and historical roots, is a process that is far less dramatic, contentious or sudden than political and cultural commentators would have us believe. The real, lived, everyday experience of multicultural society, of living together as a banal experience instead of some sort of state instigated programme, has been conceptualised by Stuart Hall (1999, in Watson and Saha, 2013) as a general process of 'multicultural drift'.

What Hall is referring to in this conceptualisation of multiculturalism is the mundane and ordinary daily interactions between neighbours from different backgrounds that are 'undetected under a particular policy perspective' (Watson and Saha, 2013:2026), but are instead captured more precisely by a general and ongoing process. The concept of multicultural drift picks up and highlights the subtle and ordinary ways in which successive waves of immigrants settle and how different groups learn to accommodate and live together. Within this conceptualisation can be read a complex, reflexive and interdisciplinary account of the ongoing impact of immigration within society. It reflects the continual flux of ethnic and cultural mixing, particularly in the post-colonial context whereupon it can be seen to unsettle the perception of homogenised and familiar constructed landscapes of a monocultural national community. One of the main points made by Hall and which is central to his conceptualisation of multicultural drift is that a movement towards a multi-ethnic and multicultural society is not the result of a concerted, top-down, governmental policy process (although certain state policies have both helped and hindered such a process); it has instead evolved as an unplanned process, gradually and over time.

As Sophie Watson and Anamik Saha point out (2013), Hall deploys a theory of multicultural drift to capture the increasing visibility and 'natural' participation of ethnic minorities in the streets as an inevitable part of British life. Visible representations of multicultural drift have become more prevalent in the post-war era. What Hall is describing is not an homogeneous 'alien' 'other' but a heterogeneous population of different minority groups located within a diverse social and cultural background and within multilayered spaces, in other words, a partial, diffused and fragmented settlement. Cameron's speech on the apparent failure of multiculturalism can be interpreted as an end to toleration by an ideologically produced homogenised population towards cultural difference. Inflammatory rhetoric of 'our values', 'excessive state support towards ethnic minority cultures', 'speaking their own language' all suggest a systematic and comprehensive process of state multiculturalism actually existing in the first place and then being systematically rejected by a homogeneous cultural and ethnic majority on their own terms.

Despite the widely publicised failure or death of multiculturalism, the reality of life in a mostly urban, post-colonial and highly globalised society is one of cultural interdependence, interrelated conviviality. Multiculturalism by its very definition describes society as being pluralistic and permanent regardless of how perpetually uncomfortable that might be for some to understand or accept. The complex power relationships and contingent, shifting and fluid relationships between different social and cultural groups is an ongoing, constant and historical social characteristic, 'in this framework, discourse of success or failure have no place' (Watson and Saha, 2013:2021).

In this sense, the occupation of Prime Minister and Home Secretary by people of colour whose ancestors originated in the Indian subcontinent proves that multiculturalism has in fact succeeded very well, yet on the other hand, it proves the complete opposite. That in fact they can only be in those positions firstly through privilege (particularly in Rishi Sunak's position as previously highlighted) by reinforcing dominant conservative narratives around the nation regardless of what they might symbolically be seen to represent, both being staunch adherents to Tory ideology, particularly Suella Braverman who is widely regarded as the most right-wing Home Secretary in recent years. The analogy is the same as when Margaret Thatcher became prime minister in 1979. Many symbolically took this to represent gender quality within the United Kingdom, yet the reality was that Thatcher was staunchly against gender equality and firmly believed in traditional gender roles for women.

Regardless of governmental policy framework and rhetoric of promoting 'shared values' or 'cultural cohesion' (interpreted through a dominant ideological perspective) Paul Gilroy has theorised (2005), a normalised negotiated ethnic difference within a conceptualised conviviality as a form of societalisation from below, where cultural differences appear ordinary rather than determining structures of sociality (Erel, 2011). This conceptualisation places the normalisation of cultural and ethnic difference at the heart of a lived, everyday experience for the vast majority who live in England's large urban centres. This not only disrupts the conservative and traditionalist discursive narrative of multiculturalism being a failure; it totally undermines it. Indeed, 'hybridity "reverses the effects of the colonialist disavowed, so that other 'denied' knowledges enter upon the dominant discourse and estrange the basis of its authority"' (Bhabha in Han, 2023:24). Hybridity and a multiculturalism provides a subversive force that challenges established regimes of power and potentially provides the opportunities for marginalised existences to become empowered.

A pluralist, inclusive, reflexive and representative identity is not only desirable, it is essential. The United Kingdom (and more specifically England) is one of the most culturally and ethnically diverse countries in Europe, and contains London which has been described by many commentators as not just highly multicultural but as a city of 'superdiversity'. Mixed race Britons represent the fasted growing ethnic group in Britain (young people are six times more likely than adults to from a mixed background); however, they are frequently left out of serious discussions concerning race or national identity. One in ten British children (according to the 2011 Census) were from a mixed-race background (Shackle, 2011), whereas the 2021 Census showed a 40% increase on that figure (Fothergill, 2022). Again, diversity and difference needs to be viewed as a norm not as an 'alien' or 'outsider' characteristic. Evidence of success in ethnic integration is therefore self-evident. The considerable numbers of intermarriage and mixed partnerships from a major study found that, 'half of Caribbean men, a third of Caribbean women and a fifth of Indian and African men had a white partner' (Modood et al., 1997:355). The result of this is that in pure numbers alone, 'dual heritage' or 'mixed' ethnicity is the fastest growing ethnic category in Britain and the third largest ethnic group overall (Thomas, 2011). Moreover, the 2021 Census showed the dramatic shifts in the population with 1.7 million people in England and Wales identifying as mixed-race, which is triple the figure for 2001 (Fothergill, 2022).

The specifically (and to some extent) quiet English success of an evolving hybrid and multicultural society has to be triumphed and become a central part of an overarching national identity. This success, as Heath and Demireva (2013) point out, on many measures of social and political integration multiculturalism has provided no evidence or negative effects on social integration. Wright and Bloemraad (2012) suggest that academic research tends to downplay null findings, but in this case, these findings carry enormous theoretical and policy significance: the most important rationale for the political backlash against multicultural policies – that they impede or hurt sociopolitical integration – appears empirically unfounded. An identity which celebrates its plurality, diversity and inclusiveness opens the possibility for social change. If the nation-space can become dominated by a reactionary and nostalgic conceptualisation based upon a sense of traditionalism and tacitly promoting racism and xenophobia, then it cannot become a progressive, diverse and inclusive social force.

The relative success and failure of the England national football team can act as a useful metaphor around cultural identity here. On the one hand, it is increasingly represented by a young and very multicultural team who can symbolically represent a modern, inclusive and progressive nation. Yet on the other hand, these elements can be compartmentalised and overlooked in favour of an Englishness that serves to embolden the conservative right. In a post-Brexit environment of economic, political and cultural anxiety, the England team can be used as a vessel to symbolically represent a sense of English doggedness, separateness, fleeting superiority and sense of historical vindication. Regardless of the ethnic or class make-up of the team the right-wing press provides tired cliches and gleeful jingoism interwoven with the conservative right fetishisation of war, empire and isolationism as cultural and political narrative. 'What dominates is the nationalistic default attachment of England's glory to the good-old-days, a blitz spirit and how England needs only itself to determine it's own future' (Cartland, 2018).

Sporting events are often used to manifest ideological sentiments, yet this doesn't need to be the preserve of the conservative right. Danny Boyle's London 2012 Olympics opening ceremony provides an example of an inclusive, positive and egalitarian sentiment (although this was clearly around concepts of Britishness) – this also providing huge amounts of outrage from the conservative right. Nevertheless, the point being that England, and this is accurate of almost all instances where the England team plays regardless of sport, is co-opted by a particular paradoxical type of nationalism regardless of who is actually representing the nation. The metaphor of the national team provides an analogy of the dominance and contradictions of conservative and right-wing narratives of the nation itself and identity politics.

## The Future Is Already Here

Mythical and illusionary concepts of England being a homogenous and mono-ethnic entity is entirely baseless, 'England is not only one of the most diverse countries in the world, it is also one of the most hybrid' (Wright, 2008:99). A shared ownership of space and place has to be recognised and seriously incorporated into any developing sense of Englishness, especially one fit for purpose within a modern and outward looking context. This is not only possible and attractive but also necessary. However, as long as a dominant sense of Englishness is bound to illusionary notions of ethnicity, tradition and an insular and defensive conservative ideology, the English, or rather, a sense of English national identity will forever be stuck in a toxic malaise of denial and self-flagellation.

A multicultural and pluralist society in England already exists; in fact it has existed for a very long time. Indeed, it can be viewed as one of the key elements that constitute the very being of England. The battle and contestation that is now upon us is one concerning the national imagination over the national space, one that is currently dominated by a conservative ideological interpretation and representation. Paul Thomas (2011) points out that increasing levels of hybridity are interrupting racialised and exclusive understandings of Englishness, meaning that Asian Muslims can be English, albeit in a narrowly defined space. This is only really applicable in very localised settings or contexts – for instance, someone of an Asian Muslim background with a strong regional accent. This (at present) would not challenge dominant discourse on Englishness but rather plays into the conservative discursive construction and ghettoises hybridity to a 'street' or rather, modern urban context alone. A key factor that is imperative to address is the contextualisation of how we view a national identity, not only historically, socially and culturally but also within the global context.

'Multiculturalism means global engagement' (Nederveen Pieterse, 2007); it signifies the social, cultural, political and economic reality of living within a general process of globalisation, which has a long and varied historical interaction with the nation. However, through conservative discourse, it is presented as a social, cultural and (to a large extent) political threat, even if as an economic process it is viewed as not only necessary but essential, inevitable and desirable. Multiculturalism is an expression and articulation of one of the many faces of globalisation. Globalisation, 'at its Sunday best, is human history conscious of itself' (ibid); this leads back to the contradictory and hypocritical ideology behind contemporary forms of a conservative conceptualisation of Englishness. It is also important to note that multiculturalism does not equate to consensus; however, what (in part) defines a conservative conceptualisation to identity is an imagined homogenised 'us', unreflective and unconscious of itself.

One of the key issues which is overlooked in the unrelenting criticism of multiculturalism is that the nation state cannot contain, or be the arbiter of, multiculturalism. It never has done and can never hope to achieve control over it. It is a complex and incremental process, much like globalisation itself of which it is a central part, as Jan Nederveen Pieterse comments, 'multiculturalism debates suffer from methodological and policy nationalism' (ibid). Concepts that are based on a traditional account of national identity cannot hold water or be relevant in a so-called era of post-nationalism. Nations as insular containers are a defunct conceptualisation, which can only promote and inspire institutional hypocrisy and lead to misguided proclamations such as 'multiculturalism is dead'.

The real failure of multiculturalism is the political mainstream and establishment's inability to grasp what it might mean outside of an ideologically narrow contextualisation of the social and cultural effects of globalisation. It can be stated that exclusion in many instances is not occasional but institutional (Nederveen Pieterse, 2007). It is not occasional because multiculturalism combines with institutionalised amnesia and the refusal to view the country's colonial past in other than a benevolent light this positions the nation as an homogenised 'us', as the benevolent 'host' as 'tolerating' and giving to 'them'. The systematic attack upon multiculturalism and the political mainstream's move to the right has only permitted a very highly regulated and constrained monocultural multiculturalism (Vidal, 2004, Wieviorka, 2004). This is entirely what is meant when the political mainstream discusses a modern multiethnic or multicultural nation. The very domination of the right within discussions of multiculturalism and immigration is always dominated by the negative effects of a so-called 'open door immigration policy' and a seemingly one-way flow of immigrants; however, what is interesting and puts such issues into context is the fact that over 5.5 million Britons (BBC News, 2022) are permanent or long-term residents abroad, yet this is something rarely discussed in immigration debates and is purposefully not recognised or mentioned as it disrupts and undermines dominant conservative narratives. Therefore, the context needs to be global not a xenophobic focus on the national as some sort of insular self-contained unit.

A multicultural society deserves and indeed needs a multicultural citizenship which should be based on the idea that citizens have individual rights, but as individuals are not uniform, that in fact, their citizenship and identity contours itself around them. Difference is a commonality within the English experience. An identity that positively includes this commonality of difference – an identity based upon positive difference, a plural identity, one that emphasises what we have in common while positively respecting difference (as difference within the English experience can be extremely wide-ranging) or as Tariq Modood comments, 'commonality must be difference-friendly' (Modood et al., 1997:355).

This stands in opposition to static and homogenous conceptions of national identity, bound by mythical and selective perceptions of history and a social and cultural community. This does not mean a weak or indifferent national identity – in fact it means quite the opposite. It is an identity that plays to the national strengths but one that requires a framework of vibrant, dynamic national narratives, all welcomed, all legitimate and representative of the nation as a whole, not just representative for an elite few. National identity can only work or successfully operate if it provides a means of belonging to one's country and if it represents the experiences of the nation, in a positive sense and on a day-to-day basis. A national identity must be respectful, not resentful, and it must build upon the identities that people value – not trample upon them.

As nations constantly change so too must identities. Nothing is static and unchanging, especially nations and national communities. The contemporary era is the age defined by fluidity and change, especially in relation to those that live within the British Isles. As Mehdi Hasan points out, 'in the 21st century, identity isn't finite; loyalties do not have to compete. Those of us who are comfortable with our multiple, non-competing identities remain bewildered by the confrontational tone of Cameron et al.' (Hasan, 2011). National identities need to be as reflective, reflexive and fluid as national stories are, 'such modulations and contestations are part of the internal, evolutionary, work-in-progress dynamic of citizenship' (Modood, 2010:63).

The crisis that English national identity finds itself in is a complex and unique 'moment'. The Conservative right, particularly since 2010, has tried to condense this 'moment' into just an economic debate about austerity or pinning social failings upon multiculturalism or immigration; however, this unique 'moment' needs to be understood as an overall social, political and cultural formation or framework. Devolution, economic uncertainty, international terrorism and the European Union have all become subsumed under an overarching centre-right conservative dominant discourse of 'common sense'. This has operated as a hegemonic settlement and ideologically dictates 'common sense' responses. Dominant conservative discourse regarding such a crisis compartmentalises, essentialises, separates and oversimplifies the issues at hand individually, or as Stuart Hall (2010) states, the whole political discourse has been 'cleansed', so that the public debate, interest and ownership becomes unspeakable. It is an ideology of 'erasure', and it provides the dominant conservative discourse with the power and conditions to steer the debate.

Just as a conservative discourse of English national identity compartmentalises and separates interconnected debates and issues, it must be recognised that ethnic, racial, national, class and cultural divisions or differences are not mutually exclusive categories within constructions of a national narrative framework – they are interlinked in a complex, historically and socially relative manner which are continuously undergoing change and flux. In this sense, 'racism in Britain cannot be fully understood unless it is located as a central dimension of a hegemonic "Anglo-morphic" ethnicity' (Anthias and Yuval-Davis, 1993:59). An ethnicity is constructed around a Christian, white, European cultural heritage, specifically around the symbolism of a selective reading of history. Ideological and political discourse from a dominant conservative perspective therefore uses this conceptualisation as being central to any construction of nation and national identity as permanent and unchanging either overtly or implied.

An important obstacle to England's and Britain's transformation into an inclusive pluralist society is that, as the Parekh Report (2000) into the future of a multiethnic Britain stated:

> Britishness, as much as Englishness, has systematic, largely unspoken, racial connotations...Unless these deep-rooted antagonisms to racial and cultural difference can be defeated in practice, as well as symbolically written out of the national story, the idea of a multicultural post-nation remains an empty promise.
> (Parekh, 2000)

The key issue concerning English national identity is that arguably there are two such general paths that are possible, the path of defensive, xenophobic, exclusivist chauvinism that harks back to imagined notions of a green and pleasant land untouched by modernity or social and cultural difference. Moreover, this provides the sire of an ideological conflict over the choice between a nation of a 'natural' global position of importance and exceptionalism, or the path of a rich, vibrant, inclusive and dynamic identity which celebrates the 'mongrel nation' that England arguably is and always has been. Either way, in the contemporary period, identity formed around the former dominates current populist debate and imagining on the issue. Tony Wright (2000) comments, it is the English that always believes somebody (usually foreign) is diddling them. It's smug, stuffy, arrogant, class-ridden and excluding. Its language is that of the 'home counties' and the 'provinces'. It says England when it means Britain. It can't see beyond the end of its xenophobic nose. It's the kind of Englishness that makes minorities feel like they might be British but never English. It's top-down and centralising, intolerant of diversity and wants to put people in their place. Unfortunately, this negative, introverted and conservative narrative and ideological framework can be seen to dominate discourse on what it means to be English and how it affects those who live in England.

Since Tony Wright painted such a dismally accurate picture of the 'less appealing' sense of Englishness, this perspective has become more extreme, not only in its xenophobic language and rhetoric but also in its consequences in terms of inequality and exclusion. Both the EU referendum and the devolution debate have also given such a discursive position both a new lease of life – in a defensive and hopelessly desperate nostalgic sense – and have begun serious discussion about life after the United Kingdom and the European Union. This has also focused minds on other 'threats' to the nation such as immigration, the threat from terrorism and further entrenches a bunker mentality towards the outside world. Extra strains on a democratic, negotiated intergrationism produce premature discussion about the capacity to be pluralistic instead of assimilative. Giving up on multiculturalism only serves to further alienate communities within society and further perpetuates alienation of minorities, even if this is not the intention of such claims and rhetoric.

English cultural parochialism that provides historical and cultural revisionism thrives on the intellectual space created by anxiety, fear and an unknown future. These anxieties may be nothing more than what H.V. Morton once called, 'the vague mental toothache of Englishness, a disquiet more often based on the feeling that one should feel anxious rather than the state of actually being anxious' (Morton, 1927). However, Paul Gilroy painted a more updated analogy when he commented that 'are we in Gosford Park, Finsbury Park, or the park and ride? The failure to just know or, rather, to just feel what the nation's favoured cultural filling should be feeds the multicultural opportunity and the melancholic outlook' (Gilroy, 2005:118).

Chantal Mouffe (2005) comments that the growth of the extreme right in many countries in Europe can only be understood in the context of a deep crisis of political identity within the background noise of a general process of globalisation; however, it can also be added that this political position is no longer the preserve of the extreme right and is related to, and fuelled by many more significant events and ideological manipulations in the contemporary period. The issues that once fed the extreme-right in Europe have become the political common ground for national debate and discussion, monopolised and dominated by the right and conservatives, for example, the disintegration and redundancy of the UK Independence Party (UKIP) within English politics. They achieved all of their objectives (led the United Kingdom out of the European Union and pulled political discourse firmly to the right particularly on issues such as immigration).

A healthy democratic society is not monopolised by one position or by one group alone; if this becomes the case, then it is all too easy for non-negotiable moral values and essentialist identities to dominate and to lead towards a destructive future path. Multiculturalism is both a reflection of a process of ongoing globalisation and a particular way of trying to manage the issues globalisation raises. Multiculturalism also provides one of the central characterisations and elements of the English experience. This general term has too easily become the manipulated scape-goat for the institutional failure to provide an inclusive sense of national community and identity that does not alienate and dis-empower minorities and diverse groups within society. Conservative and traditionalist discourses have ideologically inverted this basic term and process and has been able to accomplish this only because it dominates the discursive realm and narrative of Englishness.

Traditional party politics have become sidelined where normative meaning, symbolism and language are concerned. Simple casual narratives through a generally conservative discourse of Englishness dominate meaning, motive and understanding in relation to Europe. For example,

> 'We want our country back' is one of the most ubiquitous slogans associated with ethnic-majority nationalism, providing a rich seedbed for populist complaints about the liberal, modernising and multiculturalist values associated with elites.
>
> (Kenny, 2015:165)

Ethnic-majority nationalist sloganeering of this variety has become part and parcel of a conservative, traditionalist and omnipresent Englishness, not just within the context of immigration, multiculturalism but particularly and specifically in regards to Europe itself.

Chapter 6

# Englishness and Discourses of Europe

This chapter will seek to examine the conceptual framework of discourses on Europe in relation to contemporary concepts of Englishness. It will be argued that the dominant discourse concerning Europe is a conservative and Eurosceptic perspective. This chapter will explore normative understandings and the politicisation of Englishness in relation to discourses concerning Europe and an associated narrative that has become prominent and dominant. This chapter will not seek to provide an exhaustive account of the relationship between Europe and the nation state or the inner workings and development of the European Union, but will instead provide a specific analysis of how concepts and discourses of Englishness are constructed and created in relation to Europe and the political body of the European Union. It can be suggested that Euroscepticism is not ideologically exclusively conservative, yet it has been entirely co-opted and dominated by this position and provides a key aspect of conservative discourses of Englishness within the contemporary era. The creation of a metanarrative of Englishness will be used to evaluate the discursive prominence of a Eurosceptic perspective and how Europe has become the embodiment of a political and cultural articulation for understanding a dominant narrative of a conservative Englishness within a wider ideological framework.

In order to explore these themes in more specific detail, this chapter will be divided into six sections. The first section will argue that Euroscepticism operates as part of a wider conservative discourse of Englishness. The second section will investigate how the concept of Europe operates within the context of an historicised and essentialised discourse of Englishness. Thirdly, the rise and lasting significance of the UK Independence Party (UKIP) will be analysed in relation to discourses of Englishness and Europe. The fourth section will investigate the wider discursive significance of an 'in/out' European referendum. The multiple discourses of the Eurosceptic position, the contradictions and nuances of this position will be explored in section five. The sixth section will evaluate the significance of concepts of Atlanticism and the Anglosphere and how these ideological spaces inform a Eurosceptic approach, particularly within the context of English national identity. What is important to note is that this chapter will not suggest that this is a black and white topic area; indeed, it is characterised by

**Constructing Realities, 135–162**
**Copyright © 2024 Stuart Cartland**
**Published under exclusive licence by Emerald Publishing Limited**
**doi:10.1108/978-1-83797-545-720231007**

nuance, multiple overlapping discourses and trends that undermine and contradict one another. Nevertheless, the topic of Europe and the European Union represents a major discursive field in which dominant concepts of Englishness are constructed and which we can detect and determine dominant narratives of Englishness within the contemporary period.

## Euroscepticism and Conservative Discourse of Englishness

Conservative discourses of Englishness rely heavily upon a general, and to varying degrees anti-EU sentiment or rather Euroscepticism. Ideological conceptualisations and representations of Europe and the European Union exist as part of a wider conservative metanarrative of Englishness. Europe operates within a symbolic and interrelated framework of understanding and conceptualising Englishness alongside other key defining relationships and themes such as devolution, multiculturalism, race, globalisation and immigration. Rebecca Langlands (1999) points out that Englishness exists and operates as both a relationship and a category. It is an identity consisting of bundles of values that are thought to be intrinsic but ones which are measured against external and internal 'others'. The Eurosceptic perspective is not exclusive to the right or the conservative position. In the lead up to the 1975 European referendum, it was the Labour Party who posed the greatest resistance to joining the (then) European Economic Community (EEC), while the Conservatives and the Liberals were largely pro-Europe. Nevertheless, as a dominant discursive meta narrative, it has arguably been monopolised by this ideological position and political perspective in the contemporary era. A dominant conservative discourse however accommodates an array of varying degrees of Euroscepticism, from outright rejection and isolation from the European Union to more generally suspicious and wary positions, to a moderate and tentative position of a continued relationship with Europe, but only on very strict terms that are determined by Westminster.

A conservative and (to varying degrees) Eurosceptic discourse has become common currency within political, social and cultural narratives concerning Europe, particularly in England. Ben Wellings (2010) suggests that opposition to European integration has fundamentally informed, illuminated and shaped English nationalism for over 40 years, providing the ideological content for the most organised and dominant form of Englishness. This form of Englishness is contextually framed by time, place and events in relation to varying processes of a contextual relationship within a discourse of conservatism.

Europe, as a concept, contains deep ideological symbolism and meaning and operates as a key reference point for the creation of identities. On the one hand, Eurosceptics conflate conceptualisations of Europe and the European Union as a deeply negative, anti-democratic and anti-sovereign, ever-expanding bureaucratic superstate structure. In this sense, Europe and the European Union is conceptualised within a binary opposite understanding, yet this is a deeply ideological conceptualisation. It is an imagined sociopolitical concept which is constructed around specific ideological ideals or narratives relating back to contemporary discursive themes. It is much like national identity – a fictional construct that symbolically represents an attempt at collective imagination formation.

It can be suggested that it is not what Europe is, but how it is mediated, interpreted and represented. As a project for closer cooperation and stability, European integration instead of transcending nationalism, 'it appears to have inadvertently, despite its nationalism transcending ethos – reinvigorated nationalism through the backdoor' (Harris, 2016:245). Europe, therefore, can never lose its hold over the collective imagination as part of a wider metanarrative. Instead of diluting nationalist tensions or distinctions, the European Union has been used (within English national identity at least) to determine and characterise it.

All nations within Europe conceptualise the European Nation or their relationship with Europe differently; this can be attributed to a whole host of specific themes and factors. A particularly 'English' view on history and Europe is a largely accepted and developed myth that has promoted an inwardness and an Anglo-centricity which has dominated public life for over 400 years (Aughey 2007). This has been informed by the myth that England has always been separate and independent from mainland Europe and has always had its own national institutions, born unaided out of the national wisdom and strength of character of the English. However satisfactory this myth might be for Eurosceptics, it is 'based on a false understanding of the past' (Aughey, 2007:166). This metanarrative is built upon, yet ignores, political or economic self-interest and also ignores centuries if not millennia of close relationship and integration with continental European. This also serves to promote an entirely normalised and naturalised position of Euro-hostility within a wider framework of difference, superiority and exclusivism. This position has become so ingrained and naturalised within national narratives that it can help explain why the English in particular seem to possess such a hostile attitude towards Europe. For example, just from the 2016 EU referendum alone, England had the highest Leave vote at 53.4% (BBC, 2021). As previously discussed, while dominant right-wing and conservative discourse does not always translate or materialise at the ballot box, in this crucial instance it did.

From the Reformation in the sixteenth century, this myth has been purposefully politically and ideologically promoted and dominant. A specific English Euroscepticism needs to be grasped in terms of cultural, political and religious context of English history, 'specifically, the antiquity and political character of a sense of English national identity' (Smith, 2006). An identity as separate and exceptional as the geographical location of the cluster of the British Isles itself 'set in the silver sea'. This assumed and taken-for-granted historicisation personifies dominant conservative discourses of Englishness in the contemporary era. It is an essentialised and naturalised conceptualisation characterised by, amongst other factors, 'its insular, geographical situation' (ibid) which is used deterministically to generalise and objectivise a legitimacy of Euro-exceptionalism. A selective ideological creation and reading of English history is what a conservative sense of Englishness is predicated upon. It is one based upon a very narrow and traditional interpretation of historical events used to legitimise and justify a conservative conceptualisation of Englishness.

Relying upon figures and symbolic signposts such as Churchill, Smith's evaluative account is firmly placed within a deeply historicised account of Englishness characterised by Euro-exceptionalism, not necessarily scepticism per se, as Smith's account recalls a specific history to characterise an English separateness using a historically and culturally determinist narrative. Conservative discourses concerning Europe operate very much as a convenient and necessary 'other' to help distinguish and characterise a particular sense of Englishness. What has altered in recent years, according to Ken Spours and Diamond (2016), is that its strengths lie in a new conservative political 'double-shuffle' that has emerged over the last 10 years, combining neoliberal economics with the social and civil liberalism that has driven conservative modernisation.

Although only able to govern by a slim majority after the 2015 election, the Conservatives hegemonic political position became clear within England at the 2019 general election which was partly fought on (again) anti-EU sloganeering of 'get Brexit done'. The often conjectured contemporary image of a threat posed by Europe, specifically regarding bureaucratic regulations or cultural influence, is a key and oft repeated theme in terms of Euroscepticism which harks back to stereotypical essentialised concepts of threat posed by Europe. The conservative right overplay such scenarios of threat through emotive and persuasive image of a 'tranquil and well-ordered England threatened by continental despotism and anarchy' (Smith, 2006:435). These emotive images finding their roots in Thatcher, Acton and Burke. Oversimplified generalisations and misleading stereotypes are so well worn that the symbolism attached has become almost unquestioned and taken-for-granted; however, this is blended within a context of conservative ideological predominance, particularly in England.

For Smith (2006), English national identity is characterised by an ambivalence and disbelief in European integration, underpinned to a large extent by the Reformation. This narrative of Protestant England being the perpetual outsider from Europe is built upon selective historical myth making. Catholic France is used to generalise the cultural and religious difference of continental Europe to England, irrespective of the Protestant Netherlands or the German states. Nationalist myth specifically and very purposefully clouds political, cultural and religious memory as the ideologically constructed present is used to determine the past which then is used in turn to legitimise the present. This mythical and constructed ideal of an 'island people' is utterly politically and ideologically motivated as a means to conceptualise a homogenous and insular-idealised Englishness. England and English demographical history couldn't be further from such an image. The myth of an 'island people' is used to perpetuate and legitimise contemporary discourses. John of Gaunt's eulogy of England as the precious stone set in the silver sea is an appropriate articulation of English exceptionalism from Europe, yet one that is arguably flawed in almost every way. England has not been free from infection and disease or immune from war due to its island status, and it would be disingenuous to describe the history of its people as a 'happy breed of people' or indeed a specific race of people at all.

Island location is not evidence enough to suggest a legitimisation of English exceptionalism. The Welsh and Scots being conveniently forgotten or conflated within the English island experience. Island status provides a psychological defence or barrier to conceptually disassociate itself from those who they are not. England's relationship with the sea, although often viewed as unique or exceptional again, is used symbolically to represent status and power; however, this is neither unique nor exceptional either within the British Isles or Europe. Portugal and the Netherlands, for instance, both hold similar claims. Linda Colley (2016) points to once mighty maritime empire as constituting one of many things that Britain has in common with many other EU states, citing Denmark, Spain, France, Germany and Belgium alongside the aforementioned Portuguese and Dutch examples. However, Smith (2006) argues that a modern society and nation without an empire and with a less influential Protestantism and monarchy suffers in its quest for a distinct national identity that has become 'more problematic and elusive' (Smith, 2006:449). Moreover, Smith suggests that historical separations still destine England to be linked to, but not of, Europe, much like Churchill's claim. This can be due to the very subjectivising and essentialising top-down, traditional and conservative interpretation of history that utilises Churchillian rhetoric as a primary yet anecdotal legitimator.

For conservatives such as Roger Scruton (in Aughey, 2007), Europe and the EU 'project' represents people being set in hectic perpetual motion moving from place to place, only to discover that all places have become alike and losing in the process the local attachments that made their lives worth living. This interpretation views Europe and the European Union as a Faustian pact between English cosmopolitan intelligentsia and the European idea echoed by a general Eurosceptic conservative narrative. It is an abstract and nostalgic position based entirely upon on an ideological conservative and traditionalist metanarrative of Englishness.

Euroscepticism has undoubtedly served as an external stimulus to English self-awareness (Kenny, 2012). The normative claim of recognition of both a cultural and political conceptualisation of Englishness can be viewed as being (in part at least) articulated through Euro-hostility. European integration and governance are increasingly analysed from a discursive perspective in that they inform ideological concepts and narratives of a contemporary construction of national identity. In this regard Thomas Diez (2001) comments that 'Europe' is essentially a contested concept, in that meaning or dominant discourse is created through discursive nodal points. These nodal points attach meaning and symbolism to a particular discourse on Europe, where meaning becomes stabilised, and a dominant discourse will emerge through articulation and understanding. National narrative on contested subject topics such as Europe draws from other discursive areas, thus operating as a metanarrative. For instance, an essentialised metanarrative that draws upon particular understandings or interpretations of history inform how a discursive account on Europe may be articulated and understood within a specific contemporary context. Alternatively, an economic and free-trade discourse may offer a different discursive account of Europe as being a positive force. Here particular paradigms of understanding and frameworks for debate and discursive analysis and understanding are set in a very particular and ideologically motivated way – the debates and discussion around the trading status of Northern Ireland in relation to the European Union being a key example here where hardened discourse becomes more flexible when it meets economic reality.

It can be suggested that the metanarrative is always framed through the discursive context of the ideological field which, as previously stated, often operates through a binary understanding. For a conservative discourse of Englishness, this is framed within a generally hostile and anti-European framework of understanding and articulation using specific ideological reference points within a wider metanarrative. In many ways, Europe has become a dialogical concept; it is defined by a dominant narrative of negativity by both conservative-dominated positions of understanding and interpretation. As Gordon Brown (2016) points out, Conservative ministers all too often portray the European Union as something to be tolerated as a necessary evil rather than embraced as a force for good. However, when a dominant negative narrative of the European Union becomes so normalised, intolerance or dissociation soon becomes necessity.

## Europe and an Historicised and Essentialised Englishness

Independence, detachment, insularity and isolation of Britain, or rather England, from Europe due to its island nation status as an imagined cultural and political national barrier dominates a relationship and attitude towards and indeed operates as a popularised framework for understanding England's relationship with Europe, its history and its identity. Shakespeare's 'sceptred isle' adrift in the north Atlantic supremely detached from European politics and problems has always conjured strong mythical images of splendid isolation. This symbolic physical barrier provides and represents ideological justification to a sense of 'special' status, exclusivity and deeply impacts upon concepts of identity.

Europe and the European Union operate as the embodiment of the historicised and essentialised 'other'. For example, a defensive, traditionalist and conservative sense of Englishness is typically characterised by a Eurosceptic approach, whereas a progressive, liberal or cosmopolitan sense of Scottishness is generally far more inclusive and pro-European in character. A Conservative insistence on a course of 'hard Brexit' confirms the dominance of a national, political and social positioning which draws from common currency of xenophobia, anxiety, fear and hard-right conservative ideological dominance. Since the result of the EU referendum, the tepid and delicate pro-EU position of David Cameron has been completely abandoned in the wake of a less compromising Brexit attitude and policy direction. In many respects, Theresa May and many other fellow Conservatives were free to ride a wave of anti-EU English nationalist sentiment that they were previously denied. May's insistence of a 'hard Brexit' while installing many staunch Eurosceptics in key government positions can be viewed as a systematical attempt at monopolising a firmly Eurosceptic position; meanwhile, Nicola Sturgeon in Scotland reacted by clearly indicating that such a direction may well lead to a distinct possibility of a second independence referendum in Scotland.

It is one of the defining ideological elements within the contested nature of Englishness; political and cultural conservatism within the contemporary climate in England being dominated by insularity and xenophobia, not cooperation or openness which has already led to the end of England's relationship with one political union and seems to be heading to the end of another. The ideologically and politically constructed parameters upon which the European referendum debate was contested are symptomatic of this. Firstly, it was based upon the inherent premise of an anti-EU position. Even the 'Remain' campaign was based upon underlying concepts of British exceptionalism from and within Europe. Secondly, the entire 'Leave' campaign was dominated by the conservative right, particularly within England where they are by far ideologically strongest, any left-wing opposition to EU membership being inconsequential. Nicola Sturgeon and the SNP have been overwhelmingly in support of remaining within Europe and clearly suggested that in the event of an English dominated 'leave' result, a second Scottish independence referendum would be required as a matter of urgency. Nevertheless, the entire debate by differing levels of Conservative opposition to the European Union was personified by the 'Dave Vs Boris' caricature shortly after the referendum. This Conservative domination over a particularly ideologically and discursive matter can be viewed as symptomatic of a wider discursive dominance over concepts of Englishness and its problematical ideological relationship with outside political unions.

Necessity or pragmatism does not equate to an acceptance of European cooperation or as a place within Europe as equals; indeed, it provokes a stronger reactionary cause. According to Jeremy Black (1994), in defending the configuration of national character, politicians and ideologically motivated commentators are fighting not for selfish national interests but for the sense of the living past that is viewed as a vital component of people's understanding, acceptance and appreciation of their own society and identity. Europe represents a discursive dichotomy as a means to interpret and understand conservative and traditionalist accounts of Englishness. Its (mis)representations provide ideological representations of the self and manifestations of symbolic rejection or inclusion. As a dominating discourse, it is legitimised by specific concepts of the past and cultural representations of the present and future. This operates as an ideological necessity, which, as Hannah Arendt comments, 'legitimacy, when challenged, bases itself on an appeal to the past, while justification related to an end that lies in the future' (Arendt, 1970:52).

The dominant ideological discourse of contemporary Englishness is, as Ben Wellings (2010) points out, not explicitly borne by an understanding of politics but is instead carried implicitly by an understanding of the past. It is an historicised and ideological account read through a traditionalist prism of understanding. It is conceptualised through a framework not of economic or political pragmatism but instead through an ideological reading of the past and the attachment of mythical ideas concerning greatness, independence and a perceived 'golden era'. This conceptualisation and dominant understanding of the past as constituting and being characterised by Englishness as 'greatness' is undermined and fatally challenged by perceptions of decline in the post-war era. 'Europe' being symptomatically and symbolically linked to this falls from great power status.

The conservative and traditionalist myth of Englishness is characterised by a narrative of separateness, exemption, superiority, inwardness and a belief of a naturalness of independence and distinctness unhindered or interfered with by Europe. This can be interpreted as producing psychological satisfactions (Aughey, 2007) based upon a very subjective misrepresentation of past events. Henry VIII and the Reformation can be viewed as a key reference point, but can also be viewed within the context of the Revolutionary Wars in Europe of the 18th and 19th centuries; a narrow and decontextualised misreading of the past as a very deliberate manipulation and interpretation to legitimise a distinct sense of English (or British) separateness. A large and systematic manipulation, reinvention, reinterpretation and often pure creation of the past is entirely an ideological, political and culturally directed process, which has become part and parcel of the collective, naturalised 'memory' or story of Englishness. An Englishness of separateness from Europe has become so ingrained and naturalised that it has become almost impossible to reimagine. It can, therefore, be suggested that separateness and exceptionalism have become a propaganda cult designed to deny the historical example of England's European pedigree (Aughey, 2007).

The degree of motivating a collective imagining of the nation based upon a specific and essentialised ideological construction can be referred back to Benedict Anderson's theory of nations operating as 'imagined communities'. However, as Emmanuel Yewah (2001) comments, to think of the nation as sovereign, that is, an independent, self-governing entity, is modelled almost entirely upon monarchies that existed at the time of great historical and intellectual changes in Europe, a period of increasing religious pluralism which adds to the false notion of the nation. Nevertheless, this contradiction proves to be such an enduring conceptualisation of the nation as it ensures repeatability in changing historical and discursive conjunctures and informs strategies that rely upon well-worn and familiar historicised accounts.

The perspective or discursive framework of naturalised separateness for understanding the composition of the nation underpins a Euro-hostile, Anglospheric argument and conservative approach to a construction of an 'island nation' narrative and its attached notions of distinctiveness (ethnically, institutionally and traditionally) and isolation from Europe. This position also shows the connections between an ideological framework and an ethno-historicised narrative. As Rebecca Langlands points out, 'the coexistence of notions about "inheritance" and "otherness" in English self-identifications is perhaps most clear in the pivotal myth of the "free-born Englishman"' (Langlands, 1999). This myth refers to the defence and re-establishment of privileges against the Norman yoke and later interpreted through English civil war radicalism and 18th and nineteenth century writers such as Paine, Cobbett, Cobden, Bright, and to conservatives such as Disraeli. The Norman yoke analogy can be regarded as a 'subversive genealogy' (ibid) but also as an alien European other usurping the perceived natural right of the ethno-historicised community. It is, therefore, not a great leap to see the continuation of this theme in contemporary Euro-hostile attitudes and narratives.

The perceived threat that the nation will be absorbed into a larger political and cultural unit informs a sense of defensive Euro-hostile anxiety. Boris Johnson's (2016) comparison of the European Union with previous campaigns of European unification by figures such as Napoleon and Hitler indicates a clear historicised and essentialised account of European unification and integration. Backed by senior Conservative figures leading the 'leave' campaign such as Iain Duncan Smith, Chris Grayling and the former chancellor Norman Lamont and representing the more extreme elements of Conservative Euroscepticism, Johnson's claim of 'historical parallels' that the European Union has the same political aim as Hitler in trying to create a potential European superstate but just using 'different methods' can be viewed as an emotive yet controversial articulation of standard Eurosceptic approaches to the European Union.

What is of central importance with Johnson's comments and claims is not that it represents a broader conservative sense of Euroscepticism, as arguably it does not as he was roundly criticised by more moderate Eurosceptic Conservatives, the issue however being the complicity in the acceptance of the sentiment. Although widely criticised, this can be viewed as being largely due to the divisive and problematical use of comparisons to controversial and offensive historical figures, not the message alone. Tory MP and grandson of Churchill, Nicholas Soames (in Mason, 2016), expressed this succinctly when he suggested that Johnson had 'gone too far' and was liable for such foot-in-mouth sensationalised gaffes, crucially however not that the essential sentiment or historicised message was at fault, this widely being the response (the use of comparisons to Hitler, in particular) not the underlying Eurosceptic message. This response largely replicated and relayed through the press and media outlets – Johnson's poor use of historical figures, not the actual message he was conveying.

Although controversial, these messages purposefully played to the over-simplified and well-worn narrative of a European superstate takeover. Messages such as these also feed into narratives and discourse of a sense of enduring heritage buffeted by but always surviving the turbulence of history which also informs a perspective of a distinct and unique mythical national character. Historical examples such as the Spanish Armada, the Napoleonic Wars (particularly Waterloo) and the Second World War (in particular the Battle of Britain and the Blitz) are called upon to reinforce historical exceptionalism and survival from European threat. However, these well-worn historical narratives marginalise or very often leave out the reliance upon European partners to survive adversity. Moreover, macro-level transnational organisations such as the European Union are perceived to signal the end to sovereign autonomy of the nation state; however, European history (in particular) is littered with examples where nations have largely from their very beginnings operated in, 'alliance or contest with transnational institutions of empires, the great religions, revolutionary internationals and capitalism' (Hutchinson, 2005:168).

Within essentialised and determinist parameters of understanding, we are discursively placed into a pre-existing order, one that is (from the dominant conservative perspective) largely resistant to change. Indeed, a specifically historicised conceptualisation naturalises this order as being pre-existing and timeless; it also draws upon other seemingly timeless artefacts of the nation to legitimise itself such as landscape, but also naturalised elements of a timeless national imagining such as national institutions or architecture. Wellings and Baxendale (2015) suggest that the conviction that Britain was and is irrevocably different from continental Europe is the shared intellectual foundation of a prominent strand of hard British Eurosceptic thought. Hard Eurosceptics tend to object to Europe or the European Union on cultural and historical grounds. For example, John Redwood encapsulated the centrality of history to this approach in 2005 when he stated:

> Britain is at peace with its past in a way that many continental countries could never be [...] We do not have to live down the shame that many French people feel regarding the events of 1940-44. We do not have to live [...] with the collective guilt that Germany feels about the Holocaust [...] We do not wake up every morning like the Italians to wonder who might be in government today and which government ministers might be charged with corruption tomorrow.
>
> (Redwood, 2005 in Wellings and Baxendale, 2015:132)

This is a very ideologically subjective and narrow reading of history. Redwood's interpretation of the past is symptomatic of the dominant British (particularly English) historiography of the 19th and twentieth century which gives an uncritical celebration of Britain's military and imperial record and as a corollary a collective exceptionalism of the English-speaking Anglosphere. This approach and perspective has been at the very core of a distinctly nationalistic and historicised discourse, particularly in terms of attitudes towards Europe. This attitude is not just throwaway jingoistic commentary; it can be viewed as 'corrosive nationalist bigotry' (Mason, 2016). These accounts and narratives are replicated on a daily basis whereby it goes unchallenged and further imprints itself on the political and social environment to the extent that it becomes naturalised, normalised and legitimised.

A triumphant and uncritical interpretation of history has lent itself entirely towards a dominant conservative discourse of contemporary renewal within a context of disengagement. Statements and claims from figures such as Trevelyan or Churchill are often referred to or used as providential fact, 'we have our own dream and our own task. We are with Europe, but not of it. We are linked, but not compromised. We are interested and associated, but not absorbed' (Churchill in Wellings and Baxendale, 2015:132). This perspective and conceptualisation of European and English characteristics resonates and becomes considered objective fact and satisfactory moral evidence.

However, dominant discourses of Englishness are paradoxical and contradictory. This perspective tries relentlessly to foster a timeless and naturalness to perceived English traits and characteristics around a mythologised and ideologically constructed concept of national culture; yet under closer examination, it is nothing more than a contemporary political and ideological invention. Examples such as Morris dancing, pigeon racing, Punch and Judy, the Women's Institute and tennis as quintessentially 'English' institutions are in fact relatively modern foreign imports. We could also choose from many other banal examples such as fish and chips, tea or marmalade to highlight how taken-for-granted cultural symbolism has been appropriated by conservative and traditionalist narratives of Englishness where upon the origins have been intentionally air-brushed out.

To take this critical analysis of a myth of exceptionalism and the denial of England's European heritage one step further, a few key areas steeped in mythical symbolism can be uncovered for the ideological narratives they represent. The royal family, for example, is entirely a culmination of Europeaness, from the French nobles of the Normans, to William of Orange of the Netherlands, the German Hannoverians, the Saxe-Coburg's and even to the former Duke of Edinburgh. Moreover, The English language itself being entirely indebted to many European and indeed world languages. Also much of England's flora and fauna, which to many have a very strong distinctive symbolic value in their sense of Englishness, contain a very strong symbolic value of the deeply interconnected, European and globalised nature of England, far removed from the insular and separate 'island nation' narrative. However, they serve as pegs on to which to hang nationalist conceptualisations. Historicism, as Joan Copjec (2015) observes, operates as the reduction of society to its indwelling network of relations of power and knowledge. This is central to dominant discursive narratives of Englishness. Society and culture is reduced to conservative ideological articulations of power relations and specific ideological conceptualisations of knowledge, which is then used as a social, cultural and political narrative. Englishness depends and exists as being articulated in language and conceptualised in the imagination. Its verifiable existence (Copjec, 2015) can only operate and exist through this.

The ideological content of a conservative English nationalism has crystallised around a stance of Euro-hostility and Euroscepticism which, 'is broad enough to accommodate the opinions of those who resented bureaucratic regulation, open borders and foreign erosion of the UK's sovereignty – all understood as "national decline"' (Wellings, 2010:498). This ideological perspective can be described as post-political melancholia, where a deep nostalgia for the past is combined with a dominant narrative of Euro-hostility or Euroscepticism of the present and is packaged and articulated through a dominant conservative discourse of Englishness.

In many ways, Europe can be viewed as rescuing and providing national renewal and reinvention for many nation states across Europe for various historical, cultural and political reasons. Indeed, Europe acts as an agency of national regeneration; however, for England, the dominant perspective can be viewed as being very different as Europe and the European Union are contextualised against an historical background of industrial supremacy, world empire and victory in the Second World War. As Dean Acheson (in Brinkley, 1990) keenly observed, Britain had lost an empire but not yet found a role. The

European Union and Europe in general carries the association of perceived loss and a realisation that Britain, and in particular England, is just another nation among others, one not characterised by exceptionalism.

## The Rise and Significance of UKIP

Although UKIP as a political party are now largely an insignificance, the influence and importance of UKIP within the discursive environment around the European Union, Europe and its significance and role in a discursive lurch to the hard-right must not underestimated. The UKIP and its relatively rapid rise to popularity can be viewed as constituting a large symbolic and practical message in relation to concepts of Englishness within the context of Europe and the European Union. According to Goodwin and Ford (in Jones, 2014), around 30% of voters are believed to be both Eurosceptic and opposed to immigration, or Eurosceptic and politically dissatisfied. These themes constituted the key elements of UKIP's political message. This sentiment was built upon and continued to grow in the years leading up to the EU referendum. For example, according to the Migration Observatory at the University of Oxford, a majority of views between 2001 and mid-2016 were that immigration was named as 'Britain's most important issue' (Migration Observatory, 2020), whereas since the EU referendum Europe has become the primary concern.

Continued and persistent growth of this message can be attributed to disaffection with Conservative leadership, New Labour's legacy and the dominance of right-wing conservative discourse concerning politics, society and a national narrative. Nick Pearce suggests that, 'important connections between deepening disenchantment with politicians and the political system in this period, and the growing appeal of an English vernacular' (Pearce, 2014). This can be viewed as correlating with both a rise in support for political parties that identify with a sense of defensive English nationalism and a vote to leave the European Union. Clearly, the situation is much more nuanced and complex; however, as a general theme, there is a clear and growing disenchantment with mainstream Westminster political parties and a sense of distinct national interest on both sides of the English/Scottish border.

Moreover, this trend continued even as UKIP were only able to muster one MP at the 2015 general election, unlike the SNP (the SNP representing a distinctly pro-European and anti-Westminster narrative) who were able to seize 56 out of 59 Scottish seats. However, UKIP have in relative terms been incredibly successful. They almost single-handedly forced David Cameron's hand to provide a referendum on EU membership, which they helped to steer to a 'Leave' victory, meanwhile amassing almost 4 million votes at the 2015 general election. Their most vital success in achieving this is by popularising a simple, clear and effective message. It encourages voters to say 'no' three times: 'no' to the 'Eurocrats' in Brussels and Strasbourg, 'no' to the politicians in Westminster and 'no' to immigration. In light of this, Daniel Boffey comments that, 'Ukip is not a second home for disgruntled Tories in the shires; it is a first home for disaffected working-class Britons of all political backgrounds who have lost faith in a political system that ceased to represent them long ago' (Boffey, 2014).

UKIP are not just the party of right-wing disaffected Tories viewed to be rejecting the modernising claims of a Westminster Conservative Party leadership over issues such as gay marriage or environmental protection. UKIP attracted far more supporters who view them as an apparent cure for the fear, anxiety and disaffection that they feel, regardless of a deeper (or lack of) political message. UKIP's attraction is simple, and this can partly explain much of its success; it does away with political caveats and finer detail, yet it is devoid of substance other than to blame and exclude. Rafael Behr comments:

> Whether the grievance is focused on immigration, regulation, parliamentary sovereignty, human rights law or vague distaste for the thing called Brussels, the common theme is expropriation. It is the feeling that control of the world around you has been carried off by people who do not live like you and who do not like the way you live. If they they are not literally foreign, they are alien in the looser sense.
>
> (Behr, 2016:33)

Cold rational arguments have a limited impact on emotive narratives that target and perpetuate a feeling of resentment, disconnection and dislocation and are largely based upon ideologically sentimental images of culture. It presents a self-perpetuating ideological belief with a self-serving and unaccountable message. This reactionary and defensive position has been pushed into the political mainstream by UKIP much to the envy of many back-bench right-wing Tories. This perspective has also become normalised political terrain for debate over immigration and Europe and has pulled the Conservatives and (to a certain extent) Labour to the right over these issues and political discourse in general. At the same time, this has provided a basis for more regularised attacks on the conservative and right-wing ideological enemies and has forced a normalised narrative consisting of a position of anti-Europe, anti-immigration, anti-PC, anti-welfare state, anti-environmental protection and so on.

The UKIP message feeds off genuine feelings of powerlessness, disillusionment and disenfranchisement which should not be dismissed lightly by mainstream British, or more specifically, English political parties. For many voters, UKIP represent a rejection of mainstream politics that have largely neglected the white working class. The prism of immigration and the European Union is how UKIP filter such concerns and in turn offer a simple yet very effective message to these complex and multifaceted issues. The Clacton and Rochester and Strood by-elections of autumn 2014 can be viewed as providing an excellent example of how UKIP and the politics of xenophobia and exclusion has become centre stage in English politics.

Both by-elections were fought largely over the central issues and within the wider context of immigration and Europe. Both were won by Conservatives who had defected to UKIP, the key issue however being not that UKIP actually won these seats (both were won by incumbents with large majorities) but the social, cultural, political and ideological manner and terrain in which these contests were fought. Both campaigns pulled the dominant discourse of English politics further to the right, focusing almost exclusively on immigration and its supposedly negative effects (although both constituencies are overwhelmingly white British) and Europe and its supposedly negative effects upon British society and sovereignty.

Within this campaign, Labour pulled further to the right, specifically over immigration promising an extra 1,000 border force staff if they came into government, while the Tories were even labelled BNP-light by UKIP candidate Mark Reckless in relation to leaflets used in the campaign. The issue of immigration specifically took centre stage with UKIP being accused of suggesting that they would forcibly send back EU immigrants, a claim they later denied. With the highlight on immigration, all main political parties tried to seemingly outdo each other in how hard and uncompromising they would be on immigration which in turn sends an implied message that it is a negative process and then in turn can be viewed as further legitimising an xenophobic ideological discourse in the wider public towards the topic and to immigrants themselves. This represents a politics based upon normalised exclusion, or rather exclusionary normativeness (Zizek, 2009) and further normalises the right-wing ideological position.

Ideologically, the conservative right (embodied here by UKIP) has utterly dominated political discourse by making immigration and Europe issues of central concern, or rather the parameters within which discussion and debate is held. This also diverts attention from arguably more pressing issues that many people across England might have to deal with on a day-to-day basis such as the cost of living crisis, a collapsing NHS or other public services. The conservative and right-wing message is bloated with emotive rhetoric which is used to catch the public's imagination and provide simplistic solutions to complex issues. In his victory speech, Mark Reckless stated that UKIP would give Britons back their country, but from whom? Clearly, he is implying immigrants and European bureaucrats, but this is a dangerous and misleading message, which suggests conflict and implies that it has been 'taken' in the first place. Moreover, Europe and immigration become the assumed catch-all terms to associate with negativity and society's ills.

In an ideological sense, UKIP's impact has been felt most by the Conservative Party. UKIP's rise has split the party between those wanting to check UKIP popularity over issues such as immigration and Europe and the more moderate party members who would rather distance themselves from the distinctly right-wing message of UKIP. In the run-up to the 2015 general election, almost half of Conservative activists wanted David Cameron to forge some sort of pact with UKIP. Backbench and hard-right MPs such as Jacob Rees Mogg (who later became a front bench Minister from 2019) even suggested that the Conservatives should allow UKIP to win some seats in order to avoid splitting the right-wing Eurosceptic vote. As it transpired, the almost 4 million votes garnered by UKIP was off-set by the total collapse of the Liberal Democrat vote which in turn generally opened the door for Conservative control of most LibDem seats coupled with the annihilation of Labour in Scotland by the SNP.

A good example of the drag of the Conservatives to the right and the fractures among the Conservative Party can be seen in the deselections of two MPs (within a week of each other) in 2014, something that has happened only four times previously in the past 25 years. Both MPs – Tim Yeo and Anne McIntosh – can be viewed as typically established Tories. Both moderates endorsed by David Cameron, and both in Parliament for over 15 years. However, they were both deselected by local Tory activists (generally being older and more right-wing than the Conservative leadership in Westminster) over cumulative issues such as voting in favour of gay marriage, tackling climate change or not being Eurosceptic enough. As Tim Yeo commented on the reasons behind his deselection:

> I voted in favour of gay marriage- that wasn't a universally held view amongst my members. I have a very great commitment to addressing climate change- that's not a universally held view. I'm in favour of Britain's membership of the EU- that's not a universally held view.
>
> (Yeo in Mason, 2014)

The deepening ideological crisis within the Conservative Party represents a further crisis within English politics with discourse increasingly lurching to the right. In this sense, it can be said that the tail is most certainly wagging the dog.

This cumulative lurch to the right can be viewed as being a direct consequence of dominant forms of discourse hardening and increasingly pulling to the right over issues such as the European Union and immigration. This is put in a simplistic political framework by the likes of UKIP and can be viewed as an articulation of a sense of defensive, reactionary response to all that is interpreted as threatening, alien and out of step with a deeply traditional conceptualisation of Englishness. In relation to ideological divisions within the Conservative Party, this equates to deep splits over a trenchant rejection of a relative 'modernisation' of the party and an ideological retreat to a traditionalist position encroached upon by UKIP. This can be viewed as being representative of a wider schizophrenic crisis of identity within the Conservative Party, on one hand, a relative sense of modernisation over some social issues and embracing certain aspects of globalisation, yet on the other hand, a firmly right-wing traditionalist position led by an encroachment and narrative setting by UKIP and a reactionary militancy of party activists and grassroots members.

Ideologically, symbolic demands form the basis for much UKIP support. Regardless of how unworkable, incoherent or ludicrous the demands are, they play to the right-wing, conservative, traditionalist dominance of a discourse of 'common sense' politics which intentionally simplifies usually very complex matters. Crisis becomes opportunity to reinforce conservative messages of 'common sense' and to further normalise politics of blame and to create a sense of moral crusade against a 'PC-gone-mad' society. As Nigel Farage commented on the floods in 2014, 'ask anyone on a high street up and down the country if they'd rather their taxes went on an Indian space programme or helping pensioners in Somerset' (Daily Express, 2014).

The results from the 2014 election to the European Parliament highlight the electoral appeal of Euroscepticism to be particularly strongest in England, especially in the south. Here UKIP won a record number of seats and became the largest single party. This can be directly attributed to a strong and dominant Eurosceptic, anti-immigrant, conservative national narrative and discourse. It also provides evidence of the public's willingness to give mainstream Westminster parties a bloody nose over symbolically important issues like Europe, which it then again used as a tool to defeat Cameron's government in the EU referendum and utterly transform the political landscape.

In many ways, it is entirely accurate to characterise UKIP and the Euro-hostile position as populist in the sense of rallying a symbolic conservative and traditionalist position. UKIP attracted almost 4 million votes and achieved over 110 second places in constituencies in the 2015 general election – this is astonishing bearing in mind that essentially they are a single issue party, almost entirely located within England. As Jeremy Gilbert points out:

> In many ways UKIP is an easily recognisable phenomenon, exhibiting features which are typical of populist movements throughout history. Inchoate programmes, idiosyncratic, charismatic leaders, appeals to an assumed identity (in this case beery white Englishness) against a largely imaginary external enemy ('Europe', 'immigrants'); these have been the characteristic features of agrarian, urban and suburban populism since ancient times.
>
> (Gilbert, 2014)

There is nothing anywhere near approaching such right-wing populism in English politics from the left even with the double election of Jeremy Corbyn to Labour leader and its huge boost of membership figures. Moreover, a UKIP brand of conservatism demonstrates an ability to summon and frame popular perceived 'common sense' through political narratives and discourses and the use of everyday analogies, 'in ways that continue to elude the left' (Spours, 2016:16). This is indicative of the discursive dominance of the centre-right conservative position within England. The danger with such a dominant conservative discourse surrounding Europe (used symptomatically in relation to identity politics) is, as John Harris (2014) points out, are people on the liberal-left prepared to let England be defined as the country of kings and queens, Victorian values, the Anglican church, Margret Thatcher, Downton Abbey and Nigel Farage? Above all, the most significant challenge for an inclusive and forward-thinking narrative and discursive position within England is that 'the liberal, anti-racist, globally focussed majority of the UK population – which is currently divided over Brexit – has to reclaim the right to speak confidently about its own values' (Mason, 2016). At present, particularly within England and around key themes like the European referendum and immigration, this voice has been largely suppressed by a predominance of a conservative discourse and national narrative.

A conservative discursive position towards Englishness, exploited and perpetuated by the right-wing media, political commentators and politicians and organisations such as UKIP, can be viewed as a vernacular of injured Englishness (Kenny, 2015) or a cry for help (Denham, 2018). This acts as a vehicle for the shift towards ethnic-majority nationalism which has developed specifically in the last decade but also as a manifestation of a deepening, class-rooted sense of disaffection and resentment. That has gone from the preserve of a largely elite-based, rural identity to more traditionally working-class areas. According to Joe Kennedy (2018), this has resulted in a clamour for a sense of authenticity or 'authentocracy' by dominant discursive representations to represent '"real-people" of non-metropolitan Britain (and particularly provincial England)' (Kennedy, 2018:29). This has resulted, for instance, in Labour following this swing to the right in identity politics by risking, and indeed abandoning much of its substantive content, 'multiculturalism, cosmopolitanism, Europeanism – in order to hang on to its formal existence' (ibid), or rather, these key elements were sacrificed at the altar of populism to remain relevant in the conservative-dominated space.

Gordon Brown's infamous labelling of a Labour supporter as a bigoted woman in the run-up to the 2010 general election or the valiant effort of Jeremy Corbyn to reject conservative-right populism has been used as a stick to subdue the left and to validate claims that the left are too busy pandering to minorities, drinking craft beer or thinking about quinoa. This sense of authentocracy, according to Kennedy, 'fixates on the idea that it's despised metropolitan elites are constantly looking down their noses at the little man. They sneer at his nuclear deterrent, his poppies, his cherished imperial history, and they even sneer at his precious country' (Kennedy, 2018:134). In fact, it supposes that a critique of anything associated with a sense of authenticity, such as the white working class, is offensive left-wing elitism.

This being self-evident from the results of the 2015 general election campaign, but moreover the systematic destruction of the so-called 'Red-wall' safe Labour seats in the north of England in the 2019 general election by the Conservatives under Boris Johnson with the persistent message of 'get Brexit done' (the subtext being that anything other than support for a hard Brexit was a left-wing traitorous plot) and strong anti-immigration rhetoric. In other words, a slow and less than responsive political and constitutional make-up has failed to keep pace and placate increasing pressure brought to bear; therefore, an insular and defensive Englishness, informed and shaped by a multi-polar environment of political, social and cultural developments, has been channelled towards a conservative and right-wing end. This political manifestation has been left unchecked to dominate debate and discourse over a past, present and future conceptualisation of Englishness.

As previously mentioned, at the electoral level, the Conservatives were able incorporate the UKIP surge so that this 'third force' party hurt Labour in the north and not the Conservatives in the south (Spours, 2016). To underline the impact that UKIP has had upon the Labour Party as opposed to the

Conservatives to which many predicted would bear the brunt of its political impact, UKIP came within 700 votes of taking the safe Labour seat of Heywood and Middleton in the 2015 general election. Not only that but in Labour's traditional heartlands, UKIP seemed to perform remarkably well and seriously challenged and diminished the Labour vote. As Kenny (2015) notes, in a 2013 'Future of England' survey, this suggested that voters inclined to support the Conservatives, and UKIP are most likely to identify with Englishness. Concepts of nationhood in this respect are closely tangled up with, and partly constituted by 'a deepening disenchantment with politics and a rising sense of cultural anxiety' (Kenny, 2015:167). This can be viewed as being ideologically and politically channelled towards a more defensive, conservative and inherently Eurosceptic identity.

Working-class conservatism is nothing new and has been a feature of the political landscape since the nineteenth century; however, the populist narrative peddled by UKIP and the consequent hard Conservative right is predicated upon a mythical and seductive promise of some sort of restored democracy and restored popular sovereignty, based upon the premise of a radically redrawn relationship with the European Union and a closing of borders to immigrants. Popular disillusionment with formal politics and a sense of democratic deficit drove many voters into the arms of UKIP and the hard-right Conservatives under Boris Johnson in their 2019 general election landslide victory. With no real alternative and a national discourse dominated by the right and conservatism, Euroscepticism has become a defining political and cultural message within the fantasy realm of Englishness.

The prevalence and success of a dominant conservative discourse can be analysed in the beliefs of those intending to vote for UKIP. According to Owen Jones (2014), by and large, the vast majority of those intending to vote UKIP support re-nationalisation of the rail and energy industries want higher taxes for the rich and an increased minimum wage – all of which UKIP or the Conservatives will not, and do not, offer in any election manifesto. These are typically working-class concerns that the general population as a whole tend to share. It is therefore paradoxical that people who prioritise such issues offer support to UKIP and the Conservatives who do not share these concerns. This offers a good example of just how pervasive a right-wing conservative discourse has become, that people support political parties whose policies go directly against their own direct concerns, beliefs, values or ideals. According to research carried out by Matthew Goodwin in 2014, 81% of UKIP support believe that big business takes advantage of ordinary people, a slim majority want the government to redistribute income and an overwhelming majority agree that 'there is one law for the rich and one for the poor' (Jones, 2014). Again, these are not UKIP or Conservative concerns; they are traditionally left-wing and socialist in character. However, the rhetoric and discourse from UKIP leaning sources is one of people's insurgency against the establishment, yet UKIP stand for rolling back any progressive or egalitarian policies, couched in hard right-wing rhetoric over immigration and Europe. UKIP have highjacked radical leftist politics and have made it vessels of the hard-right, individualist, neoliberal, establishment ideals and ideology. Indeed, they pledged to slash taxes for the rich, further privatise public services and repeal basic workers' rights – themes which have been taken onboard and co-opted by the Tories.

According to Barry Smart (1992), there is no necessary relationship between social class positions and interests and identities. This can be viewed as evident in traditional working class support for UKIP in the 2015 general election or tacit support for the Conservatives. The post-Marxist analysis offered by Laclau and Mouffe (1985) becomes appropriate. This implies a state of flux and constant redefinition and avoids elements of essentialism. This also places emphasis on the unstable and changing conditions in which contemporary political struggles emerge and develop. In this regard, political relations to social identities remain open and incomplete; they are not essential or fixed. They are also, 'subject to articulatory practises in a field traversed by antagonisms' (Smart, 1992:212).

The rise and lasting influence of UKIP can be viewed and interpreted as populist nationalism and as a major political development in English politics, regardless of the longevity of the party itself. This also symbolises the growing politicisation of Englishness and the crisis of identity surrounding Englishness. There can be viewed a casual and causational relationship between Englishness and themes of Euroscepticism, devolution and 'English votes for English laws'. As Michael Kenny (2015) observes, this involves a strong idea of politicisation, which implies a uni-directional casual relationship between the adoption of a particular form of national identity and an inclination towards particular parts of the political spectrum. However, it must be emphasised that a theoretical interpretation must not be viewed as a determinist characterisation relating to concepts of Englishness but rather one contextualised by a conservative discursive dominance. Although in the early 2020s UKIP as a political movement can be described as a spent force, it has more than achieved its stated aims of shepherding an exit from Europe while also ensuring mainstream political debate and national discourse is placed firmly to the right. The 2019 general election result can be viewed as hard evidence for the success of the impact and influence of UKIP, this being encapsulated by its almost utter demise. Nationally, it only managed to garner 22,000 votes (in 2015 it managed nearly 4 million), although the anti-EU splinter party, The Brexit Party fared much better managing 644,000 votes, the point being that UKIP had achieved its goals. It had forced the Conservatives to hold a referendum on membership of the European Union, which it helped win and then propelled a very specific hard-right English conservatism to dominate national discourse, articulated by the landslide victory of Boris Jonson in the 2019 general election and subsequent administrations. Although identity politics and discursive dominance do not always translate to the ballot box or policy decisions, in this sense, it is hard to see how it did not.

## Discursive Significance of an 'In/Out' European Referendum

The promise of an 'in/out' referendum on the United Kingdom's membership of the European Union was of key importance to the Conservative Party manifesto for the 2015 general election. It can be argued that this became such a central policy partly as a means to head-off UKIP populism but also as a means of recognising a resurgence of a general mood of Euroscepticism and to legitimise and add symbolic weight behind David Cameron's demand for treaty renegotiation (situated within a narrative of British exceptionalism). Moreover, the 'in/out' referendum promise could only be made within a climate of increased Euroscepticism and a wider dominant conservative discourse of Englishness.

John Harris (2014) comments that, Euroscepticism offers a conduit for a specifically English political revolt; however, it is one characterised by people who highlight the notion of England as an angry and introverted place. Themes of a rejection of the foreigner can be viewed as a hegemonic, 'popular extremism of the centre' (Bielfeld, 1992), this being characterised by a rejection of the European Union symbolically sited within an anti-immigration context. Dominant discourses perpetrated by the right articulate and emphasise the symbolic values of a rejection of the 'foreigner' as a threat to national sovereignty and cultural distinctiveness. In this regard, the privilege and monopoly of a sense of objectivity of the conservative and traditionalist discourse of national identity reigns supreme. It is within these carefully positioned boundaries and paradigms that narrative, debate and discussion is allowed to operate.

For the very moderate and tepid 'Remain' or 'in' campaign characterised by the official government position, anything but an overwhelming majority would constitute a vote of no confidence and provide the Eurosceptic argument further evidence of its legitimacy and a platform to build on. The 'Remain' campaign needed to be positive without patronising, and aggressive without steamrolling towards inevitability. Yet as dominant discourse has arguably increasingly become more conservative and more Eurosceptic (particularly in England), it would be very difficult for it to be anything like this; instead, it almost exclusively played entirely within a negative paradigm towards Europe and any imagined future relationship with it. As pointed out, 'to win, Cameron has to fight the dragon in his party and kill it. But nothing suggests he has the stomach for that. At every sally he crumples and compromises' (Toynbee, 2015). The Remain campaign is being hobbled from the start as it was predicated upon an underlying degree of Euroscepticism.

The Remain campaign, particularly from the Conservative perspective, is very problematical in terms of politics of identity and history. Conservatives on the Remain side find themselves as almost ideological prisoners of their own creation. Dominant conservative perspectives and concepts of Englishness are predicated upon an inherent Euroscepticism, yet in political and economic terms, they are fighting to remain in the European Union. This position of a naturalised separation from Europe became the trump card for those arguing to exit the European Union, not on pragmatic economic and political grounds (although these were created) but on ideas and fantasies of uniqueness, freedom and essentialised concepts of history.

The Remain campaign was built upon David Cameron securing a significant renegotiation of the United Kingdom's formal relationship with Europe, with multiple ongoing crises' facing the European Union at the time such as Greek debt, the Ukrainian conflict, the threat from Islamic terrorism or the Mediterranean immigration crisis. Any treaty renegotiation demands by David Cameron were not only going to be of distinctly less importance but contextually trivial. Cameron also had to attempt to negotiate with politicians such as Angela Merkel who categorically stated a position of not renegotiating any key aspects of Britain's treaty membership, including a policy of free movement of people within the European Union. According to Diez (2001), policy articulations are part of discourse; therefore, Cameron's proposal of an 'in/out' referendum is an articulation of discourse which follows from the proposition that the current relationship with the European Union is unacceptable, and the Conservative government will seek to partially withdraw or seriously amend its formal relationship with Europe conceding that a Euro-hostile discourse is dominant, and that a varying degree of political and policy action is required. This discourse provides a self-perpetuating feedback loop of a conservative position towards Europe. The key point here is that Eurosceptic discourse is dominant (to some degree or another), irrespective of the European referendum result. The danger is that without any significant treaty renegotiation, Cameron was perceived as a failure and the 'out' position was boosted by a seemingly intransigent European Union and an ineffective moderate Westminster leadership.

In a more macro sense, the wider discursive significance of the European referendum has also been to highlight and reinforce dominant conservative discursive conceptualisations of the nation and narrative along 'symbolic demarcation lines' (Balibar, 2002:52). Research carried out by the Reuters Institute for the Study of Journalism found that the majority of media coverage of the referendum had been 'heavily skewed in favour of Brexit' (Greenslade, 2016) and had given far more coverage to Conservative rather than Labour politicians. Moreover, this highlights the conservative paradigm of the entire debate and narrative over nation and Europe, that the whole premise of a referendum is based upon a hostile relationship with Europe and the discourse and narrative of debate is dominated by Conservative politicians and a conservative perspective. Regardless of the outcome of the referendum, this episode underlines the discursive dominance of a conservative narration of nation, especially in relation to an ideologically significant theme being Europe.

## Paradoxes and Contradictions of the Eurosceptic Position

It is indicative of the prevailing and dominant conservative discourse that anything that can be viewed as criticising or offering an alternative perspective in relation to Europe is immediately attacked and appropriated as an indication of an outright and moral attack on 'common sense' or democracy. Rather, what has become common currency as Stuart Jefferies (2014) has pointed out is a Sun-sponsored ideological, anti-PC symbolism, a politically reactionary invention of Englishness. This populist position acts partially as an inverted political and social narrative but also as a distraction from the vast and growing inequalities within society in an economic and political sense. In a post-financial crash world instead of political debate and discourse based on accountability and fairness, we have scapegoating and insularity, 'now look where we are going: bigotry on the march and press – enforced compulsory patriotism' (Ditum, 2014).

Conservative narrative and discourse monopolises this position and characterises a hegemonic sense of national identity. This is where an ascendent, exclusive and politically subjective form of ideology becomes important. Although a dominant discourse operates as a framework for understanding Englishness, it is not absolute or unchanging, and it operates entirely within a wider political, social and cultural context. The complexity and gravity regarding conceptual frameworks of Englishness or English national identity is only apparent in the wake and fall-out of monumental events that shape its existence such as the closely fought Scottish independence campaign, changing domestic political terrain or the increasingly fraught relationship with the European Union. This also operates within a context of a domestic relationship towards ongoing processes such as multiculturalism but also interconnected developments such as ongoing levels of immigration and discursive responses. Concepts and discourses of Englishness also exist and operate within a wider context of global insecurity such as a perceived threat from Islamic terrorism, geo-political shifts of influence and power, such as tensions with China and Russian aggression, ongoing crises' within global capitalism, the threat from climate change and its related catastrophic effects upon the environment and natural resources.

Often what is understood to be English, Englishness or English national identity from the dominant conservative perspective has rested upon casual assumptions, these assumptions can be easily uncovered for the mythical, contradictory illusions that they are. Conservative concepts of Englishness and the context in which they exist – a highly interconnected and interrelated 21st century – seem to struggle to find some degree of compatibility. Contemporary developments are often portrayed as crises that are interpreted as threatening a sense of timeless Englishness, yet it may well be that this understanding of Englishness is itself incompatible with a modern, fluid, plural notion of national community. It is these characteristics which help to serve conservative notions of Englishness as a defensive and reactionary position.

Indeed, the European Union and Brexit provide the conservative right an opportunity to virtue signal its 'concerns' for the working classes, this being expressed as 'cultural concerns coalescing around immigration, patriotism and defence, rather than material ones about jobs, wage stagnation and the housing crisis. Even when employment and housing are touched on, it's to culturalise such problems by making them into a matter in which immigrants are set against the "working class," as though immigrants themselves are some kind of coddled elite' (Kennedy, 2018:25). In other words, conservative discourse recreates the concerns that the supposed homogenous 'working-class' should have or focus upon, rather than the actual lived experience of record levels of poverty and inequality within contemporary Britain that Conservative neoliberalism as actually created.

Frederic Jameson's (2007) philosophical analysis of this type of identity can be viewed as consisting of repetition, psychological desolation and tedium; that is to say neurosis. It represents a terror of the seemingly new and unexpected carrying its sameness everywhere, imprisoning the self in itself. A neurotic understanding of national identity and community must never encounter anything that it does not already know or has incorporated as constituting its identity. Arguably, all conceptualisations of national identity are based within fantasy; however, a conservative and right-wing discourse of Englishness is based within an illusion of stasis operating within a background of flux. This is where key themes of comfort and security affect and mould what can be viewed or presented as unchanging and legitimate, regardless of any sense of representativeness or relatedness. It does not need to be grounded in any sense of an experienced 'real'; it only needs to relate in a deeply symbolic manner where philosophical meaning is attached to varying points of ideological reference. For example, just three days before the referendum, the *Daily Express* ran a front page with the headline claim that 12 million Turks were poised to migrate to the United Kingdom. This headline, they later admitted, was entirely false. It can, therefore, be stated that identity can be found in the zone of indifference between psychology and logic within idealism itself (Adorno in Jameson, 2007). It is an ideological idealisation situated within psychological idealism and the context of the lived experience.

Identity formation can, within the context of social, cultural and national, prove to be very negative in character, especially when discourse is dominated by the political right. For example, the drawing closer of Europe through larger membership of the European Union and further levels of integration only serves (in many respects) to further fuel an ideological disengagement with Europe as this is interpreted by the right to add to contemporary threats to an imagined sense of Englishness. The legacy of an increasingly bitter European referendum debate and campaign is assured in terms of national narrative. The key themes of immigration and fear from the 'Leave' campaign have made this the common ground of a once repressed right that has conjoined half of the Tory party with UKIP into an anti-foreigner movement (Toynbee, 2016). Emotive and long-rooted motifs will not simply dissipate once the referendum campaign is over; indeed, they have certainly become emboldened and more entrenched.

## Europe and the British Union

Europe (in various guises) has operated as the 'other' to which a very purposefully created sense of Britishness or rather British national identity was created – now that 'other' does not bind the constituent nations of the United Kingdom together but can now be viewed as another leverage to pull them apart. Within contemporary concepts of Welsh and particularly Scottish nationalism, the European Union and Europe offer a viable union of representation away from one dominated by the English in Westminster. Europe, in many respects, has gone from a negative symbolic reference point for the Welsh and Scots to a positive point of departure, especially within a context of a reinvention of distinct national identities separate from that of England. Former SNP leader, Alex Salmond, commented that Europe is indeed very much a key issue regarding devolution, that if a primarily Eurosceptic England votes to withdraw from the European Union a primarily pro-European Scotland could not continue within a political union in its present form (BBC, 2015d). Irrespective of the referendum result, such a statement is indicative of the political and ideological significance that Europe plays and indeed reflects official SNP policy direction in its aftermath. Such sentiments were echoed by Salmond's successor, Nicola Sturgeon, who stated that Scotland cannot be imprisoned in the United Kingdom who, 'had rejected the Tories, said not to Brexit and made clear we want our future in our own hands' (Sturgeon in Brooks, 2019).

There is immense overlap of the issues of Europe and devolution where a policy of ignoring or delaying these issues will not suffice anymore. Both these key issues and processes are entirely intertwined with one another. They are not distinct or separable processes affecting the constitutive nature of England or Englishness alone. They are symptomatically interrelated with each other. However, unlike the Scots or the Welsh, from a largely English Eurosceptic perspective, Europe is equated to a loss of national sovereignty and national identity. As Krishan Kumar points out, 'the potential break-up of Britain is doubly threatening to England. Not only does it lose its raison d'être, as the core nation of Britain. It is also brought face to face with the legacy of its past attitudes to Europe' (Kumar, 2003:9).

Diez (2001) notes that concepts of Europe can operate as lenses of identity and are often used within the context of parliamentary sovereignty. For instance, a generally Eurosceptic approach views Europe as an encroachment or threat to sovereignty of the nation state. A more Euro-positive or cooperative approach, as put forward by the TUC and CBI in the European referendum campaign, was to view Europe through the lens of state, economy and mutually beneficial cooperation. There are multiple and contradictory positions even within generally pro or anti-European discourses themselves. For many on the Euro-friendly or pro-European side of the debate such as leading business organisations like the CBI, staying within the European Union is unproblematic as long as it is confined to the economic sphere and produces sufficient benefits. This was very much the approach taken by David Cameron and the Remain campaign; however, such an economic argument necessitates the free movement of goods, trade, money and crucially people. For the very moderately pro-European stance taken by Cameron, even this position was unacceptable to the majority of Conservatives as the issue of open borders, and the free movement of people is of key importance to a Eurosceptic argument. The irony being though that the ideological fantasy of sovereignty over borders and the end of EU freedom of movement has only resulted in record numbers of net migration to the United Kingdom by 2023.

## Atlanticism, the Anglosphere and Euroscepticism

A dominant conservative discourse, within the context of Europe, is riddled with inconsistencies, contradictions and counter narratives. English exceptionalism is an abstract, highly nostalgic and idealistic view of the world created through specific concepts of history and power relationships, the point being that those often harking back to some past mythical role of English exceptionalism and isolationism submerge themselves in the very process of an ideologically created sense of history and identity which is incommensurably interlinked with Europe. Nowhere is this fantasy more evident than with the enduring significance of Atlanticism and the concept of an Anglosphere and how it informs a generally Eurosceptic approach.

In many respects, Europe can be viewed as the realisation of the global position of a post-imperial Britain. Instead of Britain being a major global power militarily, financially and politically, in the contemporary era, it is not even the dominant European power. This has produced a contradictory and challenged identity based upon a power status complex. Conservative and traditionalist narratives seek to posit England in a privileged position outside of Europe. A contemporary conservative discourse which implies empire and world power generally providing a positive legacy and constituting a 'golden era' (see Nial Ferguson et al.), combined with an unapologetic stance of the impact of empire (see Cameron, Farage, Johnson et al.), positions England outside of Europe in a 'special' location, a location which distances itself as far as possible from being just another European nation among others with no specific global or regional dominance. This is where the concept of an Anglosphere and a 'special relationship' with the United States becomes apparent as an alternative community based around English foundational attributes.

A 'special status' is how many Eurosceptics would describe Britain's relationship and character as a nation within Europe. Indeed, this is precisely how Conservative MP, historian and Eurosceptic (and later Chancellor of the Exchequer under Liz Truss in 2022) Kwasi Kwarteng (BBC, 2016) characterised such a relationship and national character in an historically contextualised criticism of European membership. This perspective depends upon and utilises history as a legitimator, or rather, as an ideological positioning of nation within a specific framework of understanding. It also produces a very specifically contextualised positioning of Britain as unique, detached and, most importantly, of Europe but crucially not part of Europe.

An idealised conservative position is to engage in a process of policy discussion and re-engagement with the Commonwealth and a so-called Anglosphere as a viable alternative to the United Kingdom's involvement in the processes and politics of European integration. This theoretical position can be observed as continuation of an ideological framework within the Eurosceptic tradition, developed particularly from the late 1960s, but one specifically related to the concept of Atlanticism as an alternative to Europe. 'Despite the existence of a Commonwealth tradition on the left of British politics, the Anglosphere appeals to the right, and Thatcherite Eurosceptics in particular' (Wellings and Baxendale, 2015:123). This is contextualised within the much cherished 'special relationship' which was so well cultivated by Thatcher as a means to position the United Kingdom in a global role distinctly outside of Europe. For Conservatives on the right of the party, unlike the European Union, an English-speaking union would be characterised by deeper values such as perceived common moral commitments to democracy and freedom expressed through a common language and cultural heritage. Indeed, Thatcher argued that, 'God separated Britain from mainland Europe, and it was for a purpose' (Thatcher in Wellings and Baxendale, 2015: 131). This sentiment largely underpins right-wing conservative attitudes and wider common perspectives towards Europe and has increasingly become common currency within the mainstream of wider public opinion.

However, a so-called 'special relationship' between the United Kingdom and the United States is not a simple anti-Europe alternative. For the United States, the United Kingdom must remain firmly within Europe and the European Union, if only for the strategic means of retaining a strong and influential ally within policy proposal and in terms of trade relations. Former US president Barack Obama stated before the EU referendum that the United Kingdom must stay in the European Union to continue to have influence on the world stage (BBC, 2015a). This runs counter to the Eurosceptic narrative that UK membership of the European Union has diminished its global presence and influence. Obama also commented that the United Kingdom's membership of the European Union gave the United States, 'much greater confidence about the strength of the transatlantic union' (BBC, 2015a). This provides a multi-level discourse combining concepts of Atlanticism and the European Union as acting in concert with one another instead of being conflicting.

The centrality of a narrative set in opposition to European integration is at the heart of an increasingly Eurosceptic Englishness. The fantasy of an alternative Anglosphere represents a political and cultural response that incorporates an historicised account, close links with the United States, Canada, Australia and other Commonwealth and non-Commonwealth ex-colonies, but also a narrative of hostility and separateness from Europe. It situates history and tradition as a place of destination. The attraction and understanding of an Anglosphere is that it appears to make historic and cultural sense within an historicised account that emphasises a global role rather than being a European member state alone. An increasingly vocal strand of opinion within English Euroscepticism regards the Anglosphere as a natural and organic political community to which greater political attention should be devoted. As Wellings and Baxendale state, 'we once again need to account for the Commonwealth and the English speaking world in seeking to explain British policy and attitudes towards the EU' (Wellings and Baxendale, 2015:125). As a viable alternative to a future outside of Europe, concepts of an Anglosphere provide a necessary antidote for many on the conservative right. Indeed, this was clearly stated by Boris Johnson in the aftermath of the United Kingdom, leaving the single market and customs union when he claimed, 'we have got Brexit done and we can now take full advantage of the fantastic opportunities available to us as an independent trading nations, striking trade deals with other partners around the world' (Johnson in Boffey and O'Carroll, 2020).

This position is largely based upon a politicised and essentialised conceptualisation of traditions that operate within a narrow narrative that excludes positivity towards Europe. In this sense, history and tradition are viewed, or rather promoted, as the point of destination. This creates a solution, an alternative and a return of a position sanctified by the past, rather than being challenged by it. Links between a sense of English grievance, expressions of Euroscepticism and particular interpretations of the past merge and are articulated with an increased sense of coherence as a particularly English phenomena. Themes of a common law tradition, respect for private property, continuous representative government, a culture that nurtures civil society and entrepreneurial free enterprise, an attachment to individualism run counter to and oppose the ideological representation put forward that European government represents corporatist, socialist, corrupt and even authoritarian political cultures. Through this political, historical and cultural interpretation, an Anglosphere organisation would encapsulate a sense of Anglo-centric exceptionalism that many Eurosceptics cite as reason enough for British withdrawal and disengagement from the European Union.

Kenny and Pearce (2015) comment that the idea of an Anglosphere has become a source of increasing almost magnetic influence on conservatives. It also provides a significant intellectual framework for the 'Leave' campaign to argue for a withdraw from the European Union in an 'in/out' European referendum. The Anglosphere (and its associated concept of Atlanticism) provides a political, economic and cultural antidote to anxieties centred on Euro-inevitability. This provides substance to an ambiguous alternative, characterised by what Kenny and Pearce (2015) calls an illusionary horizon of a group of countries united by a shared political and economic culture, nourished from the roots of British parliamentary institutions, economic liberalism and Protestantism.

The idea of an Anglosphere remained on the margins of Eurosceptic political circles until the Conservatives came into office in 2010 and engaged in a discourse of European disengagement. In the years since 2010, many leading Tories have, in different ways, identified themselves with the idea of an Anglosphere as a legitimate alternative to the European Union, including David Willetts, John Redwood, Norman Lamont, Liam Fox and Michael Howard.

> During his own trip to Australia in 2013, [then Conservative mayor of London and later Prime Minister] Boris Johnson argued that when we joined the Common Market, we in effect 'betrayed our relationship with Commonwealth countries such as Australia and New Zealand'. Framing the decision to join the fledgling EU as an act of 'betrayal' was an eye-catching rhetorical flourish, even by Johnson's standards.
>
> (Kenny and Pearce, 2015)

This conservative and Eurosceptic ideological framework is couched within the interpretation that a 'Leave' vote and a subsequent exit from the European Union would represent liberation. This rationale can be viewed as constituting much of the Eurosceptic argument that the European Union is constraining, restricting and smothering the United Kingdom. For example, reinforcing historicised tropes, Jacob Rees Mogg repurposed Winston Churchill's sunlit uplands speech of 1940 by stating in Parliament that 'broad, sunlit uplands' (Rees Mogg in Hansard, 2019) await the United Kingdom in a post-Brexit environment.

Dominant discursive concepts concerning Europe, the European Union and the ideological frameworks in which they operate represent an axiomatic relationship in terms of conservative narratives and discourses of Englishness. These include historicised, essentialised and politicised concepts of Europe and their relationship to conservative metanarratives of Englishness. It must be emphasised that Europe, much like any other entity, is not stable and unchanging. It is discursively formed in relation to different nations, ideologies or institutions at different times, in different locations and within the context of different developments.

Europe operates as a framework for understanding that is always changing, either in itself, or by the creation of discursive relationships with it. General and overly simplified narratives do not give a wider understanding of the nuances and contradictory positions that Europe and the European Union provide. On the one hand, Europe and the European Union can easily be characterised as a corporate bureaucracy of homogenisation, yet on the other, it can be interpreted as a force for cooperation and progressive social change. Nevertheless, it is a very complex picture where simple black and white narratives will not suffice.

Chapter 7

# Devolution and Discourses of Englishness

Devolution, as a constitutional process and political debate, has gained prominence in contemporary discourses of Englishness. This chapter critically analyses the impact of devolution on concepts and discourses of Englishness and English national identity. Key issues explored include the notion of Englishness as a 'floating signifier' and an ideologically constructed discourse, drawing on Ernest Laclau's work. This chapter argues that devolution has fuelled an exclusive English nationalism and contributed to the fragmentation of the United Kingdom. Additionally, this chapter examines the relationship and parallels between devolution and the European Union. It posits that events, processes and discourses intertwine, shaping and influencing each other in an ongoing developmental process.

This chapter explores the ideological narratives surrounding the opposition between a Conservative-dominated Westminster and an Scottish National Party (SNP)-dominated Holyrood, focusing on the 2014 Scottish devolution referendum and the SNP's dominance in Scotland. It examines the anti-European English narrative and discourse, along with the nuanced and contradictory understandings of Britishness and the politicised interpretations of Englishness. This chapter conceptualises devolution as both an electoral and political articulation and emphasises its significance in perpetuating a polarisation of national discourses between Scottish and English politics. It also considers the consequences of English Votes for English Laws (EVEL) and its symbolic meaning. This chapter engages with key theorists such as Ben Wellings, Michael Skey, Krishan Kumar, Michael Kenny, alongside the aforementioned Ernesto Laclau. It acknowledges that concepts of Englishness and English national identity are fluid and contested, although currently dominated by a conservative interpretation and narrative. Devolution has sparked a serious debate and reflection on Englishness, future social and political realities and the potential breakup of the United Kingdom.

## Modernity, Postmodernity and the Post-Marxist Approach

The current political, social and cultural moment reflects the culmination of ideological neoconservatism spanning from the Thatcher era through New

**Constructing Realities, 163–190**
**Copyright © 2024 Stuart Cartland**
**Published under exclusive licence by Emerald Publishing Limited**
**doi:10.1108/978-1-83797-545-720231008**

Labour and subsequent Conservative administrations. Conservatism has triumphed both ideologically and economically, establishing itself as the prevailing political consensus in England, in particular. While it may seem quixotic to speak in such broad terms, the prevailing political, cultural and social climate prompts such generalisations.

Conservative ideologies have perpetuated a dominant discourse characterised by the primacy of free markets, the erosion of the welfare state and the prominence of anti-immigration policies. These discourses foster an environment that assumes and naturalises conservatism's dominance. The right-wing exerts significant influence over cultural and political commentary, employing oversimplifications, blame and reductive narratives. This perspective becomes ingrained as the prevailing 'common sense' and dominant viewpoint.

However, the ascendancy of a conservative national discourse seems somewhat incongruous in the postmodern condition, where universal solutions or answers to contemporary issues are no longer attainable. Politics, society and culture are fluid, contested and diverse. Grand narratives fail to provide comprehensive knowledge and answers for all questions. Nonetheless, it is evident that specific perspectives, positions, ideological frameworks and narratives dominate various domains at different times and in different locations.

There is nothing intrinsic or natural to suggest that a propensity to identify with English nationality is somehow ideologically predisposed to represent a traditionalist, anti-modern, defensive and conservative nationalist perspective; however, as a move away from a more multiculturalist, inclusive, progressive and outwardly looking sense of Britishness championed by the New Labour-era government, Englishness has increasingly become a location for a more defensive and reactionary form of nationalist identity. This claim can be traced back to 'various intellectual and political sources and reflects, in particular, the liberal embrace of a post-imperial civic Britishness during the later years of the twentieth century and a rejection of the post-imperial connotations of "little Englandism"' (Kenny, 2016:327).

Gordon Brown's progressive patriotism was in part 'premised upon the assumption that this was a viable container for the atavism and conservatism that subsisted within English culture' (ibid). In a more general sense, English nationalism is viewed as an attitude or lifestyle that contains conservative sentiments that run counter to a cosmopolitan, multicultural nation state and focuses upon ideologically conservative concerns. Viewing a sense of Englishness or English nationalism in generalised, anecdotal and essentialised terms can be both misleading (as previously highlighted in terms of a rich radical English political tradition) but can also create a self-fulfilling prophesy of ghettoising political and ideological opinion. It may also create an oppositional Englishness to a sense of a 'politically correct', liberal Britishness as a reactionary political stance to rally around.

Nevertheless, the general body of contemporary empirical evidence would suggest that even in terms of geography alone, for the majority of those living outside of London, Englishness is the dominant national identification when asked for just one choice. Moreover, in a political context, identity attachment outside of the major urban areas, Englishness goes hand-in-hand with the political dominance of the Conservative Party. When the contention is that Englishness is an inherently conservative form of nationalism, this is much harder to sustain in empirical terms. It must be understood that the very point is that concepts of Englishness are increasingly dominated by a conservative discursive understanding and representation which then in turn feedback into a political characterisation.

A symptomatic characterisation of Englishness still needs to be addressed if it is viewed in a deterministic manner, as Michael Kenny highlights:

> Framing Englishness as a pathological product of the United Kingdom's decline inclines politicians and citizens alike to perceive it as a regressive and insular form of identity- a retreat from the dilemmas and challenges of the modern world and the wider entanglements and alliances to which England has belonged. Such a form of understanding suggests that this species of 'narrow nationalism' needs to be contained and its potential impacts upon the working classes, in particular, negated through the cultivation of alternative ideas about universal rights and liberal values.
>
> (Kenny, 2016:332)

For many, this provides the attraction to a particular sense of Englishness. Englishness is increasingly understood as a means to disassociate and disengage with troubling political unions such as the European Union and Scotland, to free itself from constraints of political correctness, multiculturalism and an increasingly negative and toxic understanding of immigration. This has become the defining characteristics of an ideological and political conceptualisation of English nationalism, not because it is essentially determined by these characteristics but quite the opposite – because these characteristics have been deliberately associated with it through a dominant discursive process and relationship.

According to Frederic Jameson (1985), a process of self-image identity creation within a background environment of political and social flux can be viewed as an outcome or development of consumer or multinational capitalism, or rather as a cultural condition which crystallises with the transition from Fordism to flexible accumulation. What is not in doubt is the multiple pressures and factors which have led to Englishness being both thrust into wider debates and its immediacy of symbolic articulation. Although it is not explicitly articulated in terms of an emergence of a possible postmodern condition, the constitutive theoretical elements for reflection and consideration (the break-up of Britain, the end of European integration, a general process of accelerated globalisation and its various elements) clearly indicate characteristics for possible postmodern reflection and analysis.

The contemporary era can be characterised by postmodern politics of diversity, resistance and demystification which counters existing forms of ideological orthodoxy. With an apparent demystification and undermining of traditional forms of theoretical and conceptual organisation springs forth new expressions and articulations of myth and fantasy. Arguably, we inhabit an era which reveals the limitations and provisionality of social, cultural and political discourse and narrative, as Barry Smart comments, 'these developments have contributed to a "crisis of representation"' (Smart, 1992:203).

According to Smart (1992), to overcome this impasse, it is necessary to pursue a deconstructive logic of hegemony. What this amounts to is a critical analysis of 'the last base of essentialism, namely a "naturalist vision of the economy" and an associated tendency towards reductionism' (Smart, 1992:212). It is possible to state therefore that there is no necessary relationship between social class positions and interests, and that social identities are in fact relational. This can be evident, as pointed out previously, in large numbers of traditionally working class voters supporting the UK Independence Party (UKIP) in the 2015 general election or continued support for the Conservative Party. Political relations to social identities remain open, contested and incomplete; they are also not essential or fixed. Therefore a post-Marxist analysis is appropriate, one most succinctly theorised by Laclau and Mouffe (1985). This analysis implies a state of flux and contestation and avoids elements of essentialism. This also places emphasis on the unstable and changing conditions in which contemporary political struggles and discourses emerge and develop.

The ongoing separation of the constituent nations of the United Kingdom through a political, but also a cultural and social, process of devolution has in many ways exposed and undermined how outmoded and outdated forms of national identity are and have become within this context. The United Kingdom, as a project, identity or conception, is not immune to a degree of postmodernity, 'the postmodern condition of politics is plurality, a plurality of subjects, political spaces and social logics through which various forms of social and political identity are constituted' (Smart, 1992:219). Uncertainty, particularly over issues regarding identity or 'who we are' come to be the most contested, confusing and multi-conceptualised matters for immediate solution. The ongoing process, debate and issues relating to devolution in its many forms add serious weight and possibly irreversible motion to ending old perceived certainties. The notion, or idea, of certainty and stasis in regards to identity relies upon a flawed premise.

## Englishness as a Floating Signifier

The term 'Englishness' is ambiguous as it is constructed within the framework of ideologically constituted and substantiated discourses. Englishness as a term is also incoherent, challenged and contested as there are no objective, value-free definitions; it is inherently unstable and exists within a discursively challenged framework. As Laclau (1989) postulates, discourses surrounding such a word are, therefore, antagonistic as they operate largely in an argumentative context where there is a loosening of the relational systems that constitute the identity of the term. Thus, the term becomes a floating signifier where ambiguity subverts the fixity of the sign (Englishness) and makes it a contested discursive concept.

The term 'Englishness' is not independent but rather exists within a social framework. It is shaped by discourse, influenced by language systems and social identities that can be ambiguous and subject to value judgements. There are no definitive or illegitimate representations of Englishness, as its conceptualisation depends on various parameters. Identity is inherently ambiguous, unable to establish a precise difference within a closed system.

The ambiguity of Englishness arises from its central role in discourse, particularly in contested social practices and functions where its ideological substance is legitimised. Englishness operates as a floating signifier, and is to varying degrees substantiated by a process of devolution. For identity to operate, it needs to exist in relation to or in opposition against. This can be related to contemporary conservative concepts and discourses of Englishness operating and existing in relation to and largely opposed against a general social, political and cultural movement for Scottish independence (and vice versa). The existence of an opposing or conflicting conceptual ideology is essential for defining one's own ideological approach to identity. As Laclau notes, 'dialectics between necessity and impossibility that gives ideology its terrain of emergence' (Laclau, 1997:302). Englishness, therefore, constantly strives for meaning while being contingent upon other possibilities.

In a semiotic and post-structuralist sense, Englishness and English national identity can be characterised as a floating signifier; this floating conceptual term becomes signified and articulated through opposed 'discursive chains' (Laclau in Torfing, 1999). Through opposed discursive chains, a specific ideological dimension is applied and attached, 'as an alternative name for the equivalential totality which their relations constitute' (Laclau, 1997:306). This can be applied to how discursive representations operate in relation to the workings of the ideological within the field of representation and symbolic reference.

Devolution, instead of quenching and containing regional national desires, has ultimately, and increasingly, become applied to England itself in a self-perpetuating discursive and political process. This substantiates and informs political and party identity – even for historically unionist parties such as the Conservatives. In many ways, the Conservative Party have become victims of their own success of making the electorate preoccupied with a dominant discourse of fear of the English being held to ransom by the Scots under the SNP. For example, according to ex-business secretary Vince Cable (2015), the Scottish issue carried much more weight in the 2015 general election than the bedroom tax or even the mansion tax. Anxiety and fear triumphed, 'fear of being held to ransom by the Scots. This fear was carefully-brilliantly-mobilised by the Conservatives' (Cable, 2015:31). In this context, the floating signifier of Englishness is substantiated by the very purposeful creation of a binary oppositional understanding and narrative.

It is the ideological conflict over the meaning of the word Englishness that is being contested or that is open to alternative discursive representations. As a concept within itself, it is meaningless – it contains no ideological substance however, no word is or can remain meaningless. Words, and especially concepts, become sites of ideological struggle, and specific representations are articulated through discourse. In other words, there is no neutral unexpressive moral language. All identity is more or less a floating signifier. Moral, political and cultural meanings are applied and attached. By whom and constituted by which particular characteristics is the key issue.

There are no neutral expressions or conceptualisations of Englishness much like there are no neutral oppositions or contexts in which it operates or it is placed. This is a subjective, ideological and unstable process. This is also a complex process operating within a field of assumed meaning which also functions within a chain of equivalence. Here ideological discursive representations of concepts such as Englishness exist within value-laden terms and concepts such as 'right', 'wrong', 'history', 'tradition', which facilitates a justification or legitimisation of a particular ideological position. As Laclau states, 'I cannot assert a differential identity without distinguishing it from a context, and, in the process of making the distinction, I am asserting the context at the same time' (Laclau, 1996:27).

The discursive field in which Englishness is placed is as telling as the discursive content itself. To discuss Englishness in relation to the Scottish independence debate or a process of devolution, a conservative position takes up a largely defensive and reactionary approach, placing SNP calls for independence from a Conservative dominated Westminster as undemocratic, illegitimate, radical and running counter to assumed dominant narratives of an Anglo-centric and conservative history and tradition. This is largely where such debate is located and where concepts of Englishness are discursively placed.

It can, therefore, be suggested that identity is narcissistic: the subject falls in love with its own image, one of the ideal self-constructed through an image of idealisation. It is an image of the self-built upon ideological illusions of a mythical social order. It uses a process of self-legitimisation based upon its own premises and boundaries to verify and legitimise itself. It is self-informed as the reality in which it operates and provides evidence and proof in itself, for itself. It provides and constructs a reality of, 'prescriptions and promises of a juridicial, ethical, and political nature with results, one can master all of these games by mastering "reality"' (Lyotard, 1986:47). It constructs its own reality for which it generates a narrative of understanding.

## Mutually Assured Discourse

A process of devolution has accelerated and perpetuated an undermining of a primacy of Britain and Britishness as a cumulative and ongoing process. This has the knock-on effect of instead of placating nationalist calls and dispersing power as a means of decentralising government, it has spurred on, sharpened and almost made the break-up of the United Kingdom an inevitability while firmly establishing a fertile ground for the establishment of a narrative of distinct and opposing identities and national discourse. A once necessary political and economic union has been largely undermined and increasingly made an irrelevance by competing discourses and narratives surrounding devolution.

With the focus so fixated through conservative discourses on the SNP, it is no wonder that Englishness has become both politically charged and reactionary in character. Mutually assured discourse can be used as a term to identify how both the SNP and the Conservatives both did so relatively well in the 2015 general election and even better in the 2019 general election. This can also be linked back to Laclau's concept of floating signifiers – each providing a discursive narrative for the other whereby creating mutually beneficial and yet ideologically opposed positions.

A contemporary sense of crisis and the problematisation surrounding concepts of Englishness and English national identity is bound up with English political, social and cultural hegemony within the union. While concepts and identities of Englishness have been historically bound up with this project of a nation state, a process of devolution has uncovered a neglected and undeveloped national sense of self, or as Krishan Kumar comments, 'a nationalism of the state rather than of the people' (Kumar, 2001:45). Englishness remained underdeveloped, while other national identities, particularly Welsh and Scots, have flourished.

The Act of Union between the nations of England (already encompassing Wales) and Scotland in 1707 did not occur as a long overdue shared sense of Britishness; it was born out of necessity, largely politically for Westminster and economically for Edinburgh. In a top-down manner, fundamental national institutions helped to solidify a sense of Britishness and British purpose, a centralised Bank of England and a financial system based in the City of London, a highly developed professional army, Parliament, Protestantism and a formally conjoined monarchy. Unifying national domestic institutions helped foster and transform power, especially when deployed against national threats or competition. However, these institutions never formed any deep rooted, coherent, stable, all-encompassing primary national identity, as Krishan Kumar (2001) points out, the British state is the classic example of the 'state-nation', the state identified not by ethnicity or any other identifier but by the state institutions such as Parliament and monarchy. These national institutions have relatively lost their sway and have become undermined by forces of globalisation and modernity. They have also become less relevant and able to capture popular imagination; therefore, the links between nation state and identity have weakened, indeed, 'since the 1960's almost all the elements that went into making up British identity have been eroded: Empire has gone, Protestantism is in terminal decline, Parliamentary democracy is widely despised' (Driver and Martell, 2001:94). Indeed, the last twenty years represent the most dramatic phase in a long-running cumulative process of viability of the British nation-state.

Contemporary Scottish nationalism is discursively driven by calls to identity and codes of cultural belonging (Cowley, 2014). It can be generally characterised by self-determination and the positive, inclusive, outwardly looking, cosmopolitan, pro-EU, anti-austerity identity that is diametrically opposed to, and constructed against, English Conservatism. On the other hand, the 'No' campaign during the Scottish independence referendum was dominated by calls to tradition and past collective glories, coupled with a pragmatic economic argument. According to Jason Cowley (2014), the long-term, deeper and structural trends that are forcing the United Kingdom apart have been misunderstood and not taken seriously enough within the context of the union, such as the end of empire, deindustrialisation, the decline of cross-border working-class solidarity, the weakening of Protestantism and trade unions as well as a deep disillusionment and disaffection towards politics in general. As former Prime Minister Gordon Brown stated (Brown in Cowley, 2014), Britishness has lacked a central driving purpose, 'for the profoundly Scottish Brown what really unites the people of these islands is a "shared British commitment to values of liberty, fairness and social responsibility"' (Cowley, 2014:23). However, conservative discourse and political and social dominance has destroyed any sense of an egalitarian national project.

A long standing Conservative position has been that Britain equates to England, treating Scotland and Wales as Labour-supporting irrelevancies of the Celtic fringe. To all intents and purposes, Britain was understood concomitantly and interchangeably with England. This has largely and cumulatively helped the respective nationalist cause and detract from any sense of allegiance to a sense of Britishness. 'Whilst it [devolution] was designed to deal with nationalist aspirations in Scotland and Wales, it is now paradoxically, drawing attention to the curious position of the English within Britain' (Skey, 2011:108). This includes not only the English dominant status economically, demographically and politically, but also that they possess very few distinct social, political and cultural institutions.

New global opportunities and alternatives have also helped render the purpose and power of state centralism. Britain was the creation of historical circumstance, as Catherine Hall (2001) comments, the Industrial Revolution and regional industrialism, empire building and conflict all went to help form, create and solidify British purpose and identity, all of which have disappeared. The world economy and centres of power have radically and fundamentally shifted since the 18th and 19th centuries which has left unilateralism defunct and political unions built on past needs wanting.

The conditions that sustained British national identity have greatly diminished. The absence of a global empire, lack of direct military threat and waning influence of Protestantism have eroded official nationalism. Social fragmentation has eroded fixed identities and collective class solidarity. Unifying factors connecting individuals from different regions are increasingly scarce.

Devolution, though not implying a complete breakup, has been a significant historical milestone. It has exposed the contested and fragile nature of English national identity or Englishness. The authority and influence of the British nation state have been challenged and undermined, not just through devolution but also due to the conditions of our time. The forces of globalisation, deterritorialisation, reterritorialisation, detraditionalisation, individualism and post-Fordism have reshaped identities away from traditional nation-state frameworks. This ongoing process raises questions about the legitimacy of identities and problematises the relevance of older macro nation-state identities.

According to Tony Wright (2000), devolution is less about constitutional issues but rather more importantly basic accepted identity. For any arrangement to survive, it needs to achieve some degree of popular identification. A pluralistic

British identity is possible in a post-referendum political and social landscape; however, instead of the Scottish independence referendum finally solving the question of a political settlement, it has only left the English question further irritated and unresolved. As pointed out by Andrew Gamble, 'cultural identities are one thing in a multinational state, but when they are translated into political identities they risk breaking the state apart' (Gamble, 2016:366). The SNP do not hide their opposition to Scotland's continued membership of the union and command an overwhelming political dominance in Scotland. This imbalance has made English issues of pressing concern, particularly for conservatives.

Although always somewhat fluctuating, the Future of England Survey (FoES) (2014) found that, as a rule, Labour and LibDem supporters identified far less as English than British, while UKIP and Conservative supporters identified overwhelmingly as English over British. This serves to confirm the political and ideological theme and identity characteristic of contemporary claims to Englishness. According to the FoES, Jeffery et al. (2014) suggest that dissatisfaction and disgruntlement had a particular form and manifestation in England with a distinct English political attitude. This general form being most strongly represented with those who identified most strongly with an English national identity.

As an overall snapshot of English attitudes, the FoES (2014) provides a general yet firm indicator that 'English identity remains a common denominator of dissatisfaction' (Jeffery et al., 2016:34). This can be viewed as generalising dominant themes of English national identity, as indicated by the FoES being constituted by a negative approach towards key issues such as: banning Scottish MPs from voting on English-only issues, reducing Scottish spending, introducing EVEL, voting to leave the European Union and hostility towards immigration. English national identity is one which is dominated and characterised by a specific set of political and ideological attitudes. This dominant conservative sense of Englishness does not represent all within England, however areas such as London aside; it still represents a clear, distinct and dominant attitude.

Old systems of understanding the nation and place used since the Act of Union, empire and being a leading global player cannot and will not be sufficient anymore, neither will just muddling through. A new responsive modern British identity is needed and is possible if Britain is to retain any degree of popular support across its constituent nations. However, a process of devolution suggests a long overdue need for a new set of relationships (politically, culturally and socially) and identities within the British Isles between constituent nations.

## Devolution and the European Union

The European Union and devolution are interdependent and intertwined in terms of their central importance within a conservative discursive construction of identity. Drawing from evidence of public feeling from round the time of both the independence and the EU referendum, Michael Kenny comments, 'recent polling suggests that many of the English are increasingly disenchanted with the two unions to which England belongs: the EU and the UK' (Kenny, 2014). This disenchantment has been capitalised upon by a prevailing conservative discourse of English disenfranchisement, disillusion, disgruntlement, anxiety and anger and can be attributed to both a significant performance by UKIP in the 2015 general election and the vote to leave the European Union in the 2016 referendum.

Supranational bodies provide opportunities for smaller regional or national concerns to bypass traditional nation-state structures and gain influence in regional politics and the global market. Decentralised government has become increasingly common in the European context, reshaping the role of nation states and impacting national identity. While some see this as an opportunity, others perceive it as a threat. The European Union allows the 'Celtic fringe' to pursue independent paths, but it also fuels conservative and Eurosceptic arguments against an undemocratic European superstate that threatens national sovereignty. Nationalist movements like the SNP in Scotland and Plaid Cymru in Wales leverage Europe to break away from a centralised nation state and operate independently of Westminster, challenging the relevance of the United Kingdom. It's important to note that this is a nuanced landscape, not all Scottish nationalists support the European Union, and not all English nationalists are Eurosceptic. People hold multiple identities, and generalisations can be unhelpful. However, understanding how devolution interacts with external interests and fluid concepts of identity is crucial to comprehending the ongoing process.

Richard Wyn Jones (2013) comments that English dissatisfaction with the internal territorial constitution of the United Kingdom is also closely related to dissatisfaction with the current external relationship with the European Union. Even if Eurosceptic rhetoric posits Europe as a threat to British values and traditions, it is in fact those who feel most exclusively English that are more hostile to the United Kingdom's membership of the European Union. What this produces is a catch-22 situation: dominant conservative discourse to leave the European Union under the auspices of a hard Brexit only serves to bolster anti-conservative and therefore anti-British opinion both in Wales and Scotland who are far more ideologically pro-EU.

Through competing ideological expressions, Englishness becomes associated with specific identity politics. As previously highlighted, 80% of those identifying exclusively as English voted to leave the European Union, while 80% of those voting to remain identified as exclusively British. This offers a clear indication of the dominant ideological framework in which populist concepts of Englishness exist and operate in relation to broader processes and issues. For example, 'nearly 90% of people who thought immigration was bad for the economy supported leave... similarly 88% of people who thought that the country should allow fewer immigrants in supported Brexit' (Goodwin and Heath, 2016).

The existence and influence of supranational bodies such as the European Union can help promote or be used by regional national identities, especially when they are discursively positioned to be progressive and outward looking, yet they also provoke and reinforce more defensive and traditionalist national identities which can help create and perpetuate an overly simplistic yet powerful binary oppositional understandings. As commented by former Prime Minister

Gordon Brown (2015), the Tories are playing a nationalist card in England by conjuring up a Scottish menace but also politically dividing the United Kingdom by providing veto powers in the EU referendum. The key point is that whether or not veto powers are granted the debate has descended into a 'sectarian war of words' (Brown, 2015) which has raised the spectre that there are irreconcilable differences between Scotland and England.

Whether or not we witness an actual break-up of Britain what the ongoing debate around devolution throws into stark relief is the diametrically opposed discourses that run throughout the United Kingdom and respective ideological relationships to the European Union provide a clear indication of this. For example, 'Scottish nationalists do not look backwards to a nineteenth century-style nation state but forwards to a clearer Scottish location within the networks of decentralised sovereignty which increasingly characterise the emergent European polity' (Preston, 2008:717). This stands in stark contrast to the dominant English conservative perspective of not only a deeply historicised account of national identity but also the positioning of Europe, and a wider cosmopolitan position largely on the periphery of its imagined future.

The European Union offers a viable alternative (if only theoretically) to the United Kingdom, and more importantly is used symbolically to establish a clear distinction between Welsh and Scottish national discourses and conservative dominated English ones. Devolution, instead of quenching regional national desires, has ultimately and increasingly become applied to England itself in a self-perpetuating discursive and political process in which the European Union has become a key indicator of ideological dominance and direction. 'If Britain leaves the EU, Scotland would most likely leave the Union... surely even someone as focussed on shrinking the state as Cameron fears a legacy of a broken Britain, with little England offshore and adrift' (Toynbee, 2015).

## Identity and the Ballot Box

The Conservative and Unionist Party – the very embodiment of traditional Britishness – has now all but in name had to rebrand itself as the political party of England. This is largely a cumulative process. Almost the entirety of Conservative MPs in the contemporary era represent English constituencies, although this has fluctuated somewhat. Since 1997, it has struggled to hold on to a few largely southern Scottish seats and can only ever muster a handful of Welsh MPs. The Labour Party and the Liberal Democrats faired much better post-1997; however, the march of the SNP from the late 2000s onwards has all but wiped out these parties and their legitimacy in Scotland too. Krishan Kumar (2006) comments that, the greatest significance as to why the Conservative Party are the English nationalist party and why conservative discourse is so dominant within England is that the Conservatives and their associated ideological base is so utterly related to England and has therefore been swept out of the Celtic regions on a tide of self-determination nationalism. Protestantism, imperialism and industrialism are either weak or absent, while the European Union to many within England is viewed as a threat and is conflated within anti-immigration sentiment that the Conservatives have exploited and played upon.

Since 1997, and particularly since 2009, Scottish nationalism has grown immeasurably. The SNP has gone from 6 MPs and 20% of the vote to 56 MPs and 50% of the vote in just 5 years from 2010 to 2015. This tidal wave has receded to some degree with 45 MPs elected in the 2019 general election. 'The ambiguities and anomalies of devolution have been exploited skilfully first by Alex Salmond and now [then] by Nicola Sturgeon' (New Statesman, 2015). Coupled with a Tory-led and almost entirely English government in 2010 and 2015, this has played handsomely to the Scottish nationalist cause, 'rather than killing Scottish nationalism "stone dead," as former Labour MP George Robertson predicted, devolution turbo charged it' (ibid). The impact of devolution and a Conservative dominated Westminster has been nuanced; even as recently as the early 2000s, many thought that devolution had killed off Scottish nationalism for good. 'There was a tendency to depict Scotland as somehow firmly unionist until a decade or so ago, and avowedly nationalist since. In reality it had been both at the same time' (Torrance, 2015).

We must bear in mind that devolution for Wales, Scotland and Northern Ireland has not been symmetrical in character. Different histories and demands have determined the devolutionary character of these nations. For Scotland, it has been largely a recovery of an autonomous nation, distinct from an imposed English dominated rule and identity. For Wales, the Welsh language has become a main focal point, particularly in the restoration of Welsh language and history on the school curriculum and the preservation of Welsh culture. In Northern Ireland, devolution has occurred quite differently. Instead of being voted for by a majority, it has been imposed by central government, largely as an attempt to create a solution to years of bitter conflict and to promote a working relationship between Unionists and Nationalists within the province.

For the English, devolution can be viewed as representing uncertainty, loss, threat and a profound crisis of identity never before encountered on such scale. Devolution can also be viewed as reversing the very things that the English have founded and created; a modern multinational nation state with all the institutional and bureaucratic trappings. While the English busied themselves with creating or investing in a quasi-imperial or missionary identity, they were not seriously engaged with the kinds of questions other nations have had to face. This has increasingly led to a cumulative and large-scale inquiry into a national soul, purpose, place and identity in recent times exemplified by forays into investigating or claiming a new found national awareness.

England has become a victim of its own stability, success and strong traditions of institutionalism. For many countries, change, challenges and turmoil force a restructuring of archaic institutions and constitutional changes written alongside forced rethinking or realignment of who they are, 'instead, England just is' (New Statesman, 2015). In this regard, England and a sense of Englishness has long been interchangeable or coterminous with that of Britishness with all its traditional associations of empire and status as a great power. This is largely at an end and a conscious sense of what England is, its place, position and purpose separate from Britain is long overdue.

With devolution reaching the very limits of its political and institutional possibilities, the old inner Anglo union is inexorably unravelling. This process of political unravelling now requires the English to seriously consider who they are, which has been largely met with a conservative and reactionary response. Moreover, as an identity, it is contradictory, conflicting and steeped in the anxiety and sense of loss of a post-devolution landscape even if the union still exists in name. That independence was not endorsed by a majority of voters on 18 September 2014 is less significant than it appears. The independence referendum normalised bitter divisions and animosities, particularly on the English side of the border whipped up by an antagonistic, conservative and largely anti-SNP media.

Devolution has created a momentum of inevitable separation even as a referendum which sought to produce a finalised answer only produced more uncertainty and calls for separation. As David Cameron sought to prevent Scotland leaving the United Kingdom by outlining plans to guarantee the permanence of the devolved Scottish Parliament, Nicola Sturgeon threatened that the Conservative government were living on borrowed time unless further reaching devolution was forthcoming. Although Cameron stated that, 'we all agreed – as do the Scottish public – that the independence referendum should be a "once in a generation" or "once in a lifetime event. So now it is time to move on' (BBC, 2015b). As long as the SNP continues to dominate Scottish politics, they have the legitimacy to call for referendums until a result is forthcoming that settles the issue. Nicola Sturgeon already stated that in the context of a British exit from the European Union voted for by a majority of English voters, the only course of action is for Scotland to hold another referendum. The SNP, even in a post-Sturgeon era, is in a strong political position to dictate terms to a Westminster government, an institution that clearly the majority of Scots feel disconnected from and feel does not represent their concerns or wishes.

It is not just matters such as the European Union or a general process of devolution that the SNP has managed to foster a distinct discourse and narrative at odds and opposed to one of Conservative Englishness. The SNP has stated that Conservative policies on issues such as austerity, immigration and Trident nuclear weapons, which are based in Scotland, were bringing independence closer (BBC, 2015b). Indeed, the SNP has put this diametrically distinct policy approach into place with the nationalisation of Scotland's train services from 1 April 2022. In terms of ideologically based identity politics, the SNP has very purposefully and successfully positioned itself as the binary opposite to the Conservative Party and Conservative-led government in Westminster.

David Cameron's claim of a clear and decisive choice in the 2014 Scottish independence referendum rests on very shaky ground. The 'No' campaign only managed to win with 54% of the vote, whereas the May 2015 general election gave clear indication of the mood of the Scottish population by handing the SNP an overwhelming majority of seats, which it has largely held onto since. Cameron's legitimacy to comment that the referendum was a 'once-in-a-lifetime' event or that the SNP should 'move on' is seriously undermined. Constitutionally and politically, it is unlikely that a second independence referendum will take place in the immediate future, especially given every Prime Minister since David Cameron insisting that one will not be forthcoming. What is clear is the ideological differences and the huge disparities between discursive characteristics of political national identity between Scotland and a Conservative-dominated English political environment.

However, some important distinctions arise. According to Ben Wellings (2008), Euroscepticism is all but in name English nationalism. On the other hand, a distinctly pro-European stance is central to particularly Scottish national and political identity. To a large extent, Englishness can be characterised by a sense of anxiety and loss; this also feeds into Arthur Aughey's (2007) concept of 'anxiety of absence' that helps inform English concepts of place, position and future concerns within contemporary social and political developments. 'The "anxiety of anticipation" reflects a fear that England is ill-prepared for any post-UK future that its neighbours will accommodate more readily' (Bond, Jeffery and Rosie, 2010:464).

The relationship between national identity and political entitlement in England has begun to change, partly as a direct result of an ongoing and unresolved process of devolution. Susan Condor (2010) points out that English national identity or nationalism is rarely considered grounds for political voice alone. Rather, it is far more likely that English nationalism has come to the fore as a response to increased levels of recognition of (predominantly) Scottish rights to national self-determination. Therefore, it is important to disentangle political legitimacy from personal allegiance. In other words, the United Kingdom may exist as a fully functioning nation state and largely be accepted by its population as a legitimate national governmental structure, yet at the same time, it attracts very little in the way of personal allegiance in terms of national identification throughout its constituent nations.

Research carried out by John Denham (in Dunin-Wasowicz, 2019) discovered that although there is much ambiguity and cross-over between English and British identity within England, 82% of those who identified as more English than British are proud of their English identity, whereas this figure falls to just 13% of those identifying as British not English. In the same attitudinal survey, the largest group identify as either equally English and British, more English than British or English not British. Whereas over 60% of the 2021 Census respondents in Wales identified as either Welsh only or both Welsh and British (Welsh Govt, 2021). Most markedly, for Scotland, 72% of Scots primarily identify as Scottish in 2022 as opposed to 57% in 2012 (Walker, 2022).

Charles Leddy-Owen suggests that, 'for social historians such as Linda Colley (1992) and Krishan Kumar (2003), the historical submerging and potential re-emergence of a confident cultural and political sense of Englishness is indexed respectively to the rise and decline of Britishness' (Leddy-Owen, 2014:1449). This becomes apparent when compared with attitudes towards identification. This is highlighted in the British Social Attitudes 23rd Report (Aughey, 2010) which found that, between 1996 and 2006, the proportion describing themselves as British had become a demographic minority, declining from 52% to 44%. As indicated, this decline has continued unabated. Although Britishness has long been a secondary identity in both Scotland and Wales, 'the most dramatic trend was for it to become secondary in England as well' (ibid). Indeed, Krishnan Kumar (2003) found that in England, the proportion who gave British as their primary identity fell from 59% in 1997 to 48% in 2005 (in 1992, 63% of the English chose British as their primary identity). To compound this, the decline in Britishness among the English over the past decade has not been accompanied by an increasing identification with Europe or any other sort of cosmopolitan identity; rather, it has become increasingly dominated by a conservative and defensive narrative and discourse.

What is important to highlight is how a dominant and largely taken-for-granted position of an Anglo-dominated status quo has come under sustained scrutiny, partly as a result of the devolutionary process. A changing relationship has generated a palpable response within England both in terms of identity but also crucially in terms of a dominant conservative discourse, in the foregrounding narratives of victimisation, which focus on the apparent and portrayed privileging of 'other' national groups in Britain (Skey, 2011). This can be viewed as leading to a cumulative, narrow and defensive ideological discursive position. Much like dominant discourse and expressions at the ballot box, polling results around identification and nationhood can be mixed, contradictory or fluctuate; however, the constant is the dominance within a discourse of Englishness of a conservative and right-wing narrative.

The negative and defensive self-comparison with the other UK constituent nations extends to other conceptual anxieties such as an 'anxiety of imitation' (Bond, Jeffery, Rosie, 2010). Rather than England being the agenda setting core of the UK nation state, it must now ape the once peripheral nations in finding a more assertive national confidence and purpose. Although England will be compelled to replicate certain aspects of devolved power such as EVEL, from an ideological and discursive perspective, the last thing a Conservative government will do is to appear to mirror them. Within this context, English nationalism, particularly through political articulations, can be viewed as developing in terms of a response through the application of a sense of anxiety and justice which arguably feeds upon and perpetuates a defensive discourse.

A conservative discourse concerning devolution suggests it represents 'common sense', 'order' and the preservation of a traditional status quo. This calls upon familiar social, political and historical justifications directly linked to national and personal identity formations within a particular ideological prism. On the other hand, an SNP discourse suggests that it represents the wishes of the Scottish people, its desires and to free Scotland from the tyranny of an English conservative political system, within a very similar system of justification. Both are, therefore, ideological constructs wishing to legitimise and justify each opposing position. In this sense, 'politics and culture become deeply affected by this dominant pattern' (Williams, 2005:188).

Nationalism, or rather the attachment to national identity, can be viewed as a way of constructing the social reality in which we live. A notion or concept of Britishness or British national identity today is as confused, manipulated, contradictory, irrational, incoherent and contested as it has ever been. It is important that we depart from the idea that somehow a sense of British national identity is in crisis today in comparison to a mythical past age where it was strong, unifying and homogenous. This has never truly been the case. British national identity has almost always struggled to superimpose a unified, uniformed set of ideas and beliefs. As stated by Tom Nairn, 'Great Britain was quite unusually and structurally dependent upon external relations tied up with its empire' (Nairn, 1981:13). When that framework disintegrated, there is very little left to hold a predominance and purpose dependent upon such a provisional project.

It would be short-sighted to merely blame the Scotland Bill (1998) for the break-up of the United Kingdom and a sense of English grievance. In relation to identity and specifically English national identity, this has always been undefined, ambiguous and fluid mainly because a sense of British national identity for the English has largely predominated. The Scots and the Welsh, being smaller nations within the English-dominated (politically, economically, demographically, socially and culturally) United Kingdom, have always retained a generally agreed sense of identity in relation to and often against an English dominated and conflated sense of Britishness. The conflation and ambiguity between Englishness and Britishness has left the English ill-prepared and most to lose in a situation of further devolution. English national identity has not necessarily needed to exist, while the British nation state has existed as a primary and dominant political, social and cultural entity. As recently as 2007, Arthur Aughey commented that the situation seemed (so far) to be one characterised not by simmering outrage but by national equanimity, 'the English appeared to have simply put up with it' (Aughey in Condor, 2010:526).

According to Condor (2010), popular nationalist lines of argument among respondents in an in-depth survey carried out explicitly invoke an ethnic conceptualisation of nationhood in conjunction with the endorsement of political nationalism as an abstract principle.

> This stance was reflected, among other things, by the respondent displaying concern over the distinction between England and Britain (including a tendency to self-categorise as 'English' not 'British') and voicing opposition to multiculturalism and EU integration.
>
> (Condor, 2010:532)

Attitudes linking concepts of Englishness to clearly definable ideological themes and motives dominate a contemporary conservative discourse of Englishness. This is also often conflated with what Kazin (1998) terms the 'language of popularism'. This being the respondent treating such a conceptualisation of English national identity as laying claim to commonality with other 'ordinary' or 'normal' English people. This can be viewed as adopting the conservative 'common sense' position, often employed against a perceived dominant liberal or politically correct value system, which is then used in turn as ideologically oppressive towards a conservative 'common sense' or 'ordinary' position.

Moreover, English national identity, according to Owen Jones (2015), is certainly much stronger now than it ever was; however, it is too often defined negatively and defensively: as not Scottish, as hostile to the European Union, to immigrants and Muslims and the 'other' in general. The Englishness of popular radical struggle from the English Civil War, the Chartists, the Labour movement and the Suffragettes has been intentionally airbrushed out of existence by a dominant, insular, defensive and exclusive conservative discourse.

## Elections as Discursive Conflicts

The changing position and shift within England from British to an English-dominated identification can be linked to the ways in which language and discourse has been used to mark (in)equity and perceptions of inequality between England and the devolved nations within Britain. These discussions and surrounding rhetoric focus upon the political; the West Lothian question and a lack of an English Parliament, economic settlements such as the Barnett formula and the provision of welfare and grants across the different nations. This cumulates into providing a type of 'resentment nationalism' (Skey, 2011), where a dominant majority perceives its once taken-for-granted position to be undermined or under threat from minority groups, who it perceives as being granted 'special treatment'.

Within this context, a conservative domination of discourse can be attributed to playing upon fear and anxieties based upon contemporary developments that are conceptualised as a threat. Some of these have formed part of a conservative ideological position stretching back many years; however, this has become reinvigorated and sharpened with new challenges, a fear of loss of Britain due to the largely perceived quasi-Socialist SNP, a fear of loss of a position of leadership, not only within Britain (in terms of agenda setting) but also regionally within Europe, a fear of loss of a social structure legitimised and characterised by deference and tradition and fear of loss of a mythical hegemonic cultural and ethnic character under new waves of immigration. These themes were fully exploited in the 2015 general election, particularly Scottish independence and the surrounding issues regarding what the SNP specifically had been characterised to stand for. A key factor which has bolstered the Conservative position is the creation and perpetuation of fear surrounding, 'a weak, Labour-led UK government being held to ransom by the SNP' (Cable, 2015:32). The flip side of such fear mongering, however, is a boon to nationalists. A Conservative-dominated UK government with minimal legitimacy outside of England.

The ongoing process and issue of devolution, however politically mutually convenient it may be for the Conservatives and the SNP, is that 'fear and resentment now lie not far below the surface. The politics of identity rests on raw emotion, not reason' (ibid). This is inextricably tied into other pressing political and cultural issues such as Europe and immigration. Devolution, Europe and other ongoing processes all feed into a maelstrom of identity conflicts that propose simplistic solutions and understandings to complex issues. In this regard, conservatives have been left in a strong discursive position to determine and dominate the political and ideological agenda and its parameters.

Politics of oppositionality have characterised devolution discourses but has also opened the possibility of progressive political identities. According to Mark Perryman (2009), the SNP, Plaid Cymru and Sinn Fein have all cultivated different models of progressive civic nationalism which are fundamentally social democratic in character, 'yet in England progressive patriotism remain something we leave to the Celtic fringe; our politics has scarcely begun to grapple with its potential' (Perryman, 2009:42). Patriotic politics in England is dominated by a traditionalist, conservative and largely right-wing narrative built upon anxiety, loss and a backward-looking exclusivity.

In the run-up to the 2015 general election, the Conservatives sought to fully exploit a sense of devo-anxiety and the distinct possibility of a Labour/SNP coalition by playing the English nationalist card. Jones (2015) comments that such nationalist resentment cannot be stoked and then neatly be put back into a box when it has outlived its use. Indeed, such messages have been repeated in subsequent general elections. Moreover, Gordon Brown (2015) warned that the Conservatives had given up on the United Kingdom as it sought to shore up its own position by 'playing the English card'. 'If the United Kingdom collapses, it will not be because a majority of Scots are hell-bent on leaving but because the UK government is giving up on saving it' (Brown, 2015). In order for the Tories to head-off UKIP and to fully exploit a perceived threat from the SNP, they presented themselves as the English nationalist party. This shows how central the issue of English nationalism and identity has become in that the Conservatives, whose founding ethos was unionism, is now almost entirely English-based in support, representation and present themselves within a discourse of defensive Englishness.

David Cameron strategically and symbolically moved on this particular topic of concern directly after the Scottish independence referendum by proclaiming that he spoke for the 'millions of English voices now waiting to be heard' by suggesting English devolutionary powers. The Conservatives seized the moment to which many, if not the majority in England, have come to feel about identity, nation, state, representation, spending and anxieties towards the future. Even the most moderate conservative conceptualisations of identity and representation include the belief of a need to preserve and defend perceived English traditions 'and a growing belief that Englishness needs greater recognition, and some form of institutional expression' (Kenny, 2016). A deep-seated sense of grievance has festered away at the conservative-right for decades, yet it has taken the McKay Commission of 2013, the close Scottish independence referendum of 2014 and the continued SNP domination of Scottish politics to bring this to the surface in the form of a politicisation of English identity and a conservative monopolisation of Englishness.

Although the tabling of EVEL by the Conservative Party in the immediate aftermath of the Scottish referendum may be viewed as the first tangible and concrete form of a politicisation of Englishness in relation to the constitutional position of England, as a form of identity politics and competing forms of national discourse, it has been constituted by a politicised character for a long time. Cameron's claim of representing the voice of a patient yet neglected English fits very well into conservative ideological perspectives of a defensive yet assertive Englishness. With the Conservative announcement of EVEL following the Scottish referendum and a vow to give stronger devolution powers to Scotland, the Conservatives had very little to lose but to consolidate its claim to being the party of disgruntled English nationalism. This clearly reinforced by the repeated claim during the 2015 general election of the SNP as being a threat to England and holding British democracy to ransom.

Conservative narratives that the SNP would hold the whip hand over Labour in any post-May 2015 general election can be viewed as a potent enough message to have eroded and contributed to any serious chance Labour may have had in that election. This message, relayed relentlessly throughout the election campaign from a right-wing media, provided the discursive background within which the election was fought and won by the Conservatives. This only served to further exacerbate resentment on both sides of the border, 'the Tories portray the likely democratically elected representatives of Scotland as akin to agents of a foreign power' (Jones, 2015). Contradictions and hypocrisy only further embolden the SNP and help to politicise English grievances. As commented by George Eaton, 'for the first time since the campaign began, the party [Labour] unambiguously lost the "air war" as broadcasters prioritised the Tories anti-SNP blitzkrieg over Labour's "NHS week"' (Eaton, 2015:9). Regardless of the very real pain of austerity or the systematic failure of the Conservatives to meet any of their 2010 election promises, the dominant discourse was entirely controlled by the Conservatives.

Elections have proved problematical and divisive not just for the Conservatives but for all of the main UK national parties. Labour's alliance with the Conservatives in the 2014 Scottish independence referendum and their weak opposition to the Tory's on many key issues such as austerity under Ed Miliband revealed that a once taken-for-granted and mighty Scottish Labour movement all but disintegrated in the 2015 general election. The demise and all but annihilation of any British national political party north of the border severely weakens the union's bonds and signals a political de-legitimisation of the union.

Just as Stanley Baldwin and John Major conjured an idealised England of pastoral scenes of cricket and warm beer, 'from around 2004 Salmond and Nicola Sturgeon began to paint a picture of a left-wing Scotland, an anti-Tory Scotland, an egalitarian and outwardly-looking nation; an image of how many Scots liked to see themselves, if not a wholly accurate representation of who they actually were' (Torrance, 2015). This discursive representation worked along the same lines as the Conservative narrative of the SNP in the 2015 general election campaign. Both the SNP and the Conservatives used Scottish and English nationalist claims respectively to legitimise their positions. With Labour campaigning alongside the Tory's during the 2014 referendum campaign and the widespread belief that Labour had lost its soul and ditched its principles, it is quite easy to see how the SNP managed to claim the anti-Tory narrative and mantle, and the once 'red Clydebank' position from Labour – ultimately to the benefit of the Conservatives themselves.

The process of devolution has instead of quelling and ending nationalist sentiment within the separate nations of the United Kingdom enflamed it. 'The contemporary status of England and Englishness must be understood not only through comparison with other parts of the UK but, equally important, through relation to the broader – and to some degree overlapping question of Britishness' (Bond, Jeffery, Rosie, 2010:463). Although it is difficult to disentangle Englishness from Britishness, particularly in an historical context, what has become clear in recent years is that according to Bond, Jeffery and Rosie (2010), we find ourselves in an historic moment when the English have begun to develop a clear conception about the distinction between England and Britain, or rather, Englishness and Britishness. This is of fundamental political, historical and cultural significance. Arguably though, this choice has been impelled rather unwillingly upon the English to which the response has been to generally embrace a particular brand of defensive nationalism.

## Discursive Consequences of English Votes for English Laws

The passing of 'English Votes for English Laws' by 312 MPs to 270 on 22 October 2015 is one of the most constitutionally symbolic pieces of legislation passed by a Westminster Parliament in 300 years. Although designed to placate calls for some degree of legislative rebalancing of the effects of devolution and an attempt to answer the ever-lingering West Lothian question, it may however have two very serious consequences in terms of the union. Firstly, it will hasten a separation of constituent nations through official Westminster channels. EVEL was opposed by all Westminster parties except the Conservatives and UKIP, which, for many on that side of the debate, the proposals do not go far enough. Indeed, DUP leader Nigel Dodds stated that, 'the proposals neither deal with the problem they diagnose, and threatens the fabric of our union' (BBC, 2015c).

Secondly, the passing of EVEL, much like the introduction of devolution, will almost certainly strengthen nationalist claims in all constituent nations, particularly Scotland where the SNP's Pete Wishart MP told the Commons, 'Scotland is watching this and the mood is darkening. If this is an exercise in saving the union you could not have contrived of a more inept way to save the union' (ibid). The Shadow Leader of the Commons, Chris Bryant, described the move as, 'a charter for breaking up the union' (Mason and Brooks, 2015). Either way, Englishness and English-centred concerns have become the primary national identity for many within England in the last few years, 'its core concerns and dynamics are starting to imprint themselves on the Westminster political scene' (Kenny, 2012: 155). Although shocking, especially to unionists, EVEL is the natural progression for an assertive conservative nationalism, especially within the context of 'devo-max', a close Scottish independence referendum and a self-assertive, self-confident and populist SNP.

This closely mirrors a normative shift of the politicisation of Englishness concerning calls for distinct and separate powers for England within a framework of devolution. The McKay Commission of March 2013 drew upon tensions that were symptomatic of a deeper set of dilemmas facing the United Kingdom – not just whether Scottish MPs could vote on English only issues. According to Michael Kenny (2015), the English question is to be viewed as a problem of representation and governance following the introduction of devolution in the late 1990s but also in relation to a broader range of casual dynamics including deepening disenchantment with representative politics, a rising sense of cultural anxiety and a growing demand for recognition in political life.

Although the so-called West Lothian question has been present for many years and is nothing new within British devolutionary politics, couched within cumulative frustrations and anxieties, it has become a lightning rod for English nationalism. What is also important to understand is how the normative character of pushing the West Lothian question into the political long grass has become untenable, and that serious constitutional change and practice is afoot amidst a backdrop of increased English nationalism.

A fundamental issue that the McKay Commission did not recognise was a growing disquiet that the largest, most populous and economically strongest nation within the union sees itself as a victim, lacking a voice or adequate representation under current arrangements. An English backlash against the asymmetrical model of devolution introduced by New Labour in the late 1990s was not immediate in its development. Using longitudinal data supplied by the British Social Attitudes Survey, John Curtis (2009) comments that the English remained uninterested in emulating devolution and were indifferent to its effects throughout this period. The issue did not come to the fore of political debate in overt and immediate terms until the Conservative-led government of 2010 took office and the Scottish independence referendum. A growing sense of irritation is observable from the mid-2000s among the English directed at issues around the West Lothian question. This, combined with the dramatic rise in popularity of the SNP and the growth of a reactionary conservative discourse and political predominance in England, can be viewed as a source for the resurgence of Englishness, particularly of a political variety.

Examples of this conservative narrative and discourse which articulates growing unease and resentment can be seen, for instance, in the *Daily Mail* which commented that, '"England is fucked" and the most depressing illustration of this condition was the "craven way" in which matters solely affecting England were decided by those who were not English' (Fulford, 2005). This commentary of devolution oppressing the English has become a dominant narrative, particularly within conservative discourses of Englishness and its relationship to devolution. This sense of self-resentment and contempt leads not only to hastening a process of devolution but also characterises a politics of resignation symptomatic of many searching for a sense of Englishness, particularly on the right.

The political rhetoric and bemoaning language of an overtaxed, underfunded and under-represented people of England typical of English nationalists such as the Campaign for an English Parliament (CEP) has arguably become the common language and narrative of a conservative account of devolution. The underlying message of such a variety of English nationalism is more of a reluctant rather than overtly separatist nature, 'the message of CEP is that it does not want to break up the United Kingdom but wishes to see it continue in a different federated form' (Aughey, 2007:196).

Although the CEP and other English nationalist political parties and campaign groups such as the English Democrats are fringe groups, their particular and specific message and narrative has become part of the wider political debate and has seeped into seriously considered proposals for solutions to the West Lothian question and related devolutionary disparities. Fuelled by over-exaggerated concepts of fear and loss, this plays directly into wider conservative discourses of anxiety, powerlessness and anger. Although certainly not a scientific barometer for popular opinion, the right-wing press certainly influence and feed into it. For example, when *The Times* provided the headline of 'We will hold UK defence to ransom, SNP warns' (The Times, 2015), or the Sun proclaims: 'SNP threaten to hold Brexit bill to ransom unless Nicola Sturgeon gets a seat at the negotiations with the EU' (The Sun, 2017), these narratives and sensationalist rhetoric provide a simplified and entrenched ideological understanding or reference point. It also creates a feedback loop where rhetoric and narrative becomes legitimised as fact, one that politicians and social commentators feed and react to further creating an environment of intransigence.

Many within England, particularly but not exclusive to the conservative right, object to the idea that England should be treated as the residue or leftovers of constitutional change. Anti-Scottish nationalist sentiment within England has clearly been stoked and tapped into by a devo-negative conservative discourse of Englishness. The Future of England Survey (2014) indicated that in terms of political representation alone, 62% agreed emphatically that Scottish MPs should be prevented from voting on laws that apply only to England with just 12% disagreeing (Jeffrey et al., 2016). Meanwhile, it has become almost accepted as fact that the SNP will hold any political party other than the Conservatives to ransom in the aftermath of any general election, and that it is only the Conservatives who are willing to stand up to the SNP.

A defensive and conservative identification with Englishness has been encouraged and informs perceived social, economic and political disparity and inequity. The English question comes to prominence in wider Conservative circles in the guise of an upsurge of interest in the West Lothian issue, particularly following the controversy that accompanied the passage of legislation introducing foundation hospitals within the National Health Service in 2003, and the Higher Education Bill of 2004 which introduced 'top-up' fees for students. Both were contentious pieces of legislation that applied primarily to England but required the votes of Scottish MPs to secure a majority for the Labour government. The territorial composition of Labour MPs required to pass this legislation figured prominently in media coverage and wider discourse surrounding the Bills. Symptomatic of this, 'Conservative MP Tim Yeo, for instance, denounced the "constitutional outrage" which their passage represented, and a number of MPs from other parties agreed' (Kenny, 2015:155).

Shortly after this, Malcolm Rifkind (former Secretary of State for Scotland) proposed an 'English Grand Committee' composed of English MPs to deal with English-only legislation. David Cameron, after becoming Conservative leader in 2005, established a Democracy Task Force specifically to resolve the West Lothian question. Cameron has always emphasised a unionist inclination and never shared serious interest in the West Lothian question until 2014. The changing political environment however has inexorably shifted towards EVEL. The 2010 general election and continued Conservative governments, the Scottish independence referendum, the rise of the SNP and the EU referendum all providing momentum towards a specific politicisation of Englishness. Within the parliamentary Conservative Party, a significant proportion of the 2010 intake of Tory MPs identified more clearly with the idea of English grievance, a trend reflected in an ongoing shift within grassroots party opinion over key constitutional issues. This is also reflected in a poll conducted in December 2010 which found that 51% of party members thought that England should have its own parliament as opposed to only 32% of that opinion in December 2008 (Kenny, 2015).

With the Conservatives responding both to its highly concentrated support within England and a new emphasis on English concerns, it has sought to identify with a defensive and aggrieved English nationalism articulated through the passing of EVEL. Although this can be viewed as intended to protect the union and placate perceived democratic imbalances, it has fundamentally lent itself to the process of unpicking a complex political and ideological support for the union. In this sense, 'the internal cohesion of the UK is visibly weakening. Its political system is unfair, and is widely perceived as such. The institutional and cultural textures of its earlier solidarity are fraying and being foolishly destroyed' (Kettle, 2015). As a result, the constituent nations of the United Kingdom are moving in different directions. This process is occurring both rapidly yet also seemingly casually. Even the concept of EVEL six or seven years previously was very much a fringe political cause let alone the possibility of passing through the House of Commons. This process has been occurring for many years; however, it has only recently accelerated with the dominance in Westminster of English Conservatives, the political dominance of the SNP in Holyrood and the antagonistic relationship between these two ideologically diametrically opposed positions. This has also led to an apparent English abandonment of a prioritised British identity and a loosening of a containment of the power of English nationalism.

The very weight of English influence in Westminster and British politics means that England is always in general terms the dominant force. Even if legislation over economic matters is applicable only to England, its influence will ultimately affect and impact upon the other constituent UK nations regardless. However, the problem is that if federalism is the option taken, this will not be a fair and symmetrical solution, 'no federation can operate successfully where one of the units is so dominant' (Hazell, 2006:42). This would entirely be the case with a federation of the United Kingdom dominated by the overwhelming size, strength, power and concerns of the English. The campaign for an English Parliament can therefore be viewed as tantamount to a campaign for English independence. While this might not be the intended objective, this may well end up being the result. In other words, seeking to solve the West Lothian question becomes a self-defeating task; it can only be truly achieved by ending the United Kingdom as a political entity itself.

Political circumstance; the 2009 Scottish Parliamentary election, the 2010 and 2015 general elections, the 2014 Scottish independence referendum and the 2016 EU referendum have made the issue of the West Lothian question far more acute than ever before. Indeed, the Conservative landslide at the 2019 general election and the swing to the right under Johnson and Truss only widened the incompatibility between Scotland and England. A majority of English identify as English over British and serious political debate is well underway over the hidden English question contained in the shell of devolution. The once benign indifference over English national identity has been replaced by very serious political rhetoric and populist discursive outpourings.

Devolution has fundamentally changed and impacted upon the whole political nature of the United Kingdom, not just through devolved powers and the establishment of independent executives but also how British political parties operate, reach and their legitimacy. Devolution has 'thrown into question the hallowed supremacy of the Westminster Parliament, and so the whole constitutional arrangement by which Britain has been governed for the past three centuries' (Kumar, 2003:240). It has also challenged and uncovered the myths surrounding Britain and its various arrangements and exposed them as outdated and unfit for purpose in the 21st century (national events surrounding the monarchy aside).

Within this context, there has been a swift and distinct shift concerning politics of English nationalism and populist feeling. 'The BBC reported this week that a large new survey by Cardiff and Edinburgh universities shows 54% support in England for its own parliament, four times as many who disagreed' (Guardian, 2014a). Whereas figures from YouGov (2023) from Dec 2019 to March 2023 have consistency identified the 'support for a creation of a new English Parliament along the lines of the existing Scottish Parliament'. It seems clear that these developments represent a response to the Scottish independence referendum and more widely debates around devolution. It can also be viewed to represent a wish by the majority of the English not to be left out of any new devolutionary developments. This can be evaluated as being symptomatic of a negative and reactionary Englishness stoked up by the Scottish referendum but also related developments and processes.

English nationalism in previous years has remained a fringe and opportunist phenomenon. When related to the aforementioned survey by Cardiff and Edinburgh universities, it can be seen to represent a more resentful feeling in England concerning Scottish nationalist demands. This re-emphasises a conservative and defensive concept of Englishness as a general response to an ongoing and seemingly unstoppable process of devolution. A close 'No' vote in the 2014 Scottish independence referendum only ensured a resentful union built upon and held together by mistrust and acrimony with very little popular identification of a shared national project or political goodwill either sides of the border.

SNP demands for independence (particularly in light of an overwhelmingly English dominated vote to leave the European Union) and dominant discourses of distrust especially during the 2015 and subsequent general elections have fed back into longstanding Tory demands that the Celtic nations can only be treated as equals if unquestioning loyalty to Westminster is shown. As indicated with the announcement of EVEL directly after the 2014 referendum:

> There is an increasingly vocal section of the Conservative Party which has begun to speak of England and England's needs. EVEL commands great support and William Hague, charged with coming up with a solution, was criticised for not going nearly far enough in his proposals before the 2015 election.
>
> (Gamble, 2016:363)

The growing detachment of many within England from an outdated British project and an unresponsive political system has led to feelings of disconnection and alienation. From a pragmatic standpoint, the enactment of EVEL by the Conservatives can be seen as a strategy to strengthen their majority in the Commons in the short term. However, this approach fundamentally undermines the union both constitutionally and politically, permanently discrediting the Conservative and Unionist Party. While it may bring short-term triumph through an extended Commons majority, it will also deeply divide the Tories between committed unionists and opportunists seeking a quick solution to the West Lothian question, capitalising on increasing English nationalism and resentment. Owen Smith, commenting on the passing of EVEL in 2015, as 'a dog's breakfast, slopped together just before the summer recess and patently aimed at parlaying English nationalism into Tory advantage' (Smith, 2015).

The tenacious conservative resistance of its English heartland to its fate provides a catalyst and contributor to the impending disaster itself, hastening a foreseeable end. The irony and hypocrisy of a large yet incompatible socio-political-economic unit being 'better together' (to borrow a phrase from the 'No' campaign from the Scottish independence referendum) is clearly lost on many in Conservative circles; on one hand, campaigning to keep the union together, yet arguing for varying degrees of separation not only in terms of being together but also in terms of its relationship with the European Union. In many regards, it can be viewed as some sort of dysfunctional marriage – two distinct entities who have grown apart, have completely different interests and desires yet for the meantime continue the charade. Moreover, the only reason the decline of the nation state of Great Britain has operated in such slow motion is due to the very archaism of the Anglo-British state, its failure to modernise, yet its residual social strength and institutions. The Scottish mode of dominant national discourse however is one based upon an overwhelmingly politically oriented separatism, is overtly forward looking and is indifferent to themes of race and cultural ancestry, unlike its English counterpart.

English national awareness is a product in part forced from a process of devolution. The further devolution is taken to its very possibilities, the less relevant Britishness becomes and the more resentment is built up within England, further strengthening a conservative discourse of Englishness. As Tom Nairn commented, 'the more it is delayed, the more certain this awareness is to be inflected to the right, and captured by the forces feeding off the wounds and failures of decline' (Nairn, 1981:80). It is, in other words, a strong reaction to a sense of loss and decline but also a manifestation of political entitlement. There is very little room for identity and discontents to express themselves apart from a resentful and defensive conservatism.

The passing through Westminster of EVEL has helped formalise political articulations of English nationalism. This in turn has reinforced normative opposing national narratives and identities in relation to Scotland and England. Tim Edensor (2002) notes that in this regard, identity is a process, not an essence, which is continually being remade in consistent ways, through an 'internal-external dialectic', involving a simultaneous synthesis of internal self-definition and one's ascription by others. EVEL can be viewed as both an outwardly articulation of ideological, cultural and political positioning but also as an inwardly social and ideological account of a reassertive sense of Englishness. It symbolises a specific discourse on the English nation. The passing of EVEL is part of this identity formation that occurs both in the mundane and more banal but also as relatively spectacular events or statements.

Any recognition of constitutional and political changes has to take on board the responsibility of the English question. England's past has directly contributed to the constitutional and political history in which Britain's nations find themselves. England is perhaps though the least prepared and adjusted to a future of increased social, political and constitutional devolution. As Bernard Crick (1991) commented, the English must come to terms with themselves. A Britain without Scotland deprives the United Kingdom of its very reason of being; it also forces the English to consider who they are or what they might be.

Although the 'Yes' campaign narrowly lost the 2014 independence referendum, Scotland has to all intents and purposes, already departed from the union. The vast majority of Scots identify as Scottish over British, the SNP won a remarkable 56 out of 59 seats in the 2015 general election and have continued to maintain total dominance in terms of MPs returned to Westminster and the Scottish government, which is in a continued process of regaining key political and economic powers, is ruled by an overwhelming SNP majority. These key political, cultural and social shifts, alongside the increasing calls for an English only legislature, the passing of EVEL, a ruling Westminster government entirely dominated by English MPs and representing a distinct form of reassertive English nationalism, suggest that the union has become a hollow and increasingly less relevant administrative functionary.

With the passing of EVEL, a cynical charge that can be made against a Conservative about-turn on the issue of the union is that it converts a prevailing sense of English resentment and conservative discourse into political dominance at Westminster by excluding the numbers of SNP (and to a lesser extent Plaid

Cymru) MPs opposing Conservative proposals and policy. England, as a singular political entity is dominated by Conservative MPs – something that even the most unionist Tory would not have ignored when considering EVEL in the House of Commons. Nick Pearce commented that, 'political parties find it impossible to resist the temptation to succumb to party interests on matters constitutional... parties have sectional interests that they cannot easily put aside' (Pearce in Wintour, 2014). There are strong suggestions here of a constitutional fix which reduces Scotland's voice at Westminster and strengthens the Tories grip on power.

However, the Conservative Party are stuck in a bind, support and embrace a resurgent English nationalism and identification or restate the party's commitment to the union. Politically, it has committed to the latter yet discursively the previous. Nevertheless, it is clear that regardless of political formality or historical precedent, the Conservative Party are all but in name an English party, 'as Richard Weight (2002) noted, after 1997 "the Conservatives were now truly the party of one nation – England"' (Weight, 2002 in Wellings, 2008:396). Historically and ideologically speaking, it can be postulated that, 'instinctively English Conservatives were British' (Wellings, 2008:396). However, it is increasingly apparent that the Conservatives are now ideologically, politically, socially and culturally exclusively English-centred.

Shortly before the Scottish devolution referendum on 12 September 1997, Margaret Thatcher predicted the rise of an unsympathetic English nationalism similar to what can be described today as mainstream dominant discursive currency within England:

> Scottish politicians do Scots no service if they lead them to believe that they can always pick and choose the terms under which they wish to remain in the UK. They should not be surprised if the result of doing so is to awaken a resentful English nationalism, which questions other aspects of present arrangements which Scots themselves take for granted.
>
> (Thatcher in Wellings, 2008:397)

The Conservatives are staunch defenders of Crown-in-Parliament sovereignty of Anglo-Britishness; nevertheless, this identification perpetuates Scottish and Welsh alienation and turns England into, what Ben Wellings (2008) had termed 'Rump Britain'. This Rump Britain is to all intents and purposes a political veneer of the British state yet is constituted by an overarching ideological and cultural English nationalism. The Conservatives being the de facto English party, campaigning to keep the union together yet politically devolving England whilst at the same time accelerating a particular conceptualisation of English nationalism. This can be typified by, 'attitudes towards Europe, race, the English countryside and the monarchy, all served up in a historical narrative, represent the topography of Rump Britain' (Wellings, 2008:403). This helps to illuminate the backbone of conservative, traditionalist discourse as being in effect entirely Anglo-centric.

The Scottish independence referendum highlighted how problematic and confused a sense of English political and social future is compared to Scotland. This can provide the left within England an opportunity to lead the debate to build a positive, egalitarian and socially just image of a future England within or without the United Kingdom. It has become apparent that a 'No' vote will not inspire and unite a country under a shared vision or purpose. The campaign highlighted the widespread resentment from many conservative quarters over perceived special treatment given to the Scots and has only served to reinforce a defensive sense of embattled Englishness. Right-wing Tories, the conservative press and others on the right will push for further English only powers while further cementing the image of the Scots as troublesome socialists, traitorous and a drain on the national economy.

Devolution is not a new concept or political debate, but it has gained significance in contemporary discussions on Englishness. Devolution greatly influences concepts and discourses of Englishness and English national identity. Factors like the Scottish independence referendum, constitutional arrangements, political power distribution, and the rise of nationalist parties, particularly the SNP, have reinforced dominant conservative views of Englishness. These developments have also created conflicting narratives within the union. Previously peripheral debates on Parliament and English votes for English laws now hold significant importance and contribute to discussions on Englishness. The politicisation of Englishness is evident in the rapid emergence and prominence of EVEL, reflecting ideological and political divisions that have brought about substantial social and constitutional changes.

# Conclusions

This body of work began in 2011 as a doctoral thesis, since then a multitude of events have taken place that not only confirm but indicate the strength and importance that a politicised sense of Englishness now carries. Within the contemporary context, discourses of English national identity operate within a specific framework of insecurity of identity, one that is characterised by a sense of crisis and a defensive exclusivism where concepts of national identity are defined by symbolic lines of demarcation which are ideologically motivated and managed to provide a dominant sense of what England means and what Englishness represents.

As this examination has demonstrated, Englishness is firmly located within a particular conservative disjuncture. It is informed through a specific ideological-based understanding of nationalism and national identity which, although not unique to concepts of Englishness, specifically informs its particular character in relation to key topics of investigation.

The theoretically based analysis of the use of discourse and ideology has provided a means to determine and critically investigate dominant narratives, perspectives and interpretations of Englishness, identity and the forces and processes driving this within the current contemporary moment. Chapter one discussed and sought to demonstrate why discourse theory as a conceptual approach is particularly valuable and appropriate as a means to critically investigate concepts of Englishness. This theoretically based critical examination was also supported by existing and contemporary empirical sources and evidence to highlight the increasingly politicised and conservative nature surrounding concepts and understandings of Englishness. Chapter one also analysed conceptual approaches to nationalism and national identity specifically in relation to theoretically and ideologically situated accounts that characterise a conservative sense of Englishness.

The consequences of this research have produced profound if not unexpected results; an Englishness dominated and largely defined within conservative and traditionalist terms has fed and perpetuates a general national narrative of fear, anxiety and defensiveness. Past certainties of British politics have largely disintegrated, and an overwhelming sense of uncertainty has led many within England to escape to the imaginative certainties of a conservative sense of Englishness. This very particular conservative conceptualisation of Englishness

**Constructing Realities, 191–193**
**Copyright © 2024 Stuart Cartland**
**Published under exclusive licence by Emerald Publishing Limited**
**doi:10.1108/978-1-83797-545-720231009**

draws from and symbolically appropriates particular elements of tradition, history and creates a particular mythscape which is critically examined within chapter three as a means to demonstrate how an ideologically conservative narrative has become the dominant means to understand a sense of Englishness.

Chapter six and seven sought to specifically examine the impact of both the European Union and devolution upon discourses of Englishness. Here it is discussed how a conservative ideological account has come to dominate debate and discursive articulations of Englishness as a defensive response but also how conservative discourses have politicised concepts of Englishness in relation to both a process of devolution and a relationship with the European Union. This cumulative and increasingly rapid process of a distinct politicisation of Englishness can be viewed as being represented by the rise and fall of the UK Independence Party (UKIP) indexed with a shift of the Conservative Party to the right and a jettisoning of a moderate conservative ideological positioning. At the same time the conditions were created for an increasingly antagonistic disengagement from Europe culminating in the referendum and subsequent vote to leave the European Union. An increasingly acrimonious and polarised political environment within the United Kingdom is characterised by an overwhelming dominance of the Conservatives in England, the SNP in Scotland and continued calls to leave the union. At the same time we have witnessed the passing of English Votes for English Laws (EVEL) and an abandonment of Britishness as a primary national identity within England. However, as this body of work has indicated, political domination is only symptomatic of a wider and ongoing conservative discursive dominance within England.

This body of work has developed and analysed how the conservative position has become a dominant discursive narrative that its pre-eminence goes hand-in-hand with concepts or understandings of Englishness in a largely unquestioned, naturalised and normative manner. It is a perspective that has monopolised what Englishness or English national identity constitutes in many instances as a binary opposite to past conceptualisations of Britishness. This is specifically discussed in depth in Chapter four and how it has developed a particular historicised, nostalgic and defensive identity that is often defined against or in opposition to processes of the contemporary era, such as multiculturalism, immigration, cosmopolitan and inclusive narratives, meanwhile developing a particular ideologically defined interpretation of 'common sense'. Chapter five particularly examines how conservative discourse of Englishness operates specifically in relation to and as ideologically constructed accounts of political correctness and multiculturalism. This has developed in a multidirectional manner as both a top-down but also bottom-up non-linear intersectional process informing and directing a particularly symbolic interpretation of the concept of Englishness.

Within the contemporary era, there has been a sustained and ongoing process of a reterritorialisation of Englishness within the context of an assertive and emboldened conservative discursive character. This is located within a reactionary response to a general process of globalisation. Chapter two critically explores and seeks to demonstrate how a process of globalisation has deeply affected conservative notions of Englishness as an ideological (and largely) symbolic but also contradictory response. This particular theoretical field is analysed as a rapidly developing terrain of political, social and cultural flux, uncertainty and conflict as a nodal point of reference. These nodal points of reference have been specifically focused upon and exploited as a means to develop and legitimise a defensive, exclusive and reactionary conceptualisation of Englishness, one justified by particular interpretations and understandings of tradition and historicised national narratives.

This body of work has not sought to find some essentialist or determinist sense of national identity, rather it argues to move away from a defensive, negative and backward looking discourse towards a positive, inclusive and forward looking sense of community. As pointed out, identity formation is problematic and contested especially in a national sense. It is important to understand, as this work has demonstrated, not to be beholden to populism or cultural relativism. The point is not about foisting upon anyone some sort of state-sponsored version of cultural identity, rather it is about recognising the plurality of experience.

It is possible to challenge and formulate an alternative narrative and discourse, one built upon heterogeneity not homogeneity, inclusivity instead of exclusivity, progressiveness instead of reactionism, outward looking instead of being insular, positive towards future possibilities instead of one based upon anxiety and fear. However, in the early 21st century in the United Kingdom, we are in uncharted political and social terrain. Two of the external unions that have facilitated a more progressive and cosmopolitan identity have been rejected within a popular sense in England. We have left the European Union, and the days of the United Kingdom seem to be numbered. Although both of these developments represent the strength of a conservative narrative and discourse of Englishness, it is built upon myth and fantasy and informed through specific ideological constructions that can be uncovered for the socially narrow and historically shallow politicised identity that they represent.

Crucially, the point being that within society and culture, there are constantly shifting conceptualisations of who 'we' are and how these very specific constructions come about. This ultimately means that we are the protagonists but also the products of history, culture and the societies that we inhabit. The crux of the matter is not to create or define some sense of all-encompassing identity – this is both impossible and unwelcome, rather it is to give justice to the heterogeneous experience of community, life and social reality rather than it be used as some sort of ideological tool, as this book has tried to expose.

# Bibliography


Ackroyd, Peter. (2002) *Albion: The Origins of the English Imagination*, London: Chatto and Windus.

Adorno, Theodor. Horkheimer, Max. (1947) 'The Culture Industry: Enlightenment as Mass Deception', *Dialectic of Enlightenment*, Amsterdam: Querido Verlang NV.

Allegretti, Aubrey. (2022) 'Keir Starmer Walks Fine Line in Shifting Labour's Stance on Immigration', *The Guardian*, (23/11/2022). https://www.theguardian.com/politics/2022/nov/23/keir-starmer-walks-fine-line-shifting-labour-stance-immigration

Althusser, Louis. (2012) 'Ideology and Ideological State Apparatuses (Notes Towards an Investigation)', *Mapping Ideology*, ed by Slavoj Zizek, London: Verso.

Anderson, Benedict. (1983/1991) *Imagined Communities: Reflections on the Origin and Spread of Nationalism*, 2nd ed., London: Verso.

Anthias, Floya. Yuval-Davis, Nira. (1993) *Racialized Boundaries: Race, Nation, Gender, Colour and Class and the Anti-Racist Struggle*, Abingdon: Taylor & Francis.

Appadurai, Arjun. (1996) *Modernity at Large; Cultural Dimensions of Globalization*, Minneapolis: University of Minnesota Press.

Appadurai, Arjun. (2001) *Globalization*, ed by Arjun Appadurai, Durham: Duke University Press.

Appadurai, Arjun. (2003) 'Sovereignty Without Territoriality: Notes for a Postnational Geography', *The Anthropology of Space and Place: Locating Culture*, ed by Setha M. Low and Denise Lawrence Zuniga, Oxford: Blackwell Publishing.

Appadurai, Arjun. (2006) *Fear of Small Numbers: An Essay on the Geography of Anger*, Durham: Duke University Press.

Archer, Kevin, Bosman, Martin, Amen, Mark. Schmidt, Ella. (2007) 'Locating Globalizations and Cultures', *Globalizations*, vol. 4, London: Taylor & Francis.

Arendt, Hannah. (1970) *On Violence*, New York: Harcourt, Brace and World.

Armstrong, John. (1982) *Nations Before Nationalism*, Chapel Hill: University of North Carolina Press.

Aughey, Arthur. (2007) *The Politics of Englishness*, Manchester: Manchester University Press.

Aughey, Arthur. (2010) 'National Identity, Allegiance and Constitutional Change in the United Kingdom', *Nations and Nationalism*, *16* (2).

Aughey, Arthur. Berberich, Christine. (2011) *These Englands*, ed by Arthur Aughey and Christine Berberich, Manchester: Manchester University Press.

Balibar, Etienne. (1991) 'The Nation Form: History and Ideology', *Race, Nation, Class Ambiguous Identities*, ed by Etienne Balibar and Immanuel Wallerstein, London: Verso.

Balibar, Etienne. (2002) *Politics and the Other Scene*, London: Verso.

Barrett, Michele. (1994) 'Ideology, Politics, Hegemony: From Gramsci to Laclau and Mouffe', *Mapping Ideology*, ed by Slavoj Zizek, London: Verso.
Barthes, Roland. (1957) *Mythologies*, Paris: Editions du Seuil.
Baudrillard, Jean. (1994) *Simulacra and Simulation*, Ann Arbor: University of Michigan Press.
Baumann, Gerd. (1996) *Contesting Culture*, Cambridge: Cambridge University Press.
Bauman, Zygmunt. (2008) 'Identity for Identity's Sake Is a Bit Dodgy…', *Soundings on Race, Identity and Belonging*, ed by Sally Davison and Jonathan Rutherford, London: Lawrence and Wishart.
Bauman, Zygmunt. (2016) 'Zygmunt Bauman: Behind the World's 'Crisis of Humanity'', Al Jazeera, www.aljazeera.com/programmes/talktojazeera/zygmunt-bauman-worl-crisis-humanity-160722085342260.html
BBC Education. (2014) 'Social Mobility and Child Poverty Commission Study', BBC, www.bbc.co.uk/news/education-28953881
BBC Education. (2014c) 'Social Mobility and Child Poverty Commission Study', BBC, www.bbc.co.uk/news/education-28953881
BBC News. (1999) 'Tunbridge Wells: The Spiritual Home of Middle England', BBC, http://news.bbc.co.uk/1/hi/special_report/1999/02/99/e-cyclopedia/318036.stm
BBC News. (2011) 'State Multiculturalism Has Failed, Says David Cameron', BBC, http://www.bbc.co.uk/news/uk-politics-12371994
BBC News. (2013a) 'UKIP Councillor Victoria Ayling Defends Immigrant Comments', BBC, http://www.bbc.co.uk/news/uk-politics-25288162
BBC News. (2014b) 'Deeply Elitist UK Locks Out Diversity at Top', BBC, http://www.bbc.co.uk/news/education-28953881
BBC News. (2015b) 'Nicola Sturgeon: David Cameron 'Living on Borrowed Time', BBC, www.bbc.co.uk/news/uk-scotland-scotland-politics-34283944
BBC News. (2015d) 'Scotland Independence Referendum Inevitable Says Salmond', BBC, http://www.bbc.co.uk/news/uk-scotland-scotland-politics-33668002
BBC News. (2020) 'Coronavirus: Johnson on "Good Solid British Common Sense"', BBC, https://www.bbc.co.uk/news/av/uk-politics-52620312
BBC News. (2021) 'EU Referendum: The Results in Maps and Charts', BBC, https://www.bbc.co.uk/news/uk-politics-36616028
BBC News. (2022) 'Brits Abroad', BBC, http://news.bbc.co.uk/1/shared/spl/hi/in_depth/brits_abroad/html/
BBC Politics. (2014a) 'In Full: Warsi's Resignation Letter and Cameron's Response', BBC, http://www.bbc.co.uk/news/uk-politics-28657623
BBC Politics. (2015c) 'English Vote Plan to Become Law Despite Objections', BBC, www.bbc.co.uk/news/uk-politics-34599998
BBC Politics. (2015a) 'Obama Urges UK to Stay in European Union', BBC, www.bbc.co.uk/news/uk-politics-33647154
Beck, Ulrich. (2001) *What Is Globalization?* Cambridge: Polity Press.
Behr, Rafael. (2016) 'A Liberal Sigh of Disdain Could See Us Tumble Out of Europe', *The Guardian*, (04/05/2016).
Bennett, Tony. (1982) 'James Bond as a Popular Hero', *Politics, Ideology and Popular Culture 2*, Maidenhead: Open University Press.
Bhabha, Homi. (1990) *Nation and Narration*, London: Routledge.
Bielfeld, Uli. (1992) '*Popularer Extremismus der Mitte. Die Neuen Legitimations Probleme in Deutschland*', *Frankfurter Randschau*, (05/12/1992).

Billig, Michael. (1995) *Banal Nationalism*, London: Sage.

Black, Jeremy. (1994) *Convergence or Divergence? Britain and the Continent*, London: Macmillan.

Blinder, Scott. Richards, Lindsay. (2020) 'UK Public Opinion toward Immigration: Overall Attitudes and Level of Concern', *The Migration Observatory*, (20/02/2020), https://migrationobservatory.ox.ac.uk/resources/briefings/uk-public-opinion-toward-immigration-overall-attitudes-and-level-of-concern/

Boffey, Daniel. (2014) 'Senior Members Backed Pact With BNP', *The Observer*, (08/03/2104).

Boffey, Daniel. O'Carroll, Lisa. (2020) 'UK and EU Agree Brexit Trade Deal', *The Guardian*, (24/12/2020), https://www.theguardian.com/politics/2020/dec/24/uk-eu-agree-brexit-trade-deal-agreement

Bond, Ross, McCrone, David. Brown, Alice. (2003) 'National Identity and Economic Development: Reiteration, Recapture, Reinterpretation and Repudiation', *Nations and Nationalism*, vol. 9, No.3, Chichester: Wiley- Blackwell.

Bond, Ross, Jeffery, Charlie. Rosie, Michael. (2010) 'The Importance of Being English: National Identity and Nationalism in Post-Devolution England', *Nations and Nationalism, 16* (3).

Breuilly, John. (1996) 'Approaches to Nationalism', *Mapping the Nation*, ed by G. Balakrishnan, London: Verso.

Brinkley, Douglas. (1990) 'Dean Acheson and the 'Special Relationship': The West Point Speech of December 1962', *The Historical Journal, 33*, 3, https://www.cambridge.org/core/journals/historical-journal/article/dean-acheson-and-the-special-relationship-the-west-point-speech-of-december-1962/85DBA80C460E651B7A3981B511ECFF44

Brooker, Charlie. (2014) 'The News Can't Get Enough of Nigel Farage Because He Adds a Bit of Colour, Which Is Ironic Considering What He Represents', in G2, *The Guardian*, (20/05/2014).

Brooker, Charlie. (2014) 'No Wonder Cameron Wants to Celebrate the Magna Carta – Back Then Plebs Had the Same Human Rights as a Parsnip', *The Guardian*, http://www.theguardian.com/commentisfree/2014/jun/16/david-cameron-britishness-charlie-brooker

Brooks, Libby. (2019) 'Nicola Sturgeon Says Scotland Cannot Be Imprisoned in the UK', *The Guardian*, (15/12/2019), https://www.theguardian.com/politics/2019/dec/15/nicola-sturgeon-scotland-cannot-be-imprisoned-in-uk

Brown, Gordon. (2015) 'Britain's Already Fragile Union Is at Risk–Not from Scotland but Its Own Government', *The Guardian*, http://www.theguardian.com/commentisfree/2015/jun/12/scottish/independence

Brown, Gordon. (2016) 'Leading, Not Leaving', *New Statesman*, 10–16 June, London.

Burns, Judith. (2014) 'Deeply Elitist UK Locks Out Diversity at Top', BBC News, http://www.bbc.co.uk/news/education-28953881

Butler, Judith. (1990) *Gender Trouble: Feminism and the Subversion of Identity*, London: Routledge.

Butler, Judith. (2000) 'Restaging the Universal', *Contingency, Hegemony, Universality Contemporary Dialogues on the Left*, ed by Judith Butler, Ernesto Laclau and Slavoj Zizek, London: Verso.

Byrne, Bridget. (2007) 'Crisis of Identity? Englishness, Britishness and Whiteness', *Empire and After: Englishness in Postcolonial Perspective*, ed by Graham McPhee and Prem Poddar, Oxford: Bergham.

Cable, Vince. (2015) 'The Audacity of Fear', *New Statesman*, 22–28 May 2015.

Calhoun, Craig. (1993) 'Nationalism and Ethnicity', *Annual Review of Sociology*, vol. 9, http://www.jstor.org/stable/2083387

Calhoun, Craig. (1997) *Nationalism*, Buckingham: Open University Press.

Calhoun, Craig. (1997) 'Nationalism and the Public Sphere', *Public and Private in Thought and Practice. Perspectives on a Grand Dichotomy*, ed by Jeff Weintraub and Krishnan Kumar, Chicago: University of Chicago Press.

Calhoun, Craig. (2008) 'Cosmopolitanism and Nationalism', *Nations and Nationalism*, vol. 14, No.3, Chichester: Wiley-Blackwell.

Cameron, Angus. Palan, Rowen. (2004) *The Imagined Economies of Globalization*, London: Sage.

Carr, Edward Hallett. (1964) *What Is History?* Harmondsworth: Penguin.

Carrell, Severin. (2013) 'Gordon Brown: Conservatives Close to Being 'Powellite' on Immigration', *The Guardian*, https://www.theguardian.com/politics/2013/may/13/gordon-brown-tories-powellite-over-immigration#comment-23505212

Carrell, Severin. (2015) 'Sturgeon: Scrap Cuts and Trident or Face Another Vote on Independence', *The Guardian*, https://www.theguardian.com/politics/2015/sep/18/sturgeon-scrap-cuts-trident-another-vote-independence

Cartland, Stuart. (2018) 'Will England's World Cup Success Embolden Nationalist Brexiteers? You Better Believe It', Culture Matters, (04/07/2018), http://www.culturematters.org.uk/index.php/culture/sport/item/2848-will-england-s-world-cup-success-embolden-nationalist-brexiteers-you-better-believe-it

Cartland, Stuart. (2021) '2001: Revisiting the "Death" of Multiculturalism', Renewal, https://renewal.org.uk/2001-revisiting-the-death-of-multiculturalism/

Cartland, Stuart. (2023) 'Conditioning the National Discourse: Self-Censorship at the BBC', Culture Matters, (15/03/2023), https://www.culturematters.org.uk/index.php/culture/tv/item/4184-conditioning-the-national-discourse-self-censorship-at-the-bbc

Carvel, John. (2004) 'Tebbit's Cricket Loyalty Test Hit for Six', *The Guardian*, (08/01/2004), https://www.theguardian.com/uk/2004/jan/08/britishidentity.race

Castells, Manuel. (1996) *The Rise of Network Society*, Oxford: Blackwell.

Chatterjee, Partha. (1993) *The Nation and Its Fragments: Colonial and Postcolonial Histories*, Princeton: Princeton University Press.

Chatterjee, Partha. (2000) 'Whose Imagined Community', *Mapping the Nation*, ed by Gopal Balakrishnan, London: Verso.

Chesterton, G.K. (1908) *All Things Considered*, London: Methuen & Co.

Choi, Jung-Bong. (2002) 'Critical Essays and Reviews', *Journal of Communication Inquiry*, Thousand Oaks: Sage.

Chowdhury, Kanishka. (2002) 'Its All Within Your Reach: Globalization and the Ideologies of Postnationalism and Hybridity', *Cultural Logic: A Journal of Marxist Theory and Practise*, https://ojs.library.ubc.ca/index.php/clogic/article/download/191929/188886/218863

Clark, J.C.D. (1990) 'The History of Britain: A Composite State in a Europe Des Parties?' *Ideas and Politics in Modern Britain*, ed by J.C.D. Clark, Basingstoke: Macmillan.

Coates, Sam. MacDonell, Hamish. (2015) 'We Will Hold UK Defence to Ransom, SNP Warns', *The Times*, (20/04/2016), https://www.thetimes.co.uk/article/we-will-hold-uk-defence-to-ransom-snp-warns-m730kngfr7p

Cohen, Nick. (2015) 'Beware the Siren Calls of Nationalism', *The Guardian*, (02/05/2015).

Colley, Linda. (1992) *Britons: Forging the Nation 1707–1837*, New Haven, CT: Yale University Press.

Colley, Linda. (2003) *Britons, Forging the Nation 1707–1837*, London: Pimlico.

Colley, Linda. (2016) 'An Island, but Not in Isolation', *New Statesman*, 10–16 June, London.

Condor, Susan. (2006) 'Temporality and Collectivity: Diversity, History and the Rhetorical Construction of National Entitativity', *British Journal of Social Psychology*, No.45.

Condor, Susan, Gibson, Stephen. Abell, Jackie. (2006) 'English Identity and Ethnic Diversity in the Context of UK Constitutional Change', *Ethnicities, vol.6*, London: Sage.

Condor, Susan. (2010) 'Devolution and National Identity: The Rules of English (dis) Engagement', *Nations and Nationalism, 16* (3).

Cook, Robin. (2001) 'Robin Cook's Chicken Tikka Masala Speech', *The Guardian*, http://www.theguardian.com/world/2001/apr/19/race.britishidentity

Copjec, Joan. (2015) *Read My Desire. Lacan Against the Historicists*, London: Verso.

Cowley, Jason. (2014) 'A Shattered Union. Are These the Last Days of Great Britain?' *New Statesman*, 12–18 September 2014.

Craib, I. (1984) *Modern Social Theory from Parsons to Habermas*, Brighton: Wheatsheaf.

Crick, B. (1991) 'The English and the British', *National Identities, the Constitution of the United Kingdom*, ed by B. Crick, Oxford: Blackwell.

Curtis, John. (2009) *Is There An English Backlash? Reactions to Devolution*, British Social Attitudes: The 25th Report, SAGE, https://sk.sagepub.com/books/british-social-attitudes-25th/n1.xml

Daily Mail. (2012) 'London 2012 Olympics: Plastic Brits Insult Our Games', *Daily Mail*, http://www.dailymail.co.uk/sport/article-2112899/London-2012-Olympics-Plastic-Brits-insult-Games–Des-Kelly.html

Daily Mail. (2013) 'The Man Who Hated Britain: Red Ed's Pledge to Bring Back Socialism Is a Homage to His Marxist Father. So What Did Miliband Snr Really Believe In? The Answer Should Disturb Everyone Who Loves This Country', *Daily Mail*, http://www.dailymail.co.uk/news/article-2435751/Red-Eds-pledge-bring-socialism-homage-Marxist-father-Ralph-Miliband-says-GEOFFREY-LEVY.html

Daily Mail. (2014a) 'Purge of the Middle Aged Men', *Daily Mail*, http://www.pressdisplay.com/pressdisplay/viewer.aspx

Daily Mail. (2014b) 'Put UK Flood Victims First', *Daily Mail*, (11/02/2014).

Daily Mail. (2021) 'Among the Mosques: Author's Study of Muslim Britain Reveals a No-Go Area for White People, Children "Attacked for Being White", Parents Making Families Live under Taliban-like Rules an Women Who Can't Leave Home with Our Permission', *Daily Mail*, (04/06/2021), https://www.dailymail.co.uk/femail/article-9648477/Author-visited-Muslim-mosques-Britain-reveals-no-areas-white-men.html

Daily Express. (2014) 'Farage on Friday: Lets Demand EU Cashback and Divert Foreign Aid for Flood Victims', *Daily Express*, www.express.co.uk/news/uk/458527/FARAGE-ON-FRIDAY-lets-demand-EU-cashback-and-divert-foreign-aid-for-flood-victims

Daily Telegraph. (2013) 'Why Turn the Other Cheek to Those Who Hate Us?' *Daily Telegraph*, http://www.telegraph.co.uk/news/worldnews/africaandindianocean/kenya/10333477/After-Kenya-no-more-turning-the-other-cheek-to-those-who-hate-us.html

Day, Gary. (2011) 'The Changing Face of Englishness: History, Culture and Character', *These Englands*, ed by Christene Berberich and Arthur Aughey, Manchester: Manchester University Press.

Debord, Guy. (1998) *Comments on the Society of the Spectacle*, London: Verso.

Denham, John. (2018) 'A Nation Divided? The Identities, Politics and Governance of England', *Open Democracy*, (16/08/2018), https://www.opendemocracy.net/en/opendemocracyuk/nation-divided-identities-politics-and-governance-of-england/

Denham, John. (2021) 'Why Does the State Say You Can Be Black and Welsh but Not Black and English?' Centre for English Identity Politics, (11/03/2021), https://www.southampton.ac.uk/ceip/publications/ethnic-identity-in-the-census.page

Derrida, Jaques. (1967) 'Of Grammatology', translated by Gayatari Spivak. https://monoskop.org/images/8/8e/Derrida_Jacques_Of_Grammatology_1998.pdf

Diez, Thomas. (2001) 'Europe as a Discursive Battleground: Discourse Analysis and European Integration Studies', *Cooperation and Conflict*, *36* (1), SAGE.

Diez, Thomas. (2012) 'Europe as a Discursive Battleground. Discourse Analysis and European Integration Studies', *SAGE Social Science Collections, Co-Operation and Conflict*, London: Sage.

Ditum, Sarah. (2014) 'Tweeting a Picture of a House Is Not an Act of Class Warfare, Whatever the Sun Says', *New Statesman*, www.newstatesman.com/politics/2014/11/tweeting-a-picture-house-not-act-class-warfare-whatever-sun-says

Driver, Stephen. Martell, Luke. (2001) 'Blair and Britishness', *British Cultural Studies*, ed by David Morely and Kevin Robbins, Oxford: Oxford University Press.

Dunin-Wasowicz, Roch. (2019) 'Is It the English Question – Or the British Question? Three Strands of Britishness', *LSE*, https://blogs.lse.ac.uk/brexit/2019/02/14/is-it-the-english-question-or-the-british-question-the-three-strands-of-britishness/

Eagleton, Terry. (1991) 'Marxist Criticism', *Literature in the Modern World: Critical Essays and Documents*, ed by Dennis Walder, Oxford: Oxford University Press.

Easthorpe, Anthony. (1999) *Englishness and National Culture*, London: Routledge.

Eaton, George. (2014) 'David Cameron's Reshuffle Has Culled the Tory Left', *New Statesman*, http://www.newstatesman.com/politics/2014/07/george-eaton-david-camerons-reshuffle-has-culled-tory-left

Eaton, George. (2015) 'Even If Miliband Is a Second-Placed Prime Minister, It Would Still Be a Victory for Labour to Savour', *New Statesman*, 24–30 April 2015.

Eaton, George. (2016) 'Boris Johnson Backs EU Withdrawal – The Right Choice for Him', *New Statesman*, www.newstatesman.com/politics/uk/2016/02/boris-johnson-backs-eu-withdrawl-right-choice-him

Edensor, Tim. (2002) 'Conceptualising Identity', *National Identity, Popular Culture and Everyday Life*, Oxford: Berg.

Erel, Umut. (2011) 'Complex Belonging: Racialization and Migration in a Small English City', *Nations and Nationalism*, http://doi.org/10.1080/01419870.2011.574715

Fanon, Frantz. (1963) *The Wretched of the Earth*, New York: Grove.

Ferguson, Niall. (2002) *Empire; How Britain Made the Modern World*, Harmondsworth: Penguin.

Fontana, Benedetto. (2005) 'The Democratic Philosopher: Rhetoric as Hegemony in Gramsci', http://muse.jhu.edu/journals/itc/summary/v023/23.1fontana.html

Ford, Robert. Goodwin, Matthew. (2014) *Revolt on the Right*, London: Routledge.

Forrest, Adam. (2019) 'Boris Johnson Says Describing Black People as Having "Watermelon Smiles" Was "Wholly Satirical"', *The Independent*, https://www.independent.co.uk/news/uk/politics/boris-johnson-conservative-leadership-latest-racism-watermelon-smiles-satirical-a8981166.html

Fothergill, Lucas. (2022) 'Census Reveals New Chapter in Story of Mixed-Race Britain', Migration Museum, https://www.migrationmuseum.org/census-reveals-new-chapter-in-story-of-mixed-race-britain/

Foucault, Michel. (1972) *The Archeology of Knowledge*, London: Tavistock.

Foucault, Michel. (1980) *Power/Knowledge*, Brighton: Harvester.

Fulford, F. (2005) 'Why England Is F*****', *Daily Mail*, (26/11/2005).

Gamble, Andrew. (2016) 'The Conservatives and the Union: The 'New English Toryism' and the Origins of Anglo-Britishness', *Political Studies Association, SAGE*, vol.*14* (3).

Gikandi, Simon. (1996) *Maps of Englishness*, New York: Columbia University Press.

Gilbert, Jeremy. (2014) 'Populism and the Left: Does UKIP Matter? Can Democracy Be Saved?' New Left Project, www.newleftproject.org/index.php/site/article_comments/populism_and_the_left_does_UKIP_matter_can_democracy_be_saved

Gills, B.K. (2010) 'The Return of Crisis in the Era of Globalization: One Crisis, or Many?' *Globalizations*, vol. 7, No.1–2, Routledge, http://www.tni.org/sites/www.tni.org/files/BarryGills_Globalizs_special.pdf

Gilroy, Paul. (2002) *There Ain't No Black in the Union Jack*, London: Routledge.

Gilroy, Paul. (2004) *Between Camps: Nations, Cultures and the Allure of Race*, London: Routledge.

Gilroy, Paul. (2004) 'The English Identity Crisis: Who Do You Think You Are?' *The Observer*, ed by A. Hill, (13/6/2004).

Gilroy, Paul. (2004) *After Empire: Melancholia or Convivial Culture?* Abingdon: Routledge.

Gilroy, Paul. (2005) *Postcolonial Melancholia*, New York: Columbia University Press.

Goodwin, Matthew. Heath, Oliver. (2016) 'Brexit Vote Explained: Poverty, Low Skills and Lack of Opportunities', *Joseph Rowntree Foundation*, https://www.jrf.org.uk/report/brexit-vote-explained-poverty-low-skills-and-lack-opportunities

Greenslade, Roy. (2016) 'Study Confirms That the National Press Is Biased in Favour of Brexit', *The Guardian*, http://www.theguardian.com/media/greenslade/2016/may/23/study-confirms-that-the-national-press-is-biased-in-favour-of-brexit

Grierson, Jamie. (2021) 'Backlash After Priti Patel Rebukes Media Over Channel "Migrants" Label', *The Guardian*, https://www.theguardian.com/politics/2021/nov/25/backlash-after-priti-patel-rebukes-media-over-channel-migrants-label

Grimes, Darren. (2023) 'The UK's Offering Shelter to Terrorists. It's Time to Put Britons' First, Says Darren Grimes', GB News, (11/04/2023), https://www.gbnews.com/opinion/illegal-immigration-latest-terrorist-shelter-darren-grimes

Habermas, Jurgen. (1985) 'Modernity—An Incomplete Project', *Postmodern Culture*, ed by Hal Foster, London: Pluto Press.

Habermas, Jurgen. (2000) 'The European Nation-State. Its Achievements and Its Limits. On the Past and Future of Sovereignty and Citizenship', *Mapping the Nation*, ed by Gopal Balakrishnan, London: Verso.

Hall, Catherine. (2001) 'British Cultural Identities and the Legacy of Empire', *British Cultural Studies*, ed by David Morely and Kevin Robbins, Oxford: Oxford University Press.

Hall, Stuart. (1977) 'Culture, the Media and the Ideological Effect', *Mass Communications and Society*, ed by J Curran, London: Edward Arnold.

Hall, Stuart. Jaques, Martin. (1983) *The Politics of Thatchersim*, Lawrence and Whishart in Association with Marxism Today.

Hall, Stuart. (1988) 'The Great Moving Right Show', *The Hard Road to Renewel*, London: Verso.

Hall, Stuart. (1991) 'Old and New Identities, Old and New Ethnicities', *Culture, Globalization and the World-System*, ed by Anthony King, London: Macmillan.

Hall, Stuart. (1992) 'The Question of Cultural Identity', *Modernity and Its Futures*, ed by Stuart Hall and T. McGrew, Cambridge: Polity Press.

Hall, Stuart. (1994) 'The West and the Rest: Discourse and Power', *Formations of Modernity*, ed by Stuart Hall and Bram Gieben, Trowbridge: The Open University.

Hall, Stuart. (1995) 'National Cultures as "Imagined Communities"', *Modernity, an Introduction to Modern Societies*, ed by Stuart Hall, David Held, Don Hubert and Kenneth Thompson, Oxford: Blackwell.

Hall, Stuart. (1997) 'Representation and the Media', Media Education Foundation Transcript, http://www.mediaed.org/assets/products/409/transcript_409.pdf

Hall, Stuart. (1997) 'The Local and the Global: Globalization and Ethnicity', *Dangerous Liaisons, Gender, Nation and Postcolonial Perspectives*, ed by Anne McClintock, Amir Mufti and Ella Shoat, Minneapolis: University of Minnesota Press.

Hall, Stuart. (2005) 'Whose Heritage?' *The Politics of Heritage*, ed by Jo Littler and Roshi Naidoo, London: Routledge.

Hall, Stuart. (2007) 'Living with Difference, Stuart Hall in Conversation with Bill Schwarz', Soundings, http://www.lwbooks.co.uk/register.php?r=journals/soundings/articles/15s37hallschwarz.pdf

Hall, Stuart. Massey, Doreen. (2010) 'Interpreting the Crisis', *Soundings on the Neoliberal Crisis*, ed by Jonathan Rutherford and Sally Davison, http://www.lwbooks.co.uk/ebooks/The_Neoliberal_Crisis.pdf

Hall, Stuart. (2010) 'The Local and the Global: Globalization and Ethnicity', *Dangerous Liasions, Gender, Nation and Postcolonial Perspectives*, ed by Anne McClintock, Amir Mufti and Ella Shohat, Minneapolis: University of Minnesota Press.

Han, Byung-Chul. (2023) *Hyperculture*, Cambridge: Polity.

Harris, Erika. (2016) 'Why Has Nationalism Not Run Its Course?' *Nations and Nationalism*, *22* (2), Chichester: Wiley-Blackwell.

Harris, John. (2014) 'England's Identity Crisis: What Does It Mean to Be English?' *The Guardian*, http://www.theguardian.com/uk-news/2014/may/20/england-identity-crisis-english-euro-scottish-elections-ukip-patriotism

Harris, Kate. (2021) 'Five Get Cancelled! Enid Blyton's Work "Racist and Xenophobic", Says English Heritage', Daily Express, (17/06/2021), https://www.express.co.uk/news/uk/1451019/enid-blyton-racist-books-english-heritage-famous-five-noddy-secret-seven

Hasan, Mehdi. (2011) 'How We Rub along Together: When My Father Arrived in England in the Sixties, He Was Welcomed With Dog Mess through His Letter Box and Enoch Powell on the TV, Writes Mehdi Hasan. We've Come a Long Way Since Then So Why Do Politicians Claim That Multiculturalism Has Failed?' New Statesman, https://www.newstatesman.com/long-reads/2011/04/multiculturalism-british

Hastings, A. (1998) 'Connecting Linguistic Structures and Social Practices: A Discursive Approach to Social Policy Analysis', *Journal of Social Policy*.

Hatherley, Owen. (2017) *The Ministry of Nostalgia*, London: Verso.

Hazell, R. (2006) 'The English Question', *Publius: The Journal of Federalism, 36*.

Heath, Anthony. Demireva, Neal. (2014) 'Has Multiculturalism Failed in Britain?' *Ethnic and Racial Studies*, http://doi.org/10.1080/01419870.2013.808754

Heffer, Simon. (2015) 'Lessons from the Locust Years', *New Statesman*, 22–28 May, London.

Heilbronner, Oded. (2012) 'In Search of the English Psyche', English Studies, http://doi.org/10.1080/0013838X.2011.638449

Held, D. McGrew, A. Goldblatt, D. Rerraton, J. (1999) *Global Transformations*, Cambridge: Polity Press.

Helm, Toby. (2013) 'Immigration Fears Are Being Stoked by Politicians, Says Bishop', The Observer, http://www.theguardian.com/uk/2013/mar/23/immigration-fears-stoked-politicians-bishop

Herman, Luc. Vervaeck, Bart. (2007) 'Ideology and Narrative', *The Cambridge Companion to Narrative*, ed by David Herman, Cambridge: Cambridge University Press.

Hobsbawm, Eric. (1983) 'Falklands Fallout', *Marxism Today*, Jan 1983.

Hobsbawm, Eric. Ranger, Terence. (1983) *The Invention of Tradition*, Cambridge: Cambridge University Press.

Holton, Robert. (1998) *Globalization and the Nation-State*, Basingstoke: MacMillan Press.

Holton, Robert. (2005) *Making Globalization*, Basingstoke: Palgrave Macmillan.

Hopper, Paul. (2006) *Living With Globalization*, Oxford: Berg.

Hopper, Paul. (2007) *Understanding Cultural Globalization*, Cambridge: Polity Press.

Horton, Helena. (2023) 'BBC Will Not Broadcast Attenborough Episode Over Fear of "Rightwing Backlash"', *The Guardian*, https://www.theguardian.com/media/2023/mar/10/david-attenborough-bbc-wild-isles-episode-rightwing-backlash-fears#:~:text=The%20BBC%20has%20decided%20not,the%20Guardian%20has%20been%20told

Hosking, Geoffrey. (2016) 'Why Has Nationalism Revived in Europe? The Symbolic Attractions and Fiscal Capabilities of the Nation-State', *Nations and Nationalism, 22* (2), Chichester: Wiley-Blackwell.

Hough, Andrew. (2012) 'Simon Schama Attacks Downton Abbey as Silvered Tureen of Snobbery', *Daily Telegraph*, http://www.telegraph.co.uk/culture/tvandradio/downton-abbey/9022087/Simon-Schama-attacks-Downton-Abbey-as-silvered-tureen-of-snobbery.html

Hutchinson, John. (2005) *Nations as Zones of Conflict*, London: Sage.

Hylland Eriksen, Thomas. (2002) *Ethnicity and Nationalism*, London: Pluto Press.

Ipsos, Mori. (2007) *Young People and Britishness; Survey for Camelot Foundation*, London: Ipsos Mori.

Ishiguro, Kazuo. (1989) *Remains of the Day*, London: Faber and Faber.

Jameson, Frederic. (1985) 'Postmodernism and Consumer Society', *Postmodern Culture*, ed by Hal Foster, London: Pluto Press.

Jameson, Frederic. (2007) *Late Marxism: Adorno or the Perspective of the Dialectic*, London: Verso.

Jefferies, Stuart. (2014) 'Patriot Games: How Toxic Is the England Flag Today?' *The Guardian*, www.theguardian.com/uk-news/2014/nov/26/patriot-games-battle-for-flag-of-st-george-english-identity

Jeffery, Charlie, Henderson, Ailsa, Scully, Roger. Jones, Richard Wyn. (2016) 'England's Dissatisfactions and the Conservative Dilemma', *Political Studies Association, 14* (3) SAGE.

Jeffery, Charlie. Wyn Jones, Richard. Henderson, Ailsa. Scully, Roger. Lodge, Guy. (2014) *Taking England Seriously: The New English Politics, The Future of England Survey*, https://www.centreonconstitutionalchange.ac.uk/sites/default/files/migrated/papers/taking_england_seriously.pdf

Johnson, Boris. (2016) 'The EU Wants a Superstate, Just as Hitler Did', The Telegraph, http://www.telegraph.co.uk/news/2016/05/14/boris-johnson-the-eu-wants-a-superstate-just-as-hitler-did/

Johnson, Boris. (2018) 'Denmark Has Got It Wrong. Yes, the Burka Is Oppressive and Ridiculous–But That's Still Not the Reason to Ban It', Daily Telegraph, https://www.telegraph.co.uk/news/2018/08/05/denmark-has-got-wrong-yes-burka-oppressive-ridiculous-still/

Jones, Jonathan. (2012) 'From Hockney to Downton Abbey: Have Cultural Tastes Gone Conservative?' *The Guardian*, https://www.theguardian.com/artanddesign/jonathanjonesblog/2012/jan/23/hockney-downton-abbey-culture-conservative

Jones, Jonathan. (2013) 'From Hockney to Downton Abbey: Have Our Cultural Tastes Gone Conservative?' *The Guardian*, http://www.theguardian.com/artanddesign/jonathanjonesblog/2012/jan/23/hockney-downton-abbey-culture-conservative

Jones, Owen. (2014) 'Grant Schapps' Beer and Bingo' Is the Final Nail in Working Class Toryism', *The Guardian*, www.theguardian.com/commentisfree/2014/mar/20/grant-schapps-beer-and-bingo-working-class-toryism

Jones, Owen. (2014) 'Rochester By-Election: Beliefs of Ukip Voters Are Soaked in Leftwing Popularism', *The Guardian*, www.theguardian.com/politics/commentisfree/2014/nov/21/rochester-byelection-beliefs-of-ukip-voters

Jones, Owen. (2014) 'Operation Get Nigel Farage Is Politics of the Lowest Form', *The Guardian*, www.theguardian.com/commentisfree/2014/mar/13/operation-get-nigel-farage-lowest-politics-ukip-smear

Jones, Owen. (2014) *The Establishment and How They Get Away With It*, London: Allen Lane.

Jones, Owen. (2015) 'English Nationalism Is Out of the Bottle Whoever Wins', *The Guardian*, (05/05/2015).

Joseph Rowntree Foundation. (2023) 'UK Poverty 2023: The Essential Guide to Understanding Poverty in the UK', https://www.jrf.org.uk/report/uk-poverty-2023#key-findings

Kavanagh, Trevor. (2023) 'Rishi Sunak Is Battling Britain's No1 Foe – The Empire of Woke', The Sun, https://www.thesun.co.uk/news/21053474/rishi-sunak-declares-war-on-woke/

Kazin, M. (1998) *The Popularist Persuasion*, Ithaca: Cornell University Press.

Kellner, Douglas. (1992) 'Popular Culture and the Construction of Postmodern Identities', *Modernity and Identity*, ed by Scott Lash and Johnathan Friedman, Oxford: Blackwell.

Kennedy, Joe. (2018) *Authentocrats*, London: Repeater.

Kenny, Michael. (2012) 'The Many Faces of Englishness. Identity, Diversity and Nationhood in England', *Public Policy Research*, *19* (3).

Kenny, Michael. (2014) 'Rise Now and be a Nation Again?' *The Politics of Englishness, Renewal*, *22*, https://renewal.org.uk/wp-content/uploads/2020/09/englishness_roundtable_final-1.pdf

Kenny, Michael. (2015) 'Englishness Politicised?: Unpicking the Normative Implications of the McKay Commission', *The British Journal of Politics & International Relations*, *17*.

Kenny, Michael. (2016) 'The Politicisation of Englishness: Towards a Framework for Political Analysis', *Political Studies Association*, *14* (2) SAGE.

Kenny, Michael. (2016) 'The Rise of Political Englishness?' *Political Insight*, www.psa.ac.uk/print/18551

Kenny, Michael. Pearce, Nick. (2015) 'The Rise of the Anglosphere: How the Right Dreamed up a New Conservative World Order', New Statesman, www.newstatesman.com/politics/2015/02/rise-anglosphere-how-right-dreamed-new-conservative-world-order

Kettle, Martin. (2015) 'Britain Is Slowly Breaking Up Yet It Seems No One Cares', *The Guardian*, (06/02/2016).

King, Anthony. (1991) *Culture, Globalization and the World System*, Basingstoke: Macmillan.

Koobak, Redi. Thapar-Bjorkert, Suruchi. (2012) 'Open Space, Becoming Swedish: Locating the Paradoxes of In/Visible Identities', *The Feminist Review*, No.102, ed by The Feminist Review Collective, Basingstoke: Palgrave Macmillan.

Kong, L. Yeoh, B. (1997) 'The Construction of National Identity through the Production of Ritual and Spectacle: An Analysis of National Day Parades in Singapore', *Political Geography*, *3* (16).

Kumar, Krishan. (2001) 'Englishness and English National Identity', *British Cultural Studies*, ed by David Morley and Kevin Robbins, Oxford: Oxford University Press.

Kumar, Krishan. (2003) 'Britain, England and Europe. Cultures in Contraflow', *European Journal of Social Theory*, (*6*), London: Sage.

Kumar, Krishan. (2003) *The Making of English National Identity*, Cambridge: Cambridge University Press.

Kumar, Krishan. (2006) 'Empire and English Nationalism', *Nations and Nationalism*, *12* (1).

Kundnani, A. (2007) *The End of Tolerance? Racism in 21st Century*, Britain, London: Pluto.

Kwarteng, Kwasi. (2016) PM, BBC Radio 4, (09/05/2016).

Laclau, Ernesto. (1977) *Politics and Ideology in Marxist Theory: Capitalism, Fascism, Popularism*, London: Verso.

Laclau, Ernesto. Mouffe, Chantal. (1985) *Hegemony and Socialist Strategy*, London: Verso.

Laclau, Ernesto. (1989) 'Politics and the Limits of Modernity', Social Text, No. 21. *Universal Abandon? The Politics of Postmodernism*, Duke University Press, http://www.jstor.org/stable/827809

Laclau, Ernesto. (1990) *New Reflections of the Revolution of Our Time*, London: Verso.

Laclau, Ernesto. (1996) *Emancipation(s)*, London: Verso.

Laclau, Ernesto. (1997) 'The Death and Resurrection of the Theory of Ideology', *Modern Language Notes*, *112* (3), German Issue (April 1997), www.jstor.org/stable/3251278

Laclau, Ernesto. (2000) 'Identity and Hegemony: The Role of Universality in the Constitution of Political Logics', *Contingency, Hegemony, Universality Contemporary Dialogues on the Left*, ed by Judith Butler, Ernesto Laclau and Slavoj Zizek, London: Verso.

Langlands, Rebecca. (1999) 'Britishness or Englishness? The Historical Problem of National Identity in Britain', *Nations and Nationalism*, *5* (1), ASEN/Blackwell Publishing.

Leadbeater, Charles. (2016) 'Meaning over Money: How the Left Can Win Back the 'Leavers'', *New Statesman*, 8–14 July.

Leddy-Owen, Charles. (2014) 'Its True, I'm English…I'm Not Lying': Essentialised and Precarious English Identities', *Ethnic and Racial Studies*, *37*, 8.

Leggett, Will. (2013) 'Restoring Society to Post-structuralist Politics: Mouffe, Gramsci and Radical Democracy', Philosophy and Social Criticism, http://psc.sagepub.com/content/39/3/299

Lewis, Gail. Neal, Sarah. (2005) 'Introduction: Contemporary Political Contexts, Changing Terrains and Revisited Discourses', *Ethnic and Racial Studies*, *28* (3), Abingdon: Taylor & Francis.

Lewis, Helen. (2016) 'Its a Measure of How Bad Social Mobility Is in Britain That Even Our Anti-elite Movements Are Led by Elites', *New Statesman*, 19–25 April.

Lewis, Helen. (2016) 'There Is a Glaring Space in Politics for an English Nationalist Party. Who Is Going to Fill It?' New Statesman, 23–29 September.

Liew, Jonathan. (2023) 'English Cricket's Reign of Shame Exposed With Devastating Admission of Guilt', *The Guardian*, (27/06/2023), https://www.theguardian.com/sport/2023/jun/27/english-cricket-independent-commission-equity-prejudice-azeem-rafiq-racism

Lyotard, Jean Francois. (1979) *La Condition Postmoderne*, Paris: Minuit.

Lyotard, Jean-Francois. (1986) 'The Postmodern Condition: A Report on Knowledge', *Theory and History of Literature*, *10*, University of Manchester Press. https://monoskop.org/images/e/e0/Lyotard_Jean-Francois_The_Postmodern_Condition_A_Report_on_Knowledge.pdf

MacFarlane, Robert. (2015) 'The Eeriness of the English Countryside', *The Guardian*, http://www.theguardian.com/books/2015/apr/10/eeriness-rnglish-countryside-robert-macfarlane

Macklin, Graham. (2008) 'All White on the Right' *Imagined Nation, England After Britain*, ed by Mark Perryman, London: Lawrence and Wishart.

Malek, Bilkis. (2008) 'Rethinking Segregation', *Race Identity and Belonging*, ed by Sally Davidson and Jonathan Rutherford, London: Lawrence and Wishart.

Marsden, Graham. (2000) 'When Was England, England?' *The English Question*, ed by Selina Chen and Tony Wright, London: The Fabian Society.

Martell, Luke. (2008) 'Britain and Globalization', *Globalizations*, vol. 5, London: Taylor & Francis.

Mason, Paul. (2016) 'For Some Brexiteers This Is a Visceral, Life-Defining Cause. If They Lose, They Will React Badly', *The Guardian*, (24/05/2016).

Mason, Paul. (2016) 'A Regime of Crisis', New Statesman, 14–20 October.

Mason, Rowena. (2014) 'Tim Yeo Says His Moderate Views Prompted Conservative Deselection Vote', *The Guardian*, www.theguardian.com/politics/2014/feb/03/tim-yeo-moderate-tory-mp-deselected

Mason, Rowena. (2015) 'Votes or Vetoes? Betty Boothroyd Joins Experts to Blast English Laws Proposal', *The Guardian*, www.theguardian.co.uk/politics/2015/jul/16/betty-boothroyd-experts-blast-english-laws-votes-proposal

Mason, Rowena. Brooks, Libby. (2015) 'English Votes for English Laws Plan Branded "Charter for the End of the Union"', *The Guardian*, www.theguardian.co.uk/politics/2015/oct/22/commons-passes-english-votes-for-english-laws-plan

Massey, Doreen. (2014) *Neo-liberalism, Conservatism and the Social Settlement*, lecture delivered at University of Brighton, (11/10/2014).

McClintock, Anne. (1997) '"No Longer in a Future Heaven": Gender, Race, and Nationalism', *Dangerous Liaisons*, ed by Anne McClintock, Amir Mufti and Ella Shohat, Minneapolis: University of Minnesota Press.

McCrone, David. McPherson, Gayle. (2009) 'Marking Time: The Significance of National Days', *National Days*, ed by David McCrone and Gayle McPherson, Basingstoke: Palgrave McMillan.

McNeile, Cyril. (1953) *Mufti*, London: Usborne.

Modood, Tariq, Berthoud, Richard, Lakey, Jane, Smith, Patten, Virdee, Satnam, Beishon, Sharon. (1997) *Ethnic Minorities in Britain: Diversity and Disadvantage*, London: Policy Studies Institute.

Modood, Tariq. (2005) 'A Defence of Multiculturalism', Soundings, http://www.leeds.ac.uk/educol/documents/153854.pdf

Modood, Tariq. (2010) *Still Not Easy Being British: Struggles for a Multicultural Citizenship*, Stoke-on-Trent: Trentham Books.

Moore, Suzanne. (2014) 'My Idea of Englishness Is Messy, Funny, Irrational, and It Needn't Be Tainted by Empire', *The Guardian*, (25/09/2014).

Morden, Michael. (2016) 'Anatomy of the National Myth: Archetypes and Narrative in the Study of Nationalism', *Nations and Nationalism*, *22* (2).

Morton, H.V. (1927) *In Search of England*, London: Methuen.

Mouffe, Chantal. (2005) *The Return of the Political*, London: Verso.

Mouffe, Chantal. (2009) *The Democratic Paradox*, London: Verso.

Mulvey, Laura. (1975) 'Visual Pleasure and Narrative Cinema', Screen, 16.

Murray, Douglas. (2019) *The Madness of Crowds: Gender, Race and Identity*, London: Bloomsbury.
Nayak, Anoop. (2003) *Race, Place and Globalization. Youth Cultures in a Changing World*, Oxford: Berg.
Naidoo, Roshi. (2008) 'Fear of Difference/Fear of Sameness', *Soundings*, ed by Sally Davison and Jonathan Rutherford, London: Lawrence and Wishart.
Nairn, Tom. (1981) *The Break-Up of Britain*, 2nd ed, London: Verso.
Nairn, Tom. (1994) 'The Maladies of Development', *Nationalism*, ed by John Hutchinson and Anthony D. Smith, Oxford: Oxford University Press.
Nairn, Tom. (1997) *Faces of Nationalism: Janus Revisited*, London: Verso.
Neate, Rupert. (2022) 'Rishi Sunak and Akshata Murty Join UK Rich List With Combined £730m Fortune', *The Guardian*, https://www.theguardian.com/business/2022/may/20/sri-and-gopi-hinduja-named-uk-richest-people-james-dyson
New Statesman. (2015) 'Leader: Forget Scotland – Why Is the English Political Identity So Confused?' *New Statesman*, www.newstatesman.com/politics/2015/04/leader-forget-scotland-why-english-identity-so-confused
Office for National Statistics. (2011) 'Ethnicity and National Identity in England and Wales: 2011', http://www.ons.gov.uk/peoplepopulationandcommunity/culturalidentity/ethnicity/articles/ethnicityandnationalidentityinenglandandwales/2012-12-11#ethnicity-across-the-english-regions-and-wales
Office for National Statistics. (2020) 'Average Household Income, UK: Financial Year Ending 2019 (provisional)', https://www.ons.gov.uk/peoplepopulationandcommunity/personalandhouseholdfinances/incomeandwealth/bulletins/householddisposableincomeandinequality/financialyearending2019provisional
Oswell, David. (2006) *Culture and Society: An Introduction to Cultural Studies*, London: SAGE.
Oswell, D. (2012). *Culture and Society: An Introduction to Cultural Studies*, SAGE Publications Ltd, https://doi.org/10.4135/9781446215449
Owens, Craig. (1985) 'The Discourse of Others: Feminists and Postmodernism', *Postmodern Culture*, ed by Hal Foster, London: Pluto Press.
Oxfam. (2023) 'Richest 1% Grab Nearly Twice as Much New Wealth as Rest of the World Put Together', https://www.oxfam.org.uk/media/press-releases/richest-1-grab-nearly-twice-as-much-new-wealth-as-rest-of-the-world-put-together/#:~:text=Latest%20figures%20from%20Credit%20Suisse,trillion%20(%C2%A32.4%20billion)
Ozmikiri, Umut. (2000) *Theories of Nationalism*, Basingstoke: Macmillan Press.
Ozmikiri, Umut. (2010) *Theories of Nationalism*, 2nd ed, Basingstoke: Macmillan Press.
Parekh Report. (2000) 'The Future of Multiethnic Britain', *Report of the Commission on the Future of Multiethnic Britain*, Chair Bhikhu Parekh, Commission Established by the Runnymede Trust, London: Profile Books.
Paxman, Jeremy. (1999) *The English: A Portrait of a People*, Harmondsworth: Penguin.
Pearce, Nick. (2014) 'Englishness and the Dilemas of Political Leadership', Renewal, http://www.renewal.org.uk/articles/the-politics-of-english-nationhood
Perry, Greyson. (2014) 'Default Man', *New Statesman*, 10–16 October 2014.
Perryman, Mark. (2009) 'The Patriot's Game', Soundings, http://lwbooks.co.uk/journals/soundings/issue/43.html

Perryman, Mark. (2014) 'Who You Calling Ingerland?' Counterfire, http://www.counterfire.org/index.php/articles/215-sport/17088-who-you-calling-ingerland-

Pickles, Eric. (2014) 'Pickles Launches Attack on 'Militant Atheists', *The Guardian*, (07/04/2014).

Pieterse, Jan Nederveen. (2007) 'Global Multiculture, Flexible Acculturation', *Globalizations*, vol. 4, No.1, Abingdon: Taylor & Francis.

Pison, Romain. (2005) *Globalization and Culture, or How Globalization Reinforces Local Identities*, New York University. http://pisonromain.tripod.com/sitebuildercontent/sitebuilderfiles/nyu-g-rp-final_paper.pdf

Preston, Peter. (2008) 'Cutting Scotland Loose: Soft Nationalism and Independence-in-Europe', *BJPIR*, vol. 10.

Purvis, Trevor. Hunt, Alan. (1993) 'Discourse, Ideology, Discourse, Ideology, Discourse, Ideology…', *The British Journal of Sociology*, vol. 44, No.3, http://www.jstor.org/stable/591813

Rees Mogg, Jacob. (2019) Business of the House, Hansard, vol. 666, (24/10/2019), https://hansard.parliament.uk/commons/2019-10-24/debates/137302BA-0569-4C15-9F23-FF6C2DF9919E/BusinessOfTheHouse

Rahman, S. (2009) 'Muslims: Beyond the Headlines', *The Guardian*, http://www.guardian.co.uk/commentisfree/belief/2009/dec/15/muslims-open-society-institute-europe

Ramsay, Adam. (2020) 'Why Does England Vote Tory?' Open Democracy, (21/06/2020), https://www.opendemocracy.net/en/opendemocracyuk/why-does-england-vote-tory/

Rhodes, James. (2012) 'Stigmatization, Space, and Boundaries in De-industrial Burnley', *Nations and Nationalism*, Abingdon: Taylor & Francis.

Ricoeur, Paul. (1965) *History and Truth*, Evanston: Northwestern University Press.

Robertson, Roland. (1992) *Globalization: Social Theory and Global Culture*, London: Sage.

Robinson, Emily. (2016) 'Labour and the New Englishness', *Renewal*, vol. 24, 1.

Robertson, Roland. (1995) 'Glocalization: Time-Space and Homogeneity-Heterogeneity', *Global Modernities*, ed by Mike Featherstone, Scott Lash and Roland Robertson, London: Sage.

Rusbridger, Alan. (2013) 'MPs' Questions to Alan Rusbridger: Do You Love This Country?' *The Guardian*, https://www.theguardian.com/media/2013/dec/03/keith-vaz-alan-rusbridger-love-country-nsa

Savage, Mike, Wright, David. Gayo-Cal, Modesto. (2010) 'Cosmopolitan Nationalism and the Cultural Reach of the White British', University of Warwick, http://doi.org/10.1111/j.1469-89129.2010.00449.x

Say Mitchell, Dreda. (2011) 'Black Britons May Be the Last Defenders of the Union', *The Guardian*, (12/10/2011).

Schlesinger, P. (1987) 'On National Identity: Some Conceptions and Misconceptions Criticized', *Social Science Information*, vol. 26, No. 2, Sage.

Schrover, Marlou. Schinkel, Willem. (2013) 'Introduction: The Language of Inclusion and Exclusion in the Context of Immigration and Integration', Ethnic and Racial Studies, http//doi.org/10.1080/01419870.2013.783711

Schwarz, B. (1996) *The Expansion of England. Race, Ethnicity and Cultural History*, London: Routledge.

Scruton, Roger. (2000) *England: An Elergy*, London: Chatto & Windus.
Scruton, Roger. (2013) 'Identity, Family, Marriage: Our Core Conservative Values Have Been Betrayed', *The Guardian*, http://www.theguardian.com/commentisfree/2013/may/11/identity-family-marriage-conservative-values-betrayed
Shackle, Samira. (2011) 'Both Sides, Now: I Grew up Thinking of Myself as Equally English and Pakistani, Says Samira Shackle. Was I Wrong?' *New Statesman*, http://go.galegroup.com.eproxy.brighton.ac.uk/ps/i.do?id=GALE%7CA254828972&v-2.1&u=brighton_itw&it=r&p=EAIM&sw=w
Shire, George. (2008) 'Race and Racialisation in Neo-Liberal Times', *Race, Identity and Belonging*, ed by Sally Davison and Jonathan Rutherford, London: Lawrence and Wishart.
Sindic, Denis. (2008) 'National Identities: Are They Declining?' *Beyond Current Horizons*, UK Department for Children, Schools and Families, https://www.researchgate.net/publication/235759481_National_identities_Are_they_declining
Sinfield, A. (1989) 'Literature and Cultural Production', *Literature Politics and Culture in Postwar Britain*, Oxford: Blackwell.
Skey, Michael. (2009) 'We Wanna Show 'Em Who We Are': National Events in England', *National Days*, ed by David McCrone and Gayle McPherson, Basingstoke: Palgrave Macmillan.
Skey, Michael. (2010) 'A Sense of Where You Belong in the World: National Belonging, Ontological Security and the Status of the Ethnic Majority in England', *Nations and Nationalism*, Abingdon: Taylor & Francis.
Skey, Michael. (2011) 'Sod Them I'm English': The Changing Status of the 'Majority' English in Post-Devolution Britain', Ethnicities, www.etn.sagepub.com/content/12/1/106
Smart, Barry. (1992) *Modern Conditions, Post Modern Controversies*, London: Routledge.
Smith, Anna Marie. (1994) *New Right Discourse on Race and Sexuality*, Cambridge: Cambridge University Press.
Smith, Anna Marie. (1998) *Laclau and Mouffe, the Radical Democratic Imaginary*, London: Routledge.
Smith, Anthony D. (2002) 'The Poverty of Anti-Nationalist Modernism' *Nations and Nationalism*, *8* (1).
Smith, Anthony D. (2006) 'Set in the Silver Sea: English National Identity and European Integration', *Nations and Nationalism*, *12* (3).
Smith, Owen. (2015) 'English Votes for English Laws: A Tory Power Grab Dressed Up in Constitutional Jargon', *New Statesman*, www.newstatesman.com/politics/2015/07/english-votes-english-laws-tory-power-grab-dressed-constitutional-jargon
Sparrow, Nigel. (2014) 'Nigel Farage: Parts of Britain Are 'Like a Foreign Land', *The Guardian*, https://www.theguardian.com/politics/2014/feb/28/nigel-farage-ukip-immigration-speech
Spours, Ken. Diamond, Patrick. (2016) 'The Osborne Supremacy: The Unfolding Conservative Hegemonic Project and the Left's Response', *Renewal*, *24* (1).
Sturgis, Patrick, Brunton-Smith, Ian, Kuha, Jouni. Jackson, Jonathan. (2013) 'Ethnic Diversity, Segregation and the Social Cohesion of Neighbourhoods in London', Ethnic and Racial Studies, http://doi.org/10.1080/01419870.2013.831932
Sutherland, Claire. (2005) 'Nation-Building Through Discourse Theory', *Nations and Nationalism*, *11* (2).

Sutton, Trust. (2019) 'Newly Elected MPs Now More Likely to Have Been Educated at State Schools', *FE News*, (16/12/2019), https://www.fenews.co.uk/skills/newly-elected-mps-now-more-likely-to-have-been-educated-at-state-schools/

The Guardian. (2005) 'Britain 'Sleepwalking to Segregation', *The Guardian*, http://www.theguardian.com/world/2005/sep/19/race.socialexclusion

The Guardian. (2013a) 'MPs Questions to Alan Rusbridger: Do You Love This Country?' *The Guardian*, http://www.theguardian.com/media/2013/dec/03/keith-vaz-alan-rusbridger-love-country-nsa

The Guardian. (2013b) 'Where UK Immigrants Were Born: 1951–2011', *The Guardian*, http://www.theguardian.com/news/datablog/interactive/2013/dec/17/where-uk-immigrants-born-1951-2011-census-ons

The Guardian. (2014a) 'Answering the English Question', *The Guardian*, (22/08/2014).

The Guardian. (2014b) 'Cabinet Reshuffle: Breakdown by Gender, Education and Age', *The Guardian*, http://www.theguardian.com/news/datablog/2014/jul/15/cabinet-reshuffle-broken-down-gender-education-age

The Guardian. (2014c) 'Lady Warsi Resigns over UK's Morally Indefensible Stance of Gaza', *The Guardian*, http://www.theguardian.com/politics/2014/aug/05/lady-warsi-resigns-government-gaza-stance

The Guardian. (2015) 'Rupert Murdoch: Muslims Must Be Held Responsible for France Terror Attacks', *The Guardian*, www.theguardian.com/world/2015/jan/10/rupert-murdoch-muslims-must-be-held-responsible-for-france-terror-attacks

Thomas, Paul. (2011) 'All White? Englishness, 'Race' and Ethnic Identities', *These Englands*, ed by Arthur Aughey and Christene Berberich, Manchester: Manchester University Press.

Tolhurst, Alain. (2017) 'Sturge Wants a Seat: SNP Threaten to Hold Brexit Bill to Ransom unless Nicola Sturgeon Gets a Seat at the Negotiations with the EU', The Sun, (22/06/2017), https://www.thesun.co.uk/news/3861784/snp-threaten-to-hold-brexit-bill-to-ransom-unless-nicola-sturgeon-gets-a-seat-at-the-negotiations-with-the-eu/

Tomlinson, John. (2003) 'Globalization and Cultural Identity', The Global Transformations Reader, http://www.polity.co.uk/global/pdf/GTreader2e Tomlinson.pdf

Tomlinson, John. (2004) *Globalization and Culture*, Cambridge: Polity Press.

Torfing, Jacob. (1999) *New Theories of Discourse: Laclau, Mouffe and Zizek*, Oxford: Blackwell.

Torrance, David. (2015) 'The Reinvention of the SNP', *The Guardian*, (21/05/2015).

Toynbee, Polly. (2015) 'One Certain Outcome of the EU Vote? A Lonely Cameron', *The Guardian*, (16/06/2015).

Toynbee, Polly. (2016) 'Vote Leave's Campaign of Fear Will Cause Lasting Divisions', *The Guardian*, (24/05/2016).

Trickett, Jon. (2014) 'This Reshuffle Shows David Cameron Doesn't Have a Clue About Modern Britain', *New Statesman*, http://www.newstatesman.com/politics/2014/07/reshuffle-shows-david-cameron-doesnt-have-clue-about-modern-britain

Uberoi, Varun. Modood, Tariq. (2013) 'Has Multiculturalism in Britain Retreated?' Soundings, https://journals.lwbooks.co.uk/soundings/vol-2013-issue-53/article-7387/

van den Berghe, G. (2001) 'Sociobiological Theory of Nationalism', *Encyclopedia of Nationalism*, ed by A.S. Leoussi, London: Transaction Publishers.

Verdery, Katherine. (2000) 'Whither 'Nation' and 'Nationalism?' *Mapping the Nation*, ed by Gopal Balakrishnan, London: Verso.

Vidal, D. (2004) 'France: Hate and the Hijab', *Le Mond Diplomatique*, (04/02/2004).

Walker, Ben. (2022) 'Why "Scottish" Not "British" Now Leads in Scotland', *New Statesman*, (19/05/2022), https://sotn.newstatesman.com/2022/05/why-scottish-not-british-leads-scotland

Wallerstein, Immanuel. (1991) 'The Construction of Peoplehood', *Race, Nation, Class Ambiguous Identities*, ed by Etienne Balibar and Immanuel Wallerstein, London: Verso.

Warsi, Sayeeda. (2023) 'Listen to Suella Braverman and Realise: This Show of Diversity in Our Cabinet Is Not Progress', *The Guardian*, (12/04/2023), https://www.theguardian.com/commentisfree/2023/apr/12/suella-braverman-diversity-cabinet-british-pakistani-men-rishi-sunak

Watson, Sophie. Saha, Anamik. (2013) 'Suburban Drifts: Mundane Multiculturalism in Outer London', Ethnic and Racial Studies, http://doi.org/10.1080/01419870.2012.678875

Watt, Nicholas. Mason, Rowena. (2015) 'Cameron Rebukes Farage over 'Fifth Column' Charlie Hebdo Comments', *The Guardian*, http://www.theguardian.com/world/2015/jan/08/paris-attack-nigel-farage-gross-policy-multiculturalism

Wellings, Ben. (2001) 'Empire-nation: National and Imperial Discourses in England', School of Social Sciences, Australian National University, https://digitalcollections.anu.edu.au/handle/1885/41706

Wellings, Ben. (2008) 'Rump Britain: Englishness and Britishness, 1992–2001', National Identities, 9:4, https://doi.org/10.1080/14608940701737391

Wellings, Ben. (2010) 'Losing the Peace: Euroscepticism and the Foundations of a Contemporary English Nationalism', *Nations and Nationalism*, *16* (3).

Wellings, Ben. Baxendale, Helen. (2015) 'Euroscepticism and the Anglosphere: Traditions and Dilemmas in Contemporary English Nationalism', *Journal of Common Market Studies*, *53* (1), Oxford: Wiley and Sons.

Welsh Government. (2021) 'Ethnic Group, National Identity, Language and Religion in Wales (Census 2021)', https://www.gov.wales/ethnic-group-national-identity-language-and-religion-wales-census-2021-html

Werbner, Pnina. (1997) 'Introduction: The Dialectics of Cultural Hybridity', *Debating Cultural Hybridity*, ed by Pnina Werbner and Tariq Modood, London: Zed Books.

West, Cornell. (2003) 'A Genealogy of Modern Racism', *From Modernism to Postmodernism*, ed by Lawrence Cahoone, Oxford: Blackwell.

Whiteley, Nigel. (2000) *Detraditionalisation and Art*, London: Middlesex University Press.

Wigmore, Tim. (2014) 'Ed Balls' Tough Line on Immigration Only Helps Ukip', *New Statesman*, https://www.newstatesman.com/politics/2014/09/ed-balls-tough-line-immigration-only-helps-ukip

Wieviorka, M. (2004) 'The Stakes in the French Secularism Debate', *Dissent*, (Summer 2004).

Williams, Raymond. (1995) 'Dominant, Residual, and Emergent', *Critical Theory: A Reader*, ed by Douglas Tallack, Hemel Hempstead: Harvester Wheatsheaf.

Williams, Raymond. (2005) *Culture and Materialism*, London: Verso.

Winder, Robert. (2004) *Bloody Foreigners: The Story of Immigration to Britain*, London: Little, Brown and Company.

Wintour, Patrick. (2014) 'Cameron Answers 'English Question' and Conjures Nightmare for Miliband', *The Guardian*, www.theguardian.com/politics/2014/sep/19/david-cameron-english-question-ed-miliband-scotland

Woolfe, Virginia. (1938) *Three Guineas*, London: Hogarth Press.

Wright, Colin. (2007) 'Conserving Purity, Labouring the Past: A Tropological Evolution of Englishness', *Empire and After: Englishness in Post Colonial Perspective*, ed by Graham MacPhee and Prem Poddar, Oxford: Berghahn.

Wright, M. Bloemraad, I. (2012) 'Is There a Trade-Off Between Multiculturalism and Socio-Political Integration? Policy Regimes and Immigrant Incorporation in Comparative Perspectives', *Perspectives on Politics*, vol. 10, No.1.

Wright, Patrick. (1985) *On Living in an Old Country: The National Past in Contemporary Britain*, London: Verso.

Wright, R. (2008) 'Is It 'Cos I Is English?' *Imagined Nation: England After Britain*, ed by Mark Perryman, London: Lawrence and Wishart.

Wright, Tony. (2000) 'Introduction: England, Whose England?' *The English Question*, ed by S. Chen and T. Wright, London: Fabian Society.

Wright, Tony. Gamble, Andrew. (2009) 'Introduction: The Britishness Question', *The Political Quarterly*, *78* (s1). https://onlinelibrary-wiley-com.sussex.idm.oclc.org/doi/10.1111/j.1467-923X.2007.02014.x

Yewah, Emmanuel. (2001) 'The Nation as a Contested Construct', *Research in African Literatures*, vol. 32, No.3, www.muse.jhu.edu/article/29608

YouGov. (2023) 'Support for Creation of a New English Parliament along the Lines of the Existing Scottish Parliament', YouGov, https://yougov.co.uk/topics/politics/trackers/support-for-creation-of-a-new-english-parliament-along-the-lines-of-the-existing-scottish-parliament

Younge, Gary. (2000) 'On Race and Englishness', *The English Question*, ed by Tony Wright and Selina Chen, London: The Fabian Society.

Younge, Gary. (2013) 'Globalization's Scapegoats', *The Nation*, http://www.thenation.com/article/174237/globalization-scapegoats

Younge, Gary. (2015) 'This Polarised Debate Won't Help Us Move on from Charlie Hebdo', *The Guardian*, (12/01/2015).

Yuval-Davis, Nira. (1987) 'Marxism and Jewish Nationalism', *History Workshop Journal*, no 24 autumn 1987.

Yuval-Davis, Nira. Anthias, Floya. (1989) *Women-Nation-State*, London: Macmillan.

Yuval-Davis, Nira. Anthias, Floya. (1993) *Women-Nation-State*, Basingstoke: MacMillan.

Zizek, Slavoj. (2000) 'Class Struggle or Postmodernism?' *Contingency, Hegemony, Universality Contemporary Dialogues on the Left*, ed by Judith Butler, Ernesto Laclau and Slavoj Zizek, London: Verso.

Zizek, Slavoj. (2009) *Violence*, London: Profile.

Zizek, Slavoj. (2011) *Living in the End Times*, London: Verso.

Zizek, Slavoj. (2012) 'The Spectre of Ideology', *Mapping Ideology*, ed by Slavoj Zizek, London: Verso.

Printed and bound by CPI Group (UK) Ltd, Croydon, CR0 4YY
22/11/2023
08193432-0002